An End to Allegiance

Individual freedom and the new politics

GEOFFREY SAMPSON

Temple Smith/London

320.5
S192e

First published in Great Britain in 1984
by Maurice Temple Smith Ltd.,
Jubilee House, Chapel Road
Hounslow, Middlesex, TW3 1TX

Sampson, Geoffrey
    An end to allegiance.
    1. Libertarianism—United States
    I. Title
    320.5'12'0973   JC599.U5

ISBN 0 85117 253 9
86-725

Typeset in 11 point Plantin by Tellgate Ltd., London WC2
Printed and bound in Great Britain at
The Camelot Press Ltd, Southampton

An End to Allegiance

Contents

For MED

Preface

I happen to be a university teacher by trade; but this is not meant to be an academic sort of book, so I have not weighed it down with the apparatus of footnotes and scholarly references that professional academics use in order to impress each other. Publications which I have relied on heavily in constructing my argument are listed at the back of the book. Where I have quoted some writer in passing, or referred to an item from a newspaper or magazine, I do not give chapter and verse in my text because I believe most readers will not want it. Nevertheless, if any reader wishes to check up on a particular point, he is very welcome to write to me and I will supply details of my source.

I owe a debt of gratitude to the University of Lancaster for allowing me the period of leisure during which the book was written; and I owe a bigger debt to Vera for putting up with me while I was writing it. I thank Chris Tame for many useful comments on the manuscript; he should not be taken to agree with my views. And finally I should like to thank Ingleton Parish Council for its contributions to my political education. Matthew vii:19.

Ingleton, Yorkshire
4 January 1984

1/Straws in the Wind

This book is about a revolution in political attitudes which is taking place in our time. Many people are participating in that revolution; few of them recognize it for what it is. All over the Western world, in the final quarter of the twentieth century, people are becoming convinced that ordinary individuals can run their own lives better than any corps of benevolent mandarins or Big Brothers can do it for them. Authority in all its forms is distrusted as never before in modern history. Even the most democratic of States are coming to be seen by their subjects as both incompetent and unfriendly; similar attitudes are emerging towards subsidiary authority-structures such as the learned professions.

By the early 1980s, few adult Britons can fail to have noticed symptoms of this growing mood. The temptation is to shrug it off as just the latest of those shifts of fashionable opinion which succeed one another as decade follows decade and pass away without having effected more than minor changes in the political landscape. To some extent (the suggestion would run) people are choosing to move from one to another of the options which have all appeared on the political menu since our great-grandfathers' days; for the rest, they are chafing and grumbling at annoying inevitabilities which, not long ago, it was usual to put up with quietly.

This view, I believe, is mistaken. What it fails to take account of is the emergence of ideas and theories which, if they succeed in winning acceptance, are destined utterly to transform the menu of what is politically possible. It has often been noticed that in the 1950s and 1960s political theory was a fairly dead subject: all the big questions seemed to have been settled once for all. In the last ten years, among people who think analytically about social issues, politics has become one of the

liveliest of subjects; and this is largely because of the increasing
r_mber of thinkers and writers who are evolving an ideology
which harmonizes with the popular mood of opposition to
authority, and takes that principle to extremes of which the man
in the street has not yet dared to dream. 'The ideas of
economists and political philosophers,' according to John
Maynard Keynes, 'are more powerful than is commonly
understood. . . . Practical men, who believe themselves to be
quite exempt from any intellectual influences, are usually the
slaves of some defunct economist.' Some of the views I shall
discuss in this book would be dismissed by most contemporary
voters, even those whose opinions tend in a broadly similar
direction, as so far beyond the bounds of what is realistically
thinkable as to be scarcely sane. But all that proves, surely, is
that these ideas were not current fifty or a hundred years ago,
when today's common sense was an interesting, novel body of
thought. If thinkers are staking out a coherent set of positions in
virgin intellectual territory, and if the population at large has
started heading in the same direction, what reason is there to
expect the marchers suddenly to stop short and turn back to
where they came from?

My suspicion is that the movement presented in this book
heralds the most significant break in the continuity of political
evolution for more than a hundred years. If it continues to
gather strength and support, it must end by turning our
political landscape upside down. I surmise that the ideas
discussed below will make the twenty-first century at least as
different from the present, in terms of the kinds of social and
economic relationships obtaining among individuals and the
organizations of their society, as our age is from Victoria's.

Why do I say that the public mood is changing?

The most obvious symptom is the change in political
complexion of governments, throughout the democratic world
but nowhere more strikingly than in Britain.

Only a few years ago it was still true that if we had a major
party standing for political innovation it was the Labour Party;
the Conservative Party eschewed theories or ideology, and in
practice its policies just trailed a decade or two behind those of
Labour which seemed, during much of the 1960s and 1970s, to

have become the 'natural party of government'. Since Margaret Thatcher took over the Conservative leadership in 1975, friends and opponents of the party alike concede that it has become the radical party, the party of ideas, the party where one finds a willingness to call accepted wisdom into question; and the electorate has responded in two General Elections which produced large Conservative majorities. One might well retort that Margaret Thatcher's radicalism seems to have become a matter of talk more than action – her first administration achieved precious little in the way of 'rolling back the frontiers of the State', and as I write (a few months after the 1983 election) her government seems to have fairly thoroughly lost its way. But the point is that Margaret Thatcher's promises are evidently what the electorate want to hear. The stridently aggressive rhetoric in which she identifies herself with the little man struggling to build a future for his family amid a sea of red tape and overpaid official do-gooders would have been little more than an embarrassing joke twenty years ago; in 1979 it made her Prime Minister.

The nature of the Conservative Party is changing at the grassroots. No longer is it dominated by polished members of the landed gentry: these people are being shouldered aside in the constituency associations by men in off-the-peg suits and loud ties, garage proprietors, pub landlords. The Labour Party seems to be abandoning any serious intention of regaining power, and as things stand at present it is hard to believe that, at the next election, it will not give place to the SDP-Liberal Alliance as the other main party. The so-far nebulous policies of the Alliance are divided between a purely conservative desire to maintain the postwar *status quo* of balance between collective and individual decision-making while somehow eliminating the problems that become part of that *status quo*, and an attempt to purloin the Thatcher causes of enterprise, competition, and deregulation while avoiding the Thatcher reputation for unfeeling harshness. The newly-elected Alliance leader, David Owen, outlined party policy in autumn 1983 in terms which differed in scarcely any important respect from Mrs Thatcher's views.

Comparable political changes are occurring throughout the

West. In the USA, Jimmy Carter was succeeded by Ronald Reagan, whose rhetoric about the evils of big government may have proved hollow in practice much sooner and more thoroughly than Margaret Thatcher's, but who was certainly seen at the time of his election as a proponent of ideals very like hers. The more radically anti-Big-Government candidate in the 1980 Presidential election, Ed Clark, got over a million votes; his Libertarian Party was founded only in 1971, but already by 1976 the *Congressional Quarterly* classified it as the third-largest US party. In Germany, CDU has replaced SPD; and so on, almost wherever one looks. France seemed to swim against the tide in 1981 by electing the socialist François Mitterrand, but within a couple of years Mitterrand was jettisoning his socialism wholesale – in a television speech in September 1983 he declared the class war dead, lauded the profit motive, and described the level of taxation which he himself had introduced as 'intolerable'. In Paris, that nursery and hotbed of left-wing intellectuals, the crop has finally failed. 'For many of those who took part as students in the great would-be revolutionary happenings of May 1968,' as the *Times* noted in August 1983, 'not only communism but socialism itself has now become an object of contempt.' The *Times* quotes a contemporary French philosopher, Jean-Edern Hallier, as maintaining that 'socialism and culture are metaphysically contradictory and historically irreconcilable.' According to *Le Monde* a month earlier, 'relations between the Socialist State and French thinkers are at absolute zero.'

Obviously, no change in attitudes as fundamental as the one I am describing occurs instantaneously. Here and there changes of government have run counter to the trend – in Sweden, and in Spain; perhaps something of the kind will crop up in Britain in due course. But it is plausible to see such cases as waves which disguise but do not alter the fact that a tide has turned.

Changes of government are a particularly obvious index of the change in mood. But many symptoms of the new outlook are only tenuously connected with the left-versus-right dimension of politics, and some of them have very little to do with the traditional agenda of government at all. Consider a few straws in the wind.

When in 1970 the Austrian-Mexican intellectual Ivan Illich published a tract, *Deschooling Society*, which advocated the wholesale dismantling of organized compulsory schooling as we know it, ordinary middle-of-the-road types (if they heard of him at all) dismissed him as a wild-eyed fantast perversely determined to attack established institutions for the sake of attacking. In September 1982 the *Times* reported on a growing movement among ordinary middle-class British parents who are educating their children at home (and fighting the State for permission to do so) because they do not like what schools do to their children.

Ten or twenty years ago, the black economy was something that 'nice' people in Britain were scarcely aware of, and were liable to be shocked by if they did happen to encounter it. Nowadays, no middle-class householder who needs a job done is in the least surprised to be offered one price for payment by cheque and another for cash. Small tradesmen no longer feel hesitant about making the suggestion, for they know they will not be 'shopped': morality has changed, and we no longer believe that we owe the State its tithe.

Not long since, doctors were the twentieth-century priests, deferred to with awe as they worked their miracles. In 1980, a GP writing in *World Medicine* quoted a poll showing that the proportion of patients who trusted their doctors had plummeted in a single year from the already-low level of fifty-odd per cent to under forty per cent – why is it, he asked, that 'patients who were once ready to put their lives unquestioningly into the hands of their GP now wouldn't buy a used car from him?' Public disillusion with the medical establishment had reached such a pitch in 1980 that one of the leading articulators of that disillusion, Ian Kennedy, was invited to give the BBC Reith Lectures. A few years later, claims that homeopathy and simple folk therapies are superior to orthodox high-tech medicine have become a media cliché, and in 1983 practitioners of 'alternative therapies' founded a British Holistic Medical Association which nobody regards as good for a laugh.

Rioting French youth in May 1968 were demanding a Marxist revolution, or something very like it; youth across the West decorated their walls with posters of Che Guevara, or looked towards China as a mysterious Oriental civilization believed to be practising true Marxism-Leninism uncontaminated by Soviet deviation. At the beginning of the 1980s, the new locus of political riots by the young was – of all places – Switzerland, where the State intervenes less in daily life than, arguably, anywhere else in the world; and the youngsters who rampaged through Zürich made it clear that they had no more time for socialism than they did for the multinational financial empires which are prominently represented in Swiss cities – their allegiance was to anarchism. They demanded a place where young people could live without being required to acknowledge the sovereignty of the elders of Canton Zürich. (Switzerland being Switzerland, they came surprisingly near to getting it.) Meanwhile, China is busy building Holiday Inns and expensively chic restaurants to cater to the tourist trade.

In Britain, people who would have 'done their bit' in the Second World War without question and been proud of it are suddenly joining the nuclear disarmament movement in large numbers. The ladies being hauled out of the path of missile-carriers at Greenham Common are not just the loony-feminists the media love to interview, but ordinary mums and grans as well. This change of heart cannot be explained simply by the special horrors of nuclear warfare, because we have known about those for more than thirty years. But people sense now that the State has become too concerned with its own survival in a future holocaust, and too careless of the lives of the citizens it is supposed to serve.

Even people who objected to Big Government used to see local government as a provider of unglamorous but useful services, and at worst a collection of fairly harmless bumblers. Nowadays local-government responsibilities have grown so vast that bumbling has ceased to be harmless. According to the scriptwriter of a Central TV series about local government, *Muck and Brass*, 'Most people in our society wander round being discontented most of the time and not knowing why but it's because the system, including local government, is working against them all the time.' Decisions to spend millions of pounds of ratepayers' money go through on the nod with little awareness of their implications for the citizens affected, while a problem about Women's Institute jam-making is referred to Whitehall. 'They're all such pompous self-important little men,' commented the director of the series after studying his subjects in real life. In 1981 the National Consumer Council reported 'a very high level of unhappiness with attitudes of local council staff '. Paul Johnson, ex-editor of the *New Statesman* and ex-socialist, is more outspoken about local government: according to him, its 'inefficiency and contempt for ordinary people is perhaps the biggest single outrage in Britain today'.

There is no lack of evidence for this new mood of hostility towards authority, of refusal to defer. But most people who share this mood do not yet see themselves as part of a political movement, because they look towards the past rather than the future. People who see that the State has grown over-mighty talk in terms of shifting social arrangements back to the way they were in some vaguely hinted-at golden age before things went wrong; but when was this golden age? In the 1950s, when postwar American aid and large markets in an Empire that was only beginning to turn into a Commonwealth gave Britain a sudden prosperity which silenced social criticism? Those conditions could not last. In the *Belle Epoque*, when Britain invented the concentration camp in the course of fighting a cruel and unjust war against South African Boers, and when at home society was divided as never before or since into 'haves' who lived and breathed snobbery and material ostentation versus 'have-nots' who had to be bought off by placing their trades unions outside the framework of law which governed the rest of society? In the early nineteenth century, when press gangs tore men away from home and family, often never to see them again, and paper and newsprint were taxed heavily in order to suppress the spread of popular education? Margaret Thatcher talks of the need to return to 'Victorian values', and some values which marked the Victorian period, such as thrift and enterprise, were in harmony with her own ideals; but the Victorian age was also, for instance, a time when women were totally subordinated legally to men, and middle-class family life was governed by a rigid, stifling propriety and religiosity, whose effects were tempered for males by the existence of a vast army of prostitutes, many of them children.

Looking backwards is never an inspiring stance in political life. At any period there are shortcomings in society's arrangements. If people are unhappy about the current state of their society, their only serious answer is to think about how they would like to see it organized in the future, and to work forwards to that ideal. No doubt we will never quite attain anybody's political ideal, but only when we have something inspiring to aim at do we make any real progress.

The current juncture is in fact a very odd one in political history; practising politicians, temporarily, are in the vanguard of political thought. When the parliamentary Labour Party came into existence in 1906, its members were sustained by a vision which, however practical and coherent it may or may not have been, was certainly very different from anything known from the past. Socialist ideas were quite widespread among educated Britons at the end of the nineteenth century, and it is difficult to believe that Labour politicians could have succeeded in the humdrum work of parliamentary and, soon, governmental activity without the support of a sizeable segment of the public who shared their understanding of the distant goal towards which the petty compromises of day-to-day parliamentary activity were meant to lead. Yet, at present, Margaret Thatcher and some of her colleagues in government seem to be considerably more aware of the ideas with which this book is concerned than almost any of their supporters in the country at large. One can exaggerate this awareness; the extremer versions of the ideology no doubt go unread at Westminster. But for instance Friedrich Hayek (to name the thinker whose views would possibly command the most unanimous respect among the intellectual grouping I am concerned with) certainly is a familiar and well-respected figure, both as a person and as a writer, for quite a number of our current political leaders. By the standards of many of the people to be discussed below, Hayek is a moderate; but by the standards of most voters, even Conservative voters, he is so extreme as to be out of sight. Columnists in serious papers regularly demonstrate their ignorance of Hayek's thought by lumping him together with Milton Friedman as 'monetarists'. (If 'monetarism' means anything, then Hayek is the opposite of a monetarist.)

Surely, this situation cannot last long. The normal place for politicians in a democracy is bringing up the rear in the march of public opinion, tempering the idealism of the leaders of social thought with the compromises that are inevitable when ideals are translated into practice. Politicians frame their manifestos to appeal to voters' existing motives; they cannot normally do much to change voters' values (and arguably they should not try). Either the shift in mood whose symptoms I have sketched is destined to peter out as a temporary aberration, or else the ideas we shall examine must soon enter into the mainstream of public thinking.

What are these ideas? This entire book is my attempt to answer that question, and even this answer will certainly be inadequate. But, to squeeze an ideology into a nutshell, one might say the following:

All, or almost all, matters involving conflicts of interest between people are inherently capable of being decided peacefully by voluntary negotiation. Whenever any matters are capable of being settled in this fashion, both expedience and morality alike always, or almost always, require that they should be. It is never, or almost never, either morally permissible or practically advantageous to allow institutions to impose decisions on individuals, either by appeal to political 'loyalty' and 'legitimacy' or by threat of force – irrespective of how wise and benevolent the people manning those institutions may be.

An important class of matters to which these principles are relevant are the issues traditionally identified as 'economic'. There are strong moral and practical presumptions against allowing State power to play any role in determining patterns of investment, employment, income distribution, or ᵗhe like. Individuals must be left to negotiate all or almost all such matters privately; what 'negotiation' means is that one party agrees to exchange something he controls for something controlled by another party; therefore all, or almost all, property (i.e. control over economically-relevant resources) must be privately owned.

But economics as traditionally understood imposes an arbitrary division between 'economic' and 'non-economic' aspects of human life. The same arguments which suggest that authority must not interfere with private negotiations involving money and money's worth suggest equally that authority must not impose decisions on individuals in domains to which money is entirely irrelevant.

All this does not amount to a recipe for universal happiness or individual self-fulfilment. There is no such recipe. It amounts only to a framework within which individuals can seek to realize whatever admirable or unadmirable values they hold. It does not guarantee that their quest will be rewarded; on the contrary, it is guaranteed that individuals will often make mistakes, sometimes serious mistakes, from which they will suffer. But only if individuals are allowed to make their own mistakes and suffer for them can people become wiser and societies more prosperous.

These principles, likewise, do not amount to a recipe for equality between individuals, either materially or in terms of the degree of emotional satisfaction derived from life. Again, there is no such recipe. It is guaranteed that some individuals will be materially better off than others in a society conforming to these principles, but the same is true for any other possible arrangement of society. A society in which individuals are responsible for their lives turns *relative* deprivation to good purpose by using it to fuel a rise in *absolute* levels of prosperity; in a society which subordinates individuals to authority, deprivation is merely arbitrary deprivation. As for emotional satisfaction, different individuals' emotional rewards cannot be reduced to a common measure; but if, as is often said, happiness is a by-product of working towards a goal rather than something attained when goals are achieved, then a society organized on voluntarist principles gives individuals the best chance of self-fulfilment, while a society based on authority which frustrates their independent initiatives must reduce that chance.

I have defined these principles at a high level of abstraction; but perhaps I have said enough to suggest how novel, in terms of the recent map of politics, is the grouping of particular social prescriptions that follow from them. Hostility to State interference with private property, and preference for private rather than collective provision of economic wants, is in British terms a Conservative preoccupation, and some of my remarks may have suggested that what I am talking about is simply the politics of the 'dry' wing of the Conservative Party. But Conservatives, wet or dry, tend also to be champions of the police, and enthusiastic about the enforcement of traditional morality in domains such as drug-taking. The principles I have outlined imply coolness at best towards the existence of police forces, whose only *raison d'être* is to enforce State authority, and they suggest that the individual ought to be as free to experiment with cannabis – or, indeed, with heroin – as with the consumer goods offered by 'legitimate' big business.

The movement with which I am concerned genuinely is breaking the mould of politics, to use a much-abused cliché. In its attitude to economic life it is well to the 'right' of any parliamentary Conservative; on non-economic issues it adopts what are traditionally seen as left-wing positions, if they are associated with any traditional political grouping at all. Where, in the traditional Conservative-versus-Socialist political spectrum, would one place a group who favour abortion without legal control and unrestricted immigration, but oppose laws against sexual and racial discrimination? – who favour extending civil rights to children, and favour nuclear power too? – who welcome gay liberation, and warmly approve of business? The assumptions of recent Western political thinking make these attitudes seem dissonant. Members of the movement under discussion see them as harmonizing; they are all concerned with increasing individual freedom.

I have finally used the word 'freedom'. It is time to give the movement I am talking about a name. As it happens, that poses problems.

Historically, the combination of disrespect for authority with stress on the virtues of private enterprise and free trade in the economic domain characterized the Whig side of British politics; the established attitudes and institutions which the new movement opposes have much in common with Toryism in its traditional sense. The term 'Whig' is still occasionally used in connexion with the practice of politics: Cecil Margolis sits as a Whig member of Harrogate District Council, stressing that he opposes the paternalist kinds of local government activism favoured by his Conservative colleagues as much as he does the policies of more socialist members. Given the ambiguities of contemporary political vocabulary, it might be tempting to revive the term 'whig' as a clear label for the subject of this book, but there are difficulties: the word 'whiggish' has a somewhat frivolous air in the late twentieth century, and it is perhaps inappropriate to use a word tied as specifically as 'Whig' to British history, when the movement I am discussing is thoroughly international. (More people adhere to it in America than in Britain, and by now it has flourishing little outposts even in places like Iceland and the Faeroes.)

Our Whig party evolved into the Liberal party, and 'liberal' is another standard political term for a position which emphasizes the freedom of the individual in contrast to collective or State authority. Again the usage is problematic, for two reasons. One is the continued existence of the Liberal Party today; there is an inevitable presumption that 'liberalism' must relate to the policies of the Liberal Party, whereas in fact that party has changed out of all recognition since acquiring its name. This problem is not too serious: it does not seem to worry anybody that the Conservative Party is now less conservative than the opposition. But the other difficulty is that 'freedom' is one of those political hurrah-words – perhaps the chief one – which is redefined by almost all groups so as to make it apply to themselves, and since 'liberal' etymologically means nothing more specific than 'free' the word 'liberal', too, has acquired very different connotations at different times and places. Particularly remarkable is the development the word has undergone in the USA, where, according to one American commentator on public affairs, the term 'liberalism' now connotes 'aggressive use of central government power', and 'liberals tend to favour equality more and liberty less' than their opponents!

This may seem too absurd etymologically to take seriously. Yet the fact is that in the USA, where 'socialism' commonly counts as a dirty word, so many people now use 'liberal' as a euphemism in order to insinuate socialist proposals into public debate that Americans supporting the very un-socialist movement I am concerned with almost always feel it necessary to differentiate themselves from 'liberals'. Sometimes they call themselves 'true liberals', but that sounds question-begging. Sometimes they call themselves 'classical liberals'; but this inevitably suggests a focus on the past rather than the future, whereas, as I have already said, any serious political movement must – and this movement certainly does – spend most of its time looking forward rather than back.

Many Americans (and some others) solve these problems by using the word 'libertarian', a term adapted from the vocabulary of turn-of-the-century French anarchism. This usage too is problematic. In line with its origins, the term 'libertarian' has a meaning more specific than simply 'favouring individual freedom as against collective or State power'. If someone calls himself a 'libertarian', there is a fairly strong presumption that he is an anarchist, someone who believes that human societies can and should manage without *any* States at all – in other words, who believes that every occurrence of the phrase 'all or almost all' in the statement of principles on page 17 can unproblematically be replaced by 'all'. Some members of the movement discussed in this book are anarchists, but most are not; they accept that States are needed to do certain jobs that only States can do, while refusing to regard their State in the way that a small child regards his parents, as an appropriate focus of unquestioning loyalty or allegiance. For members of the movement under discussion, States are just institutions which, like hospitals or service stations, do not-very-pleasant but useful tasks either well or badly. If a State – or a car repair shop – carries out its proper functions efficiently and cheaply, they may offer it gratitude along with their fees for services rendered; in neither case do they welcome it taking over their lives.

By no means everyone who calls himself 'libertarian' is an anarchist; but many of the people who use the term are at least fairly close to the anarchist position, whereas only a small fraction of this book will deal with such extreme views.

Therefore I prefer to avoid using 'libertarianism' as a general label for my topic. But I avoid it also because I find it strikingly ugly; and I do not see why members of this movement should have to put up with an ugly, secondary derivative from the root 'free', leaving the more basic and attractive derivative 'liberal' for another use, since their right to this word was established first. It may be that socialists have chosen to redefine 'free' in such a way that, for them, an individual who makes no significant long-term decisions and consumes goods and services all of which are provided by the State has more 'substantive freedom' than someone who is responsible for piloting his own way through life and consumes fewer goods and services along the way; but they cannot require others who think differently to respect this verbal hi-jacking, which unquestionably amounts to a violent change in the meaning of 'freedom' irrespective of whether one approves or disapproves of socialist principles.

Accordingly, I shall use the terms 'liberal' and 'liberalism' to describe the political movement whose nature has been sketched, and I shall use these terms in no other sense. In this I follow the lead of some of the most eminent members of the movement, including Milton Friedman and Friedrich Hayek.

Contemporary opponents of liberalism often use phrases such as 'right-wing' or 'the New Right' to describe the movement. As I have already suggested, those aspects of the liberal movement which coincide with the 'right' of current politics are specifically the economic aspects. Liberalism as a whole cuts across the standard contrast between Conservative right and socialist left, and it seems misleading and question-begging to use either of these terms in connexion with it – they just serve to enforce the assumption that political debate must always be confined to the same sterile one-dimensional spectrum. But the term 'right' is misleading also in a more ominous way. The 'right' in politics has historically stood for a position which defended entrenched privilege and asserted that an individual's lot in life should be fixed in terms of birth and status. Political currents of this kind exist today, in the shape of nationalist and racialist movements which seek to force individuals into inferior positions because of the place they were born or the colour of their skin; such movements are properly described as 'right-wing'. Opponents of liberalism find it convenient to make the word 'right' cover everything that is not 'left', and thereby make liberalism seem to be a natural ally of some of the most morally objectionable political attitudes of our age. But the truth is that liberalism is entirely hostile to 'right-wing' politics in this sense: for a liberal it is simply immoral for civil rights to be withheld from an individual because he is not white-skinned, or for a job of work to be reserved for a resident of Britain if the same job could be done more efficiently and cheaply by a resident of Singapore. To my mind anyone who insists on using the words 'right' and 'left' in connexion with liberalism is just muddying the waters of political debate.

It is time to put my cards on the table. I am a liberal. That does not mean that I approve of all the views to be discussed in this book; I don't. Liberalism is a complex, evolving political movement; there are many things happening in it that make me giggle, and others that make me grimace. I shall not try to gloss over those things in the pages that follow. Nevertheless, my criticisms of individual liberals, though sometimes severe, will be made from a broadly friendly standpoint. Instinct and intellect alike convince me that the best hope for humanity is to move towards a position somewhere within the array of social ideals that we shall examine. Perhaps one needs to be in broad sympathy with a movement if one is to interpret its complexities successfully: I mention the point so that the reader can make his own allowances for my sympathies.

Most of the chapters that follow will deal with an individual figure or a particular trend within the broad spectrum of liberal thought. But, first, let us remind ourselves how we got where we are now.

2/The Planners' Nemesis

At the end of 1940, Britain had its back to the wall. A few months earlier, the evacuation from Dunkirk had shown to all that the nation was now more defenceless in the face of an enemy than it had ever been since the Norman Conquest. Night after night, that autumn and winter, German bombs pounded British streets to rubble. Living on an island too small to feed its population, dependent on convoys crossing thousands of miles of submarine-infested ocean, Britons were perpetually hungry and cold. Food rationing began in November; by next May the individual's allowance of cheese was down to one ounce a week. The entitlement to eggs fell to thirty a year. People sometimes found themselves burning their furniture, for want of any other fuel to cook or heat with in the bitterly cold winters that succeeded one another in the early part of the war.

Anyone who walked up the hills above Dover could see, across twenty miles of water, territory controlled by a power which was harnessing modern technology to the service of a nightmarish brutality that people had supposed extinct since the Middle Ages. Englishmen, who took it for granted that civility and good humour could be maintained despite political differences, found themselves on the verge of defeat by a regime whose treatment of citizens whose faces did not fit included their use as raw material in the manufacture of soap. Hitler's Germany was not only a State whose wickedness had few parallels, but one of the most successfully aggressive ever: in April Hitler had conquered two countries in a single day, and by now virtually all of Continental Europe was either controlled by Germany, allied with Germany, or leaned towards Germany in its neutrality. Britain stood alone in fighting against Nazism. It had no allies left.

At this moment, Englishmen and Englishwomen turned to

contemplating the new Britain they would build after they had won the war, as none of them – publicly – doubted that they would. The *Picture Post*, a large-format magazine whose text was enlivened by masses of high-quality photography, was at threepence a week the 1940s' equivalent of television, interpreting the nation to itself, making patterns for Everyman out of the inconsequentialities of daily life. The issue for New Year, 1941, had a single theme: 'A Plan for Britain'. It opened with a picture of a Welsh coalminer, with his fifteen-year-old son and their sheepdog, Sam, gazing out over a hillside. 'They look down the valley scarred by colliery refuse. They look on the mines, idle in the midst of war. In their hearts lives faith that we are moving towards better things.'

Tom Hopkinson, the editor, reminded his readers of the missed opportunities at the end of the First World War: what was wanted was 'imagination, planning, an idea of the country we wanted to make, and a passionate – actually passionate – determination to make it. Those qualities, when they were needed, were not there.' The same thing must not happen again, and this was the time to plan a 'fairer, pleasanter, happier, more beautiful Britain than our own', if there was to be any hope of realizing it when victory arrived.

The first article was a testimony to the failings of the old Britain. It was written by the miner, Bert Coombes, whose picture appeared above it – he had sent it in to the magazine saying 'I have written something about life today, as it looks to me and my mates. Is it any good to you?' Mr Coombes had begun life as a farmer and been forced off the land by falling prices: 'It came to the point where the price for swedes wouldn't cover cartage to the station,' so he had to move eighty miles to a new life as a miner. Now, for reasons not made clear in the article, the coal-pits too were at a standstill; ready as he was to do dirty and dangerous work for a fair reward, he had no work to do. And his son, a natural mechanic, was idle too – 'the country doesn't want his skill or his labour.' Coombes's piece does little in the way of analysing the roots of the problems besetting him and his family and neighbours, but it commands respect as a poignant expression of the rottenness of a society in which resources were wasted while basic human wants went unmet. The blunders of the 1930s had 'finished for ever the tradition of a class that was born to govern; and educated to believe that only the best was good enough for them . . . there must be great changes in the men and women who run this country. There must be new ideas and new methods.'

The rest of the magazine offered the analysis and the concrete ideas for the future which Coombes glimpsed only dimly. A young Oxford economics don, Thomas Balogh (now Lord Balogh), explained how a 'national plan to make the best use of our resources' would operate scientifically to guarantee work for all. Julian Huxley and Dr Maurice Newfield wrote about the need for a National Health Service, which would offer preventive medicine to the masses rather than merely trying to cure maladies once they had arisen. J.B. Priestley wrote of the need to shorten the working week so that working people would have time to become involved with the creative arts. A.D. Lindsay, Master of Balliol, writing below a photograph of two supercilious young lads in top hats and Eton suits doing their best to ignore a group of scruffily-clad urchins standing next to them, discussed the 'evil' of fee-paying schools, and the need to raise the school-leaving age and make the higher reaches of education available to all classes. And so on. 'Planning' in the usual modern sense – town planning – was discussed by Maxwell Fry, who had worked in partnership with the world-famous German modernist Walter Gropius in the 1930s, and was to become Vice-President of the Royal Institute of British Architects in the early 1960s. Fry's chief photograph illustrated the idea that 'modern materials' and 'modern brains' can produce 'such wonders as this road-junction outside New York' (a night scene of a sodium-lighted cloverleaf, then unknown in Britain). Artists' impressions contrasted part of a typical town as it then was – 'jerry-built streets . . . not enough light and air', 'roads too narrow, too crooked for modern transport' – with the same town remodelled in the planned Britain of the future: 'courts and alleys are swept away,' with airy blocks of flats towering towards the sky in a parkland setting. 'The roads are straight and wide.' Here and there it was already possible to see what could be done: Leeds had 'abolished 23 acres of obsolete housing at one sweep,' and an inset photograph shows a view across a broad plaza towards one of the as-yet-uninhabited nine-storey ribbons of modern housing that had replaced them. Fry offers a choice: postwar Britain could struggle on with such obsolete, chaotic hangovers from the past as private ownership of land, which 'made nonsense of town planning,' or it could opt for mass welfare achieved through central direction. But the choice was no choice: 'The New Britain must be PLANNED,' announces Fry's title in enormous capitals. And the same contrast, of beneficent State planning versus individualistic 'chaos', echoes and re-echoes throughout the magazine.

The editor predicted that these ideas would become 'common ground among all political parties'. And, as we know, he was right.

The Welfare State concept was not invented in the Second World War. The idea that a society should be organized on the model of a family, whose members work for one another's benefit as much as for their own, predates history – the smaller the society, after all, the easier it is for its members to maintain the personal bonds of sentiment that encourage them to live communally rather than individualistically. In the post-mediaeval West, the revival of that concept and the work of developing it and reconciling it with modern living conditions has come to be called socialism. Socialism as a body of intellectual doctrine originated in the writings of Saint-Simon in the Napoleonic period, and was developed as the nineteenth century advanced by many thinkers, including most famously Karl Marx. In Britain, as it happens, socialism as an intellectual theory made only a limited impact; but that is not because it was rejected in favour of a rival doctrine. Free-trade thinking survived longer here than elsewhere; but the trend of opinion swung in the same way in Britain as on the Continent, though British socialism tended to be more a matter of emotions, and of perception of particular, concrete problems, than of fine-drawn theorizing.

Where Germany had Karl Marx, we had Charles Dickens, whose influence in shaping British perceptions of social evils would be hard to overestimate. For a hundred years Dickens was (perhaps still is) the one novelist that everyone read – the novelist that the science student boasted of reading in order to establish that he was not dead to the world of culture. Dickens's novels portray worlds of which many readers lacked personal experience, in vivid contrasts of black and white whose implausibility did nothing to detract from their grip on the imagination. How many readers of *Hard Times* can have been impervious to the message that mill-owners and their class are ruthless hypocrites, while manual workers such as Stephen Blackpool are decent and upright? How many readers of *Nicholas Nickleby* can have resisted the suggestion that leaving the education of the young to private arrangements was a recipe for cruel, mindless child-farming? E.G. West has shown that nineteenth-century parents even in the poorest strata of society were strikingly willing to find money for the education of their children, and took great care to seek out good teachers; he argues that the 1870 Education Act actually inhibited the rise in educational standards that had been occurring before the State intervened. But the careful academic research of a West has little power to combat the potent myths of a Dickens. People are oddly unsymmetrical in their attitudes to novelists like Dickens who work by means of caricature. When he portrays a scene of merry good-fellowship, at the Pickwick Club or on Christmas Day at the Cratchits', we are all cynical enough to realize that he is laying it on too thick – we know from our own experience that social life always involves tensions as well as jollity, that nothing is ever that perfect; but when he paints people or institutions in sombre tones, we are readier to forget our scepticism and believe him. Dickens, and many other novelists of the age, reserved their darkest hues largely for the owners of capital and for the process of industrialization. In doing so, arguably, they heavily distorted the facts. Perhaps the strongest of all fictional expressions of nineteenth-century industrial cruelty was Frances Trollope's *Michael Armstrong*; J.M. Jefferson has pointed out that this book was based on an identifiable non-fiction source which there is reason to believe was deceitful.

If many Victorian novelists and their middle-class readers shared a dislike of industrialization and a willingness to exaggerate its evils, this may be explained by a romantic preference for the rural England that was disappearing. They could see the ugliness and squalor that were one side of industrialization (and these things were real enough; early-nineteenth-century Manchester was no garden suburb). They could not see the equally real benefits conferred by the cheapness of mass-produced consumer goods – novelists belonged to the minority of the population who could take the basic material amenities of life for granted. Rural poverty could look quite picturesque to the patrician outsider who viewed it from a distance; but, in harsh reality, 'rural life could often be the cruellest, most impoverished and most insanitary life of all.' Standards have risen, and we would not like to live in an early-Victorian industrial town now; yet something caused people at the time to flock to such towns from the countryside. (The idea that recruits to the urban working class were forced off the land by the Enclosure Acts is a myth: G.E. Mingay points out that most rural cottagers had no commoners' rights, and the rights that did exist before the enclosures were usually insufficient to offer a livelihood.)

The phrase 'cottage industry' has nowadays acquired idyllic connotations, and we feel that the transfer of manufacturing from rural households to large, regimented factories must have degraded the workers involved. But the people who knew eighteenth-century cottage industry at first hand knew that it was no kind of idyll. Ivy Pinchbeck has shown that the lot of women, in particular, was greatly improved by the transfer of manufacture from the home to the factory. As Martin Pawley points out, 'Freedom from direct servitude, a flexible private economy based on money instead of food, work which was comparatively highly paid and which women and children could also do, all conspired to encourage the poor to leave the land. . . . It was *population concentration* which made the defects of the old patterns of living suddenly manifest; disease, high infant mortality and short life expectancy had always been the lot of the poor. . . . ' The social conscience which was one of the attractive features of the Victorians led them to document the miseries of early industrial England fully and factually in a series of Royal Commission reports; pre-industrial life was seen through a factless haze of romantic nostalgia.

This romanticism was very obvious in the case of William Morris, leader of the Socialist League and founder of the Arts and Crafts movement. His *News from Nowhere*, published in 1890 and one of the most influential tracts of British socialism, depicted a future communist Britain as a mediaeval dream-world unsullied by the problems of housing, feeding, and clothing a modern population. In his poem-cycle *The Earthly Paradise*, Morris exhorted his readers to

> Forget the snorting steam and piston stroke,
> Forget the spreading of the hideous town,
> Think rather of the pack horse on the down,
> And dream of London, small, and white, and clean,
> The clear Thames bordered by its gardens green.

People nowadays who associate socialism and communism with urban, industrial life often fail to realize how strong a streak of utopian romanticism ran through the ideas of many of the founders of socialist thought. Friedrich Engels believed that English labourers before the Industrial Revolution were men of leisure, so healthy in mind as well as body that they never even allowed themselves to take too much to drink. Karl Marx expected communism to do away with the division of labour altogether; anyone will be able to 'hunt in the morning, fish in the afternoon, rear cattle in the evening, produce literary criticism after dinner'. And Marx's vision of communism seems restrained by comparison to Trotsky's, who looked forward to the day when 'The average human type will rise to the heights of an Aristotle. . . . And above this ridge new peaks will rise' – to say nothing of Fourier, who expected the seas to turn to lemonade and wild beasts to lose their ferocious nature.

By the end of the nineteenth century, though, even practical men were shifting towards belief in the need for State organization of society, impressed by the example of Bismarck's Germany which was rapidly overtaking Britain as the world's leading industrial power. In 1895 the future Edward VII announced that 'We are all Socialists nowadays.' Surely His Majesty would have been hard put to it to expound Marxist theory, but in the sense in which he meant his words they were true. Thinking, intellectually-influential men and women by the end of the century were convinced of the need for the State to expand its field of action far beyond its fundamental roles as defender against foreign aggression and guarantor of the laws –

roles which are essential State functions, in the sense that an organization not fulfilling them could not count as a 'State'. Expedience and morality alike required States to assume responsibility for a wide range of activities previously run largely by private arrangements – provision of education and medical services, insurance against unemployment, illness, and old age, housing, industrial investment, and many others. Naturally there were some thinkers who took a relatively extreme line and others who held out against the new orthodoxy, but it seems fair to say that the hold-outs were just that – people who were slow to abandon traditional beliefs. There was no systematic, positive intellectual alternative to socialism at the turn of the century, or for many decades afterwards. The first such countercurrent is the movement to be described in this book, and that is barely a dozen years old.

Although, intellectually, socialism had been 'in the air' for a long time, and many isolated steps – some of them quite large ones, such as the 1870 Education Act already mentioned – had been taken in a socialist direction, it was the Second World War which decisively converted the population at large to the idea of a full-blown Welfare State. The war generated a massive apparatus of central State direction of daily life: it conjured up armies of officials on a scale previously unknown in Britain. This apparatus was created in order to marshal all of Britain's resources into the service of an overriding goal. The British State between 1939 and 1945 had just two aims: to keep the civilian population alive at a minimum tolerable level, and to conquer the Axis; and the population shared those aims. If ever there was a just war, the war against Nazism was just – not in all aspects of its prosecution, but certainly in its ultimate purpose; and it was perceived by the average Briton as being just. When so little food was coming into the country, of course it was necessary to instal a complex rationing scheme to ensure that everyone got their share: the population demanded it. When the homes and perhaps the bodies of one's friends and relatives were being smashed daily by enemy bombs and artillery, of course one put up cheerfully with a myriad official restrictions and directives, as part of one's personal contribution towards the defeat of Germany. Niggles, even anger about individual

acts of officialdom that seemed idiotic or pointlessly harsh –
these reactions were frequent enough. But they led to no
general feeling of conflict of interest between the individual
citizen and the State. How could there be such a conflict? – the
British State was simply an agency for planning and
coordinating the efforts of individual citizens towards the goal
which virtually all of them passionately shared.

And this perception of the State long outlived the war which
had produced it. The war was won: planning had been seen to
work. If it was worth accepting State direction in one's daily life
in order to achieve the purely negative goal of defeating an
enemy, how much more worthwhile, surely, to accept it in
order to promote the positive goal of a better life for oneself and
one's fellow-citizens. 'We planned for War – now let us plan for
Peace,' so ran the slogan. That special issue of *Picture Post* was
surely one of the most accurate historical prophecies ever. The
Beveridge Report of November 1942, setting out a scheme of
'cradle to grave' State protection against the evils of sickness,
poverty, unemployment and ignorance, was the best-known of
a series of official reports dealing with different aspects of the
same theme. Words were translated into action: the Education
Act of 1944 might have been designed on the basis of the *Picture
Post*'s education article, the Town & Country Planning Act of
the same year went far towards meeting Maxwell Fry's
objections to private ownership of land by removing owners'
discretion over land-use while leaving the technical title to
property in owners' hands. The 1945 election produced a
landslide for the Labour Party, who were perceived as the party
most dedicated to Welfare State ideals; but those ideals, as Tom
Hopkinson had rightly predicted at New Year 1941, were now a
consensus, and through the 1950s and 1960s the Conservative
Party was scarcely less enthusiastic than Labour about
maintaining and developing the machinery that had been
installed in the immediate postwar years whereby the State
provided for all aspects of welfare.

This machinery was financed by high and steeply progressive
rates of taxation, rising at many periods to ninety-eight per cent
on income and, in real terms, to well over a hundred per cent on
capital growth, causing control over the investment of society's

resources to be transferred increasingly from private to public hands. It became common sense that the only way in which a modern society could operate was by entrusting all the big decisions to a cadre of benevolent, high-minded and disinterested officials, leaving the majority of the population to carry out routine functions at work and to entertain themselves after hours with the leisure facilities provided for them. If some wealthier citizens grumbled, it was easy – and, often, accurate – to dismiss that as representing personal selfishness and nothing more. Political philosophy as an intellectual discipline withered away, as the fundamental conflicts of interest that had wracked earlier centuries came to seem obsolete. Politics in a modern nation was not concerned with questions of State legitimacy and the individual's duty of allegiance, but with unphilosophical questions about the efficient running of various social services.

Since the middle 1970s that consensus has broken up. We have seen, now, what happens when the visions of that *Picture Post* plan are translated into reality, and we know how empty was its promise that the State could let us escape from economics into a secure, prelapsarian world sheltered from the harshnesses of life.

The old-fashioned 'courts and alleys' were torn down in city after city, and replaced by the tower-blocks and pedestrian precincts envisaged by Maxwell Fry. Those concrete plazas that looked so sunny and appealing in the 'artist's impressions' turned out to be windswept, rubbish-strewn breeding-grounds for vandals. Life in flats high above street level proved to involve psychological tensions that no one had anticipated; young mothers found themselves condemned to daily sentences of solitary confinement, cut off from the spontaneous contacts with neighbours that are inseparable from ground-floor living, frightened of the petty crime and filth in the corridors, and unable to keep an eye through the kitchen window on children playing outside. Repeatedly, the worst of these buildings have proved so uninhabitable that the local authority which built them at vast expense has had to demolish them long before paying off the loan by which they were financed. Narrow, crooked town streets have been replaced by wide roads which speed up traffic: at the cost of wrecking the complex, fragile web of relationships which make a district a human community rather than a mere area on a map. Contractors and councillors on the take, like the Tom Craig and Reg Palmer of TV's *Muck and Brass*, have made a killing out of 'comprehensive redevelopment', and architects have boosted their egos by realizing grandiose dreams in the shape of buildings they would not consider living in themselves, leaving ordinary people to scuttle about concrete deserts like beetles which have lost their way on a marble floor.

When the National Health Service was inaugurated, Beveridge's theory was that it would involve a heavy initial expense while the nation's backlog of maladies was treated, after which costs would fall back to a manageable level as the preventative rather than merely reactive approach to illness enabled the health of the population to be maintained at a high level. Almost forty years later there is no sign of demand slackening, and no one any longer imagines it ever will: 'The existence of shortages is inherent in any system of medical care which is more or less free at the point of access,' to quote a 1979 report by the Office of Health Economics. In October 1983 a junior health minister admitted that a thousand kidney patients are dying each year for want of treatment; more than once a month a child dies because he has had to wait too long for a bone-marrow transplant. Non-emergency conditions, often quite distressing to the sufferer, can involve years of waiting before one's turn for treatment arrives. Many doctors and others who work for the NHS strive with dedication to do a good job, but the system fails to support them. The costs of the service have risen by leaps and bounds in real terms, but extra spending has not achieved extra value: between 1965 and 1973, the number of staff employed by the service increased by 28 per cent, the average number of hospital beds occupied daily *fell* by 11 per cent (though there was no lack of patients queueing). Astonishingly, by 1976 there were actually fewer hospital beds in Britain than when the NHS took over in 1948. And anyone who hoped that the Welfare State would help to foster the dignity of Man must surely be depressed by the experience of visiting an NHS hospital as an out-patient. Amid a dreary décor, patients are moved from queue to queue like children too young to look after themselves. What needs to be done medically is done, but (if my own experiences are representative) there is little of the respect and attentiveness we take for granted in a commercial relationship where the retailer is glad to have our custom. In 1977 the Environmental Health Officers' Association reported on a survey of hospitals which found the food-handling areas of 153 of them to be so dirty that they would have been prosecuted if they were not immune from prosecution, being Crown property.

With the growth of medical knowledge, the emphasis in medicine has moved away from the GP whose bedside manner was as significant a part of his equipment as the limited resources of his black bag, and away from the cottage hospital which eased its patients' sufferings even if it could not cure them, towards high technology which depersonalizes the patient, turning him or her into raw material for ingenious medical processing. Expectant mothers, for instance, often find that maternity homes run childbirth as a five-day-a-week production line, and mums who threaten to go into labour over the weekend are 'induced' by artificial methods. Questioning such practices is very difficult when the layperson is faced not only with the mystique of doctors' professional authority but also with the awareness that one is not a paying customer. But the State does not always allow citizens who are disenchanted with medical practice to reject its attentions. Mrs Michelle Radley had had a baby in an NHS hospital and was repelled by the experience, so when her second was expected she and her husband asked their Regional Health Authority to arrange for a home delivery. When the Authority imposed impractical conditions (for example, private hire of a stand-by ambulance, and fumigation of the room), Mr Radley by-passed them by studying midwifery and attending his wife himself; following which, in August 1982, the Health Authority had him fined £100 under a law designed for a different purpose. (My second daughter was born in my unfumigated bedroom, with the nearest ambulance many miles away, in 1978, and has a row of baby-show prizes to prove that she did not suffer from the experience; there is evidence suggesting that since 1968 home deliveries may on average have been safer than deliveries in maternity homes and hospitals.)

In the educational field, the school-leaving age has been raised, and raised again. The selective system of secondary education was replaced by a 'comprehensive' system which opened the door to the late developer to find his own level. Universities have been expanded at State expense, and a host of new universities created, together with a series of local-authority-operated polytechnics to provide the less academic, more vocationally-oriented higher education that the Master of Balliol saw as necessary in 1941. To what end? Schools vary, but one does not have the impression that children are on the whole better-educated than they used to be; certainly many parents are convinced that educational standards are falling, and the word 'comprehensive' has acquired connotations of ill-bred, ignorant loutishness. Individual teachers are often hard-working and sincere, yet many of the schools they work in do not deliver the goods. Personal impressions are subjective and unreliable; but statistical research on exam results, too, suggests that reform of secondary education has severely worsened the performance, not just of those children who would have been grammar-school pupils, but of the average child. (A 1979 survey compared results in two socially-similar Manchester boroughs, one of which retained selection while the other had 'gone comprehensive': the average pupil in the selective borough obtained 52 per cent more passes at grades A to C at O Level, 31 per cent more at A Level. Even the secondary modern pupils tended to out-perform the comprehensive pupils in subjects such as English.)

Unlike individual parents, the State can lavish unlimited resources on the upbringing of a child, if it chooses to do so. At a DHSS centre for delinquent children in Brentwood, costs in 1977 amounted to the phenomenal sum of £20,000 per year *per child*. (This centre got into the news when it emerged that some of its staff made a practice of running errands to the tobacconist for their under-age charges, taking them out drinking, and fornicating with them.) But the State's priorities do not always coincide with a parent's. At age four the son of Claire Tomalin, literary editor of the *Sunday Times*, had above-average intelligence but a physical handicap which confined him to a wheelchair; because of his handicap, the Inner London Education Authority refuse to provide him a place at any but an understaffed special school which teaches no science and where no child takes exams beyond CSE (the ILEA explained to Mrs Tomalin that her child's initial IQ was 'artificially' high because he comes from an 'advantaged' home, and that she must expect it to fall). Many parents fear that schools nowadays are often concerned more to indoctrinate children in half-baked political attitudes than to educate them in any real sense. It is remarkable how many parents are finding the quite massive costs of private schooling for their children, despite having at the same time to pay through taxes for the State system: one man sold his house and moved into a caravan in order to keep his three boys in a private school.

As for universities, their arts faculties are often resented as extravagant luxuries, self-indulgent finishing-schools where the most favoured sector of our youth spends an agreeable three years living off taxes paid largely by their less fortunate fellow-citizens and putting off the need to earn a living, going on in some cases to do 'research' which is often wholly fatuous and even in the more respectable cases could adequately be carried out in the spare time of a paying job. People are more willing to respect the polytechnics and the science faculties of universities; yet the ostensible motive for State support in their case is the general benefits to be derived from a technology-led revival of Britain's economic performance, and this new industrial revolution has obstinately refused to materialize. (Perhaps I am too impatient; in 1983 there are signs that the information-technology field might really achieve for Britain what other industries have tried and failed to do in the past. If there is one individual who can be taken as representative for this particular 'sunrise industry', it is surely Sir Clive Sinclair, inventor and marketer of the pocket calculator, the home computer, and the flat-screen television. Like George Stephenson and Isambard Kingdom Brunel, Sir Clive did not undergo higher education; his electronics is self-taught.)

A State social security system guarantees the individual a modest income in case of illness or unemployment. But the State's terms seem designed to foster dependence among its claimants, rather than to encourage self-reliance. A man who loses his job and tries to keep his hand in by working for no pay commits an offence against the Supplementary Benefits Act, and this is no hypothetical legal quibble: people caught doing this are regularly convicted as criminals. A writer who was forced to give up work through illness but then succeeded in selling an idea for a future book to a publisher during his convalescence was not merely required to repay the State benefit received but convicted of an offence against the Social Security Act. On the other hand, for people who have no interest in supporting themselves and prefer shamelessly to play the system, rewards can be quite high. In 1980 two Italian teachers published a booklet called (in Italian) *How to live in England paid for by the English State*. The booklet, which sold well, explained that a visitor to Britain should register as unemployed on arrival, and claim rental expenses by buying a rent book and getting a friend to sign as 'landlord'; after which he or she could embark on the menu of discretionary payments – 'for example for new clothes for you and your children, for heating, if you are moving and must buy furniture. . . . If you are refused you can appeal and stand every chance of success, as the commission which decides is composed of people who do not work for social security.' Overall, the booklet concluded, a savvy visitor ought to be able to milk the State for about £200 a month. (Even after more than three years of 'Thatcherism', in November 1982 an unemployed man pointed out in the *Times* that if it were not for part-time earnings by his wife his State benefits would be equivalent to an annual pre-tax income of £9,000, substantially more than he expected to earn when he found a job.) In 1983 a GP announced that he was convinced that some of his girl patients were deliberately becoming pregnant in order to get access to the range of State benefits available to the unmarried mother. The truth of such a charge is near-impossible to establish, but many inhabitants of contemporary British society did not find it implausible.

The Welfare State is an expensive State; so taxes are heavy. However, the weight of taxation might be tolerable if the pain of being a taxpayer were limited to parting with cash – but it is not. The injustice and inhumanity of taxation in modern Britain distorts our lives and oppresses us in ways that have little to do with spending foregone. Both for a business and for the individual, extra time and effort spent reorganizing activities so as to reduce tax bills is commonly the most financially-rewarding way to use resources – yet this kind of work is in itself wholly unfulfilling and unproductive, it contributes no goods or services whatever to the national pool. There is a great deal one could say about the impact of taxation on business. But what arouses people's political passions is its impact on people. The collection of income tax has become an affair in which, behind closed doors, individual citizens are stripped of their human dignity. A proportion of the population sees nothing of these things: someone who simply draws wages or a salary and takes no commercial initiatives of his own may be only vaguely aware of the tax that is deducted from his earnings before he receives them. To anyone who contributes enterprise to society, rather than merely executing a function prescribed by an employer, the Inland Revenue shows a different face. When it suspects a discrepancy – sometimes tiny, and often mistakenly – its implacable, Kafkaesque harassment can drive taxpayers to breakdown, even suicide.

The author Vincent Brome was required to locate ex-girlfriends he had lived with ten or fifteen years earlier – and in some cases parted from on bad terms, as couples will – in order to beg for signed confirmations that they had contributed to his living expenses. If anyone else suggested such a proceeding, one would knock him down; but with the Inland Revenue one must swallow one's manhood and obey – the taxpayer is treated as guilty of earning income unless he can prove his innocence, and rates of tax are such that few people can afford to say 'Here, take the extra money and leave my private life alone.' In my experience, employees of the Inland Revenue tend to be grey, socially-inadequate personalities who in a decent society would be tactfully shunted away from positions giving them power over others; but the State must staff its tax-gathering operation somehow. When my tax inspector summoned me before him (not because of underpayment or failure to provide information, but exclusively so that I could receive a dressing-down for the insufficiently respectful tone of my correspondence), the merest polite hint was felt sufficient to conclude the interview:

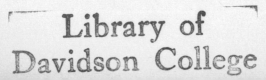

'Take care, Mr Sampson; I should be very sorry if we found ourselves needing to take a closer interest in you.' The words might have been lifted from some cheap thriller about the Gestapo. The artist H.M. Bateman 'actually saw an [income-tax] official dribbling at the mouth, at the thought that he could do exactly what he wanted with a person.' Disenchanted recruits to the VAT control service in 1978 described their experience of induction courses on which a higher officer 'spoke of the "untold delights" of witnessing the trader trembling with fear on his arrival'. For Englishmen, the knock on the door at midnight used to be an evocative symbol of foreign tyranny. Nowadays, for the shopkeeper or other small trader it heralds the arrival of the bully-boys from VAT control, who are empowered to enter premises by force if necessary and ransack them for evidence of fraud, and who know the best hours to catch their victims with defences down.

The Inland Revenue appears to recognize no constraints of decency on the methods used to achieve its ends. David Kelly, a Harrogate antiques dealer, scorned underhand evasion and openly refused to pay a particular levy which he regarded as morally unjustifiable. After a spell in goal failed to break him, in 1977 the Revenue proceeded to find a legal way of threatening his mother with prison in order to force him to give in.

It is no answer to say that people who pay their taxes honestly need have no fear. In the first place that is just not true: tax rules are so insanely labyrinthine that impeccably honest people are every week being driven to distraction or the tranquillizer-bottle by worries that some aspect of their affairs may prove to involve unforeseen tax liabilities which they will be unable to meet. And it can be very difficult not to become an offender: in the case of VAT, for instance, returns must be submitted every quarter on the dot, and in the eyes of the law illness or a dilatory accountant are no excuse for lateness. But, furthermore, few of us any longer hold a view of our duties to the State which bears much relation to what six-hundred-odd middle-aged men and women whom we hear on the radio brawling like third-formers in a problem school have declared to be 'the law'. (Would one advise a friend not to fear muggers because, provided you hand over your wallet without demur, they will leave you unharmed?) It is not as if our legislators feel bound to share the burdens they impose on the rest of us; again and again in recent years laws have been juggled so as to exempt MPs in general or ministers in particular from the consequences of new tax measures. And how can anyone respect a tax system which, for instance, requires many couples to pay thousands a year extra because they have committed themselves to providing a stable home life for their children by marrying rather than simply living together?

Britain fought the Second World War to win it. In the course of fighting it, many brave and not-so-brave Britons were sent to their deaths; the act of declaring war made that inevitable. That said, the State devoted great resources to preserving the lives of its civilian citizens. A year before the war began, thirty-eight million gas-masks had already been issued; the entire output of the Scottish jute industry was being used to make sandbags. Air-raid shelters were distributed free to householders with gardens. Many millions of children, pregnant women, and mothers with babies were evacuated from cities to safe areas; by the beginning of the war one and a half million people staffed the Civil Defence services.

If Britain's integrity is threatened by a war now it will be a nuclear war, and in a nuclear war there will be no 'safe areas'. Our safety now, the State tells us, lies in deterrence rather than in any measures that might be taken if deterrence fails; some local authorities have distributed leaflets to householders telling them how to rig up makeshift fallout shelters in their kitchens, but beyond that we are left to our own devices – a government-sponsored report on medical services after a nuclear attack recommends, for example, putting those suffering from radiation sickness out of their misery by smashing their skulls with a large stone.

There is a grim logic to this attitude; but the State does not apply that logic to itself – government has no intention of perishing through radiation sickness. After the Soviet invasion of Afghanistan I asked some local worthies in the village where I live whether any thought had been given to preparation for war. We are a remote, sheep-farming area, and I could well have understood that the subject might have appeared too hypothetical and apocalyptic for local government to grapple

with; but not a bit of it. The District Councillor in the group
began to expound the plans with enthusiasm and (I suspect) less
discretion than he should have. Immediately after an attack,
until communications with the District capital twenty miles
away are re-established, our village will be governed from the
cellar of a named pub; from there, a neighbour who chairs the
local Bench will rule us with just two punishments at his
disposal, 'the lash, and death'. Further plans provide for the
orderly reintegration of government through district and
regional to national levels (in 1982 our local paper, whose front
page usually concentrates on ads for grazing rentals and stock
auctions, got into hot water through an unaccustomed bout of
investigative journalism which leaked the District Council's
secret plans to provide its personnel with a nuclear bolt-hole).
'All this is impressive,' I commented to our councillor, 'but
what is going to be done for the rest of us?' He looked blank. A
few months later, military exercise 'Square Leg' drew national
attention to the situation; as the *Times* commented, 'there are no
shelters or evacuation plans for the public, the Government has
spent its money mainly on the means of preserving a skeleton of
government.'

In February 1983 the Defence Minister, Michael Heseltine,
showed some indignation at suggestions that American nuclear
missiles in Britain should be under dual-key control; America is
our ally, he pointed out, and allies trust one another not to act
without mutual consultation. Knowledgeable American
commentators soon put him right: if a decision is made to fire
the missiles, that decision will be made by Americans alone. As
Henry Kissinger has put it, 'it will not be in anyone's interest if
the chief protector of free world security is hamstrung by
bureaucratic procedure. . . . ' Yet our governors still insist that
a dual key is unnecessary (according to reports circulating in
Washington, Mrs Thatcher requested it from President Reagan
in confidence and accepted no as an answer). Apparently those
who rule us care more about the gentlemanliness of their
relationship with their American opposite numbers than about
the rational fears of tens of millions of their subjects.

In the bad old Britain that Bert Coombes and the *Picture Post*
wanted to see swept away, society (as they saw it) was divided

into two camps: a mass of struggling, exploited workers, and a boss class brought up to believe that 'only the best was good enough for them', who lived well by dint of screwing down their employees' wages and throwing them out of work for the slightest reason. It was not just inefficient but downright immoral to leave the deployment of the nation's resources of human strength and talent to a host of private owners of capital, who – even if no more than averagely selfish by nature – could not be expected to take much account of the needs either of society as a whole or of their employees. The commanding heights of the economy, at least, ought to be removed from private ownership and become the property of the British nation, to be run for the benefit of the nation as a whole and of the individuals who devoted their lives to working in them.

And so it came to pass. Bert Coombes did not have very long to wait; coal was the first industry to be nationalized. I still have a picture-history of Britain which I was given for a boyhood birthday – the usual kind of slightly-naive compilation paying more attention to the triumphs than the moments of disgrace. Almost the last picture is one taken on New Year's Day, 1947, showing a group of sturdily-beaming miners in Derbyshire surrounding a notice announcing that 'This Colliery is now Managed by the NATIONAL COAL BOARD on Behalf of the People.' Other industries, such as electricity and steel, soon followed. And a series of new industrial-relations laws has vastly increased the bargaining power of employees and their representatives as against the owners of those industries which remain in private hands, so that for instance it is now very difficult for an employer to dismiss an unsatisfactory employee. (In 1978 a man used his job on the night shift at Vauxhall Motors in Luton as an opportunity to take off shoes and socks in a quiet corner, pull a blanket over himself, and catch up on his sleep; Vauxhall dismissed him and claimed that they would be a 'laughing stock' if they took him back, and they were fined £7,319 for failing to do so.)

But these changes in the position of the worker have turned out to be no sort of recipe for industrial harmony. No doubt some nineteenth-century employers were harsh to their workers – though it is known that many were highly enlightened and actively concerned to provide good working conditions, long before there was any public pressure on them to do so. But when the tables are turned and employees are given the leading role in deciding what happens at work, it seems that they are capable of being fully as cruel to one another as any Gradgrind ever was to them.

In March 1979 there was a methane explosion in a mine at Golborne, Lancashire; three miners were killed instantly, and eight survivors were horribly burned (over the next few days, all but one of them were to die). They were taken to Withington Hospital in Manchester, which has a special burns unit. Hospital ancillary workers belonging to the National Union of Public Employees happened to be striking for higher pay, and their pickets at Withington turned back deliveries of oxygen and other medical gases vital to the miners' treatment, impervious to 'pleading' by the hospital administrators.

Nor do workers show greater mercy to those whose weakness makes them wholly dependent on the goodwill of society's breadwinners. In May 1977 participants in a local hospital-workers' strike over work rotas prevented food deliveries to a hospital for mentally-handicapped children, and to another hospital for geriatric patients. (At the latter, five girls with food-parcels broke through the picket line amid showers of sticks and abuse.) At Broadgreen Hospital, Liverpool, another hospital-porters' strike in pursuit of higher pay, in May 1982, proceeded by 'blacking' surgical operations. Wanting to limit the public odium incurred, the strikers' shop steward made an exception for emergency operations, but the decision about what counted as an emergency was his alone: he crossed five cases off a list drawn up by a consultant surgeon where he regarded immediate surgery as imperative, threatening 'appropriate action' if the surgeon went ahead nevertheless. The regional organizer of his union supported him, explaining that it is 'very easy for people who work in hospitals to distinguish what is an emergency and what is not just by looking at the patient'.

Bert Coombes complained about employers depriving men of the right to work when work was waiting to be done. Now, employees do this to one another. Some examples are trivial: in 1981 an eighty-three-year-old woman arrived by taxi at Gatwick Station, and the taxi driver tried to carry her luggage onto the platform for her. The ticket collector prevented him: no one but a railway porter was allowed to do this work, and, though there were currently no porters, taxi drivers were forbidden to come onto the platform in case, one day, there might be some. Other examples are far more serious. A large goods distribution centre was built at the major rail junction of Didcot, with a view to getting better use out of the rail network by transferring containers offloaded from ships to Didcot and forwarding the contents from there rather than distributing them by road from ports. But in 1977 the dockers declared that this work belonged to them; railwaymen were eager to operate the Didcot centre, but it could not be used because any forwarding agent using Didcot would find all his work 'blacked' at any port.

This case involved conflict between groups of workers. More poignant is the treatment by organized labour of individuals.

Mr Smith was a toolsetter for Jaguar at Coventry. In 1976 he had been working for them for sixteen years; his shop steward, Mr Stapleton, had twice had occasion to reprove him for working too hard. In October, because a dispute had arisen with the management, Mr Stapleton came to Mr Smith's workplace and ordered him in an offensive tone to stop work. Before doing so, Mr Smith allowed himself to take two minutes to screw a cap on part of his machine. At union insistence, for this two minutes' insubordination towards the guardian of his interests he was demoted by Jaguar and, when he refused to accept demotion, sacked. As the union convenor put it to the Industrial Tribunal to which Mr Smith appealed, 'Mr Smith is a quiet, reserved man who had probably made up his mind he was not going to conform . . . in a factory like Jaguar . . . one man being awkward can cause tremendous difficulties. . . . In any organized society we all have to conform and do things we are not particularly in favour of.'

Back in 1964 a lad just out of school went to work at a dye works in Baildon, Yorkshire; there had been a strike which he understood to be over and done with, and he stayed in the job for about three months. Unknown to him, the firm was still blacked. Fourteen years later, now a thirty-two-year-old father of three, the man was recognized, stripped of his union card, and, since his current employer operated a closed shop, sacked.

Union officials refused to discuss the matter with the press.

The State-enforced shift of bargaining power away from employers towards employees was meant to let workers stop feeling like pawns, subject to the arbitrary whims of a higher authority. But collective bargaining requires an organization to do the bargaining: the effect of the power-shift has been to transform trades unions into a new and sinister source of authority. No longer are workers' aspirations represented to employers by men chosen from the shopfloor by their mates for their ability to express their shared views. Nowadays, trades unions are rich and powerful institutions; running them is a profession in its own right, and one far removed from the work of their membership. Trades union leaders like to impose closed-shop agreements on their members' workplaces, enabling them to devote less effort to winning and retaining members, and legislation in the 1970s made it increasingly easy for them to achieve this. In mid-1974 the leaders of a small printers' union called SLADE decided they needed to expand. Over the following months they approached a series of firms more or less remotely connected with printing and announced that they required the entire workforce to join SLADE, the alternative being use of the 'blacking' weapon to bankrupt the firms concerned. (As SLADE's negotiator put it on one occasion, 'You join by 10 o'clock tomorrow or you're out of business.') The threat was not idle: managements were forced to herd their workers into SLADE despite, in some cases, massive votes to reject SLADE's approach.

Trades unions are classified legally as provident societies, giving them advantages such as tax exemption, and there was a time when a chief purpose of unions was to help members in sickness, old age, and unemployment. In 1976 less than 6 per cent of the income of Clive Jenkins's ASTMS was spent on benefits to members, 94 per cent going on administration – including running the union staff college in a country house near Bishop's Stortford, where trainees are offered own-label wines. (The total spent on benefits to members by the National Union of Bank Employees that year was £3.) The largest union, the Transport & General Workers Union, has spent £6 million building a 'Leisure Centre' on Eastbourne sea-front, a 133-

bedroom luxury hotel reserved for the union and likely to be used by few of its rank-and-file members; it has bought a hotel in London specifically for the use of its officers. Union leaders are as jealous of their privileges as *Ancien Régime* aristocrats; shortly before he was elected General Secretary of the TGWU, in February 1977, Moss Evans advocated a return to the seventeenth-century system of State licensing of newspapers, in order to force them to be more respectful towards trades unions. Even the magazine *Marxism Today* recognized in August 1982 that union officers are now an 'elite' motivated more by love of an easy life than by care for their members' interests. A Conservative MP interested in industrial relations spent several days at a large plant in South Wales, at the end of which he took the chief shop steward out to a convivial lunch. The shop steward chatted freely about his hopes of rising from shop floor up through the local and, ultimately, national union hierarchy. At the end of the meal the MP drew his guest's attention politely to the fact that he had not mentioned the members he was supposed to represent. The answer was brief: 'To hell with them.'

The citizen's welfare includes security from crime; and a State cannot assure its citizens' welfare without preserving itself from subversion. The 'sharp end' of the State is the police force. Historically, police are a novelty in Britain. In theory, even today, a policeman is no more than someone paid to uphold the law by doing things that anyone can do in his private capacity. In 1829 Sir Robert Peel issued instructions to his new force of Metropolitan Police, which recruits still have to learn by heart:

> The constable will be civil and obliging to all people of every rank and class . . . particular care is to be taken that the constables of the police do not form false notions of their duties and powers . . .

Obviously, the very existence of organized police forces guarantees that they will form a subculture of their own, that a policeman will inevitably be much more than just a citizen who happens to spend his time enforcing the law. The BBC's genial PC Dixon of Dock Green was an idealization, belonging to a period when the media deferred to British institutions in a way that is now obsolete. Yet the image was not wholly false. In the 1950s, police really were a part of the communities they policed: they patrolled on foot or got around on push-bikes in the country, and they were known as individuals to the residents of their beat. Their uniform alone set them apart from others on the street; foreigners would marvel at the fact that, even when pursuing armed criminals, British police carried no guns.

In the 1970s, bobbies turned into cops. The police nowadays speed about in garishly-painted cars with science-fiction electronic sirens, and materialize in the shape of hostile strangers at an incident provoking their attention. In 1981 the Metropolitan Police decided something needed to be done about street crime in Brixton; rather than stepping up the tiny amount of foot-patrolling going on there on a regular basis, they mounted a temporary 'Operation Swamp' in which an army of policemen were suddenly drafted in to stop and search potential muggers. In one week, 943 people were stopped and searched, 118 arrested, 75 charges brought – which implies 825 unjustified friskings and 43 wrongful arrests. (In the following week Brixton erupted in the worst riot in recent British history.) There are far *more* police now than before: over the twenty years to 1982, the effective strength of the Metropolitan Police doubled (including its civilian employees, who now do many tasks that used to be covered by the police themselves). Police spokesmen like to suggest that such increases are necessary to cope with a massive growth of crime – but in fact the only kinds of crime that are seriously on the increase are categories such as mugging and stealing from parked cars, for which the only relevant policing is the bobby on the beat. Serious crimes such as homicide, rape, fraud, forgery, and receiving are on a falling trend in London.

In March 1979 the chairman of the Police Federation blamed the increasing violence of criminals for the fact that, as he put it, the police had had to 'take over the role of executioner', having shot three people dead in as many months. Perhaps there is some justice in his point of view. But in 1983 it was found unnecessary to discipline a group of police who had surrounded an unarmed man in a Mini and repeatedly shot him because they mistook him for a suspect; this must surely suggest that the police are becoming too trigger-happy altogether?

Each of us has his own sticking-point. To me it happens to be the identity card issue which epitomizes the changed nature of the British State.

In Continental countries which I know, citizens are required to register their address with the police, and in many countries citizens must carry cards by which the police can identify them. This has always seemed to me an obnoxious system; I used to be proud to think that, in Britain, it is none of the police's business to keep track of everyone's whereabouts. I remember my mother telling me how, after the war, the police wished to retain the system of identity cards that was introduced as a wartime emergency measure, and how the idea had to be abandoned when citizens burned their cards to demonstrate their refusal to cooperate.

Well, yes. But virtually anyone who might be interesting to the police needs a driving licence. Driving licences used to be little red booklets issued by county authorities, serving their ostensible functions and nothing more. In 1976 the local licensing system was replaced by a centralized system: the new, green licences are all issued through a massive computer installation in Swansea. In the bottom right-hand corner of the new licences is printed the holder's birthdate: not very relevant for driving, but the pairing of name with birthday is the way the police keep track of individuals. But how nice: the Driver and Vehicle Licensing Centre has anticipated the sensitivities of ladies at the wheel, and of the rest of us who see no reason to make it easy for nosy cops to check us out, by printing a dotted line across that corner of the licence and inviting the holder to snip it off. So gallant . . . until you realize that the 'Driver Number' at the top of the licence contains the same digits in a simple permutation. If a driving-licence holder changes his address, he is required to report the change to the DVLC at Swansea immediately; and the DVLC transmits an update of these records to the Police National Computer at Hendon on a daily basis. In turn, the policeman on patrol can get access to the PNC data within minutes via his radio link with the computer-terminal operator in his station. Personally I would much prefer an honest system of compulsory registration direct with the police, so that we all knew where we stood.

In case any reader is naive enough to imagine that the police use these records strictly to check whether individuals are entitled to drive, I might add that phone calls overheard in police stations have shown that the Police National Computer version of the vehicle files incorporates information such as individuals' membership in the Anti-Blood Sports League, the National Council for Civil Liberties, or the Gay Activists Alliance. The Thames Valley force has gone a stage further: since 1974 it has maintained (and attempted to keep secret) a computerized bank of data about persons living in its area, with room for dossiers on a quarter or more of the adult male population. One man's file includes a statement that he 'fancies small boys', based on gossip overheard by a policeman's wife in a village shop.

I have tried to make my general points more vivid by quoting individual examples. There is nothing exceptional about the few I have space to mention. It would be easy to fill this book with comparable cases from my files, which are drawn from newspapers and magazines in wide circulation and do not represent any laborious delving into inaccessible byways of information. The kinds of phenomena I have discussed form the very warp and weft of British public life in the 1970s and early 1980s. Many people are able to close their eyes to these things. Members of the State salariat often choose to read newspapers which give little prominence to such issues, and they persuade themselves to take the State's activities at face value, as genuinely contributing to the welfare of the population. Often they have highly agreeable and rewarding careers which are entirely dependent on the continued existence of the Welfare State: every regime has its bought men, who very rarely, I imagine, are consciously aware that they have been bought. But for any intelligent person with eyes to see, and whose judgment is not distorted by dependence on the State, it has become hard in the 1980s not to recognize the pattern behind jigsaw-pieces like the ones I have quoted.

The Welfare State was a noble idea in its way. But it rested on an unexamined premiss: the premiss that a corps of mandarins would be capable of organizing the details of individual citizens' lives more satisfactorily than the individuals could do for themselves, so that it made sense to entrust our resources to the experts and let them get on with the job. That *Picture Post* editor never discussed the question of whether his contributors would be able to make good on their grand promises. He did not need to discuss it; the man in the street in the 1940s was humbler and more deferential than today, and eminence in professional fields such as architecture or scholarship evoked automatic respect. Now we have tried giving the experts their head, and everything they touch has turned to dross. There is no need to postulate bad faith. With few exceptions, the Platonic guardians we have put in charge of our lives are genuinely anxious to do good, but they are utterly incapable of achieving the goals mapped out for them. Unwittingly they have built a monster they cannot control.

Small wonder that ordinary, decent, middle-of-the-road Britons have become disrespectful or actively hostile towards expertise and authority in all its forms. There are still a few people about whose reaction to the bankruptcy of Welfare-State socialism is to advocate ever more extreme collectivist creeds, by-passing the Labour Party and sporting the unamiable clenched fist of the Socialist Workers' Party. Others, particularly in the Liberal Party, argue that the problem lies in the size of the units of government, and urge that our troubles will be solved by pushing the locus of political decisions down from national to local levels. (I find this idea quite implausible, considering that the lower one goes in the hierarchy of government the less restraint is used in the exercise of power. At national level there is some feeling for constitutional limits on executive action and the rights of the individual against his rulers, while the kind of local busybodies who offer themselves for election to parish councils tend to see the few statutory powers entrusted to them as gifts from God to be used just as they wish and opposition as *lèse-majesté*.) But it is striking how many people nominally committed to collectivist brands of politics are nowadays arguing against all the consequences that flow from collectivism in practice. Evan Luard (then Labour MP for Oxford) published a book in 1979 advocating *Socialism Without the State* – an idea that seemed as contradictory to me when I finished the book as it had seemed before, but Luard makes it clear that he finds life under the Welfare State as intolerable as do those of us who have been less responsible for administering it. In 1982 Patricia Hewitt, now looking after Neil Kinnock's public relations, published *The Abuse of Power*, a valuable guide to ways in which the State has escaped from parliamentary control in imposing an ever-deepening tyranny on the individual. Professor Alec Nove's 1983 book *The Economics of Feasible Socialism*, while purporting to sketch a realistically possible 'socialist' future, is devoted mainly to making very clear that socialism as normally understood, whether in Marxian theory or East European practice, rests on hopelessly confused intellectual foundations.

Socialism won't wash with Britons any longer; the Welfare State has come to feel like a senile parent, foolishly attempting to organize his adult children's lives as if they were still five-year-olds. The liberalism of the mid-nineteenth century eventually failed, because as an ideology it was confined to an educated elite while the mass of simple people still took for granted a mediaeval model of society as a family in which they were the children; when the poor gained political power, they enforced policies appropriate to that paternal model. But now the traditional proletariat is melting away, and most people display educated, middle-class attitudes. We don't want to be harsh to the aged parent; it gave us a good start in life from Magna Carta onwards, and we still like taking foreign visitors to see Buckingham Palace. But we are grown-ups now. We have our own lives to lead; we have outgrown allegiance.

There is a terrible irony in the nature of the society which has been built on principles formulated in the war-wracked Britain of forty years ago. Consider the following:

. . . the State shall make it its first duty to promote the industry and livelihood of citizens. . . . The activities of the individual may not clash with the interests of the whole, but must proceed within the frame of the community and be for the general good. We demand therefore: abolition of incomes unearned by work . . . nationalization of all [monopolies] . . . that the profits from wholesale trade shall be shared out . . . extensive development of provision for old age . . . The Common Interest before Self.

These words come close to being a description of the Britain we live in. They are quoted from the manifesto of the National

Socialist German Workers' Party, commonly called the Nazi
Party. No one would be such a fool as to equate Welfare State
Britain with Nazi Germany; the horrific aspects of Nazism, its
slaughter of racial minorities and brutal suppression of dissent,
are unknown here. But these features, although by far the most
notorious aspects of Nazism, were not its essence. The average
German who supported the Nazis in the 1930s did not do so
because he wanted Jews to be exterminated in gas chambers; he
did so because he wanted Germany to become the kind of
society which *Picture Post* held out as the hope for Britain, and
he believed the Nazis were most likely to bring this about.
Glancing through that number of *Picture Post* with the benefit
of forty years' hindsight, it is striking how close its vision of the
good society was to the vision approved by the regime Britain
was fighting. Healthy young men and women frolic by a
swimming pool, as if in a piece of propaganda for the Strength
Through Joy movement – but where are the proportion of fat
and old bodies that must exist under any system? A crowd hikes
off into the countryside like German *Wandervogel* – but what
about the people who prefer to stop indoors, listen to records,
and smoke cigarettes? Those massive concrete structures of the
future: how reminiscent they are of the grandiose architectural
schemes which Hitler and Albert Speer planned for the Reich.
(On both sides of the war there was enthusiasm for the way in
which the Blitz was clearing the ground for a planned utopia; in
1944 Maxwell Fry condemned the futility of insisting that
towns should be allowed to evolve naturally by describing how
'the bombs . . . blew a whole silly theory sky high with the
blast,' and he was echoed by Josef Goebbels in February 1945:
'the bombs . . . have only smashed the prison walls. . . . In
trying to destroy Europe's future the enemy has only succeeded
in smashing its past.') The cover of the magazine is devoted to a
massive close-up of a group of bonny, bouncing babies,
inheritors of the New Britain. Unconsciously, the
photographer has chosen a shot in which every child in the
foreground has fair hair.

And what of that Welsh miner and his son, staring wistfully
into the future above the magazine's lead article?

In 1979 someone found the son, Peter Coombes, now a

coach-driver in his fifties. His father, it turned out, was scarcely an average miner moved to unaccustomed literary activity by the plight of his family and his 'mates'. In reality he was a writer by avocation (a book of memoirs had been published by the Left Book Club in 1939, and a big sea chest was overflowing with rejected manuscripts). His statement that he had been laid off work by the colliery which employed him had been, it seems, a falsehood. Nor did Bert Coombes have any reason to claim that his country had rejected his son's natural aptitude as a mechanic – when the article was written Peter had already started work as a garage hand. Bert Coombes, it appeared, was a self-dramatizing, self-pitying, self-centred bully: that moving photograph of father and son gazing into the future from a Welsh hillside, posed for the benefit of the Coombes's visitors from the London literary world, was the first and last occasion on which the father ever tolerated the son's company beyond strict necessity. After his death, Peter discovered that Bert Coombes was not even his father's real name. Everything about that *Picture Post* story was a sham. As sham as the promises of a better life in a housing unit nine floors above a sodium-lighted urban clearway.

3/Return of the Invisible Hand

The central idea shared by all liberals, whatever else they may disagree about, is the excellence of the market as an organizing principle for society.

Homo sapiens is a gregarious animal. Few aspects of our lives are completely private, in the sense that they do not depend in any way on others' cooperation and have no implications at all for others' welfare. Almost everything we do is a communal enterprise. A bachelor, relaxing alone with his record collection of an evening, can do so because people (perhaps long dead) wrote the music; other people learned to play instruments (which other people again manufactured); more people made record-players and records – and, indeed, further people made the armchair he sits in, built and repaired the house sheltering him, and so on, endlessly. A shepherd trudging the fells to look after his flock may not see another human from beginning to end of his working day, but his work has a purpose only because in due course people unknown to him will be turning wool into suits which other people will wear. It is a truism that society is an interdependent, immensely complex web. A decision made at any point transmits its implications from thread to thread of the web in ever-ramifying chains of consequences which reach out to touch even members of the society who are very remote from the decision point.

This being so, there is no possibility of individuals conducting their lives without reference to the decisions of other individuals. The question is not whether this would be desirable: it is not possible. An individual, or a small group of individuals, engaged in productive work can choose to organize their work this way or that way, but almost any such decision will have implications for the nature of the inputs to the work – the materials they are busy processing into something else, the location occupied to do the job, the number of people that are needed to do it, and so forth – together with implications for the nature of the products. One individual's or group's products are another individual's or group's inputs; consumers cannot choose what range of goods to consume without reference to what is being made available by producers, and producers in turn are dependent on others' output. Even a creative artist uses materials. In any human society there must be *some* means, perhaps efficient or perhaps inefficient, perhaps morally admirable or perhaps abominable, by which the activities of its members are coordinated – which resolves the various choices that individuals might be disposed to make in isolation into a set of decisions that are compatible taken as a whole, so that nobody is processing or consuming anything which does not exist because it has not been produced.

There are two contrasting principles by which this coordination can be achieved. Any actual society uses a mixture of the two, but the proportions vary greatly from one place and time to another. The principle which, arguably, seems most natural is the principle of planning and command. The task of finding an efficient and fair solution to the coordination problem is an immensely complex task, so a competently-staffed organ of State is charged to work out a satisfactory solution, and the State delegates to this body the authority to impose its solution on individuals in their roles as producers and consumers. The opposite principle is that of the market. Under this principle, the State claims no authority to dispose of the various resources within society, each of which is controlled instead by some particular individual or voluntarily-established institution. No overall plan of coordination is formulated, and instead a pattern of coordination emerges spontaneously as individuals attempt to satisfy their wants as consumers by engaging with others in voluntary exchanges of the resources under their respective control (including their labour).

The right to control and dispose of a resource is what we commonly call 'ownership' or 'property'; so we may describe the contrasting principles by saying that the pure market solution requires even the physical, inanimate resources of society to be treated as individuals' private property, while the pure command solution requires even people in their productive capacity to be treated as State property. Each of these implications seems unattractive to many people; as already suggested, many societies occupy something like a halfway house between the two extremes.

Liberal-minded commentators sometimes talk as if the market approach were innately natural to humans, whereas the growth of State intervention and the command system for resolving the social coordination problem were a twentieth-century innovation. This seems to me a profound mistake. Surely, if the problem of coordinating millions or tens of millions of individuals' lives is as difficult as I have suggested, the natural thing is to suppose that a satisfactory solution requires a great deal of careful and well-informed thought. If we want to minimize waste and to maximize the extent to which people's multifarious actions serve each other's needs, then painstaking and detailed planning seems to be called for. Perhaps plans can never be perfect, but imperfect planning must surely be better than just sitting back and leaving everything to the accidents of billions of decisions made by millions of independent individuals few of whom know, or care, very much about the implications of their decisions for society in general. Certainly there are plenty of cases of command systems whose plans realize values other than fairness and efficient satisfaction of the population's wants; but, if we want these values to be realized, it would seem that we need a carefully-organized command system to do it, since a market system is not guided by any overall aims at all. Any wise man tries to plan his own affairs, rather than just drifting at the mercy of every momentary gust and current in life. Surely we owe it to ourselves and to one another to arrange for society's affairs to be organized at least as carefully as we organize our own?

This, I should have thought, would be virtually anyone's instinctive response to the contrast between command and market principles; and historically the application of the command principle was until fairly recently limited mainly by the technical limits to the capacity of pre-modern States to make and impose detailed economic plans, rather than by any doubts about the theoretical virtues of the command principle. In Britain we have been moving during the last century away from the market and towards the command principle, and the very sophisticated information-gathering resources available to a modern State make it possible for the command principle to be implemented nowadays to an extent that would not have been feasible a century or two ago. But, from a longer historical perspective, it seems to be the command principle which is traditional and the market principle which is a novelty. In the seventeenth century Louis XIV's finance minister Colbert set out to regulate French industry to a degree of detail that has scarcely been approached in twentieth-century Britain even in wartime: his thousands of pages of *règlements* went as far as to dictate the number of threads in each width of cloth.

Not until two hundred years ago was the remarkable idea first propounded that the market system is actually better than the command system at achieving the very goals which motivate the command system's idealistic supporters. The classic statement of the virtues of the market was Adam Smith's *Wealth of Nations*, published in 1776. As Smith put it, in a market system based on private property each participant 'neither intends to promote the public interest, nor knows how much he is promoting it . . . he intends only his own gain, and he is in this . . . led by an invisible hand to promote an end which was no part of his intention. . . . By pursuing his own interest he frequently promotes that of the society more effectually than when he really intends to promote it.'

Smith's 'invisible hand' is for liberals a key concept in understanding the functioning of society. Any attempt to invoke State power to modify society's workings, liberals argue, is likely to lead to results which are the opposite of those intended. Society is a delicately-balanced, self-regulating machine, and if we find that things are going amiss in some area of society the liberal's reaction is to look for a cause in terms of unnecessary State regulation of some activity, or failure to parcel out some collectively-held resource into a set of private property rights – and certainly not to institute new laws or regulations in an attempt to cure the malady by force.

Why should anyone believe such an implausible idea? That is

a longish story. First, let me try to make the idea less implausible by illustrating it via a concrete example: the housing shortage.

Let us go back, one last time, to the case of Bert Coombes, the Welsh miner of Chapter 2. The reader will remember that he began life as a farm worker, and moved to a mining area eighty miles away when farm work ceased to pay. He did not describe the actual move itself as a major step, and probably it wasn't; in those days it was easy to find rented accommodation if someone decided to up sticks and move across the country for work or any other reason. That is not true now. As somebody recently put it, in the 1980s a decision by a man in humble circumstances to move to a job beyond commuting distance from his current home requires something akin to a military operation. In 1978 a Walsall paper noted that even middle-class people such as teachers and nurses coming to jobs in its area were being forced to live in the Salvation Army hostel because no alternatives were available; and there was nothing special about Walsall. The problem exists nationwide, and it has one paradoxical cause: well-intentioned State action to improve the lot of private tenants.

Early in the twentieth century, nine out of ten British families lived in privately-rented housing (the tenth family being owner-occupiers). Rents were settled by the ordinary laws of supply and demand, until the First World War upset the normal functioning of the market. There was then a sudden unprecedented inflation (after a hundred years during which the value of money had been close to constant) and rents began to soar alongside other prices. In 1915 rents were frozen at the immediately-prewar levels, as a compassionate emergency measure to last no more than six months after the end of the war.

(Whatever the details of the economic situation which sparked off the original rent controls, two points are worth noting. The emergency in which they appeared, irrespective of its moral rights and wrongs, was one wholly of the State's making: private individuals do not declare world wars. And although rents may have risen abruptly in money terms – as various prices do in periods of high inflation, by definition – it is scarcely credible that landlords could have raised rents in real terms to levels at which large numbers of people were forced into homelessness, since that would have implied large numbers of houses standing empty and yielding no income to their owners: who would have gained by that?)

That emergency measure has outlasted the war which provoked it not by six months but, in one form and another, by more than sixty years.

After the First World War, landlords were allowed to increase rents by a specified percentage, but this was not enough to compensate for wartime inflation. So, naturally, the supply of new houses for rent began to dry up as rent control made housing a relatively unprofitable investment. To cure the shortage, the law controlling the powers of local government was changed to encourage local councils to go into the housing business.

Council housing was (and is) exempt from legal rent control; but that scarcely matters, since it is subject to a different sort of control via the ballot-box. A local council which raises rents hurts its tenants' interests in a very clear and public fashion, and gets into political difficulties accordingly. It is much less likely to lose votes by subsidizing its housing from the rates, because ratepayers are not in a position to keep track of all the different things their money is spent on and how far they each represent value for money, without engaging in a research effort which few of them have time for. (In any case, while council houses are all occupied by residents with votes, a large proportion of the rates are paid by businesses without votes.) By 1976 the *average* local authority's rents were so low as barely to cover the costs of maintenance, allowing nothing towards repaying the capital. Some were much lower (though since 1979 the Conservative central government has forced councils to raise them somewhat). Naturally, councils acquired long queues of would-be tenants eager to take advantage of this bargain – queues in which it takes months or years to reach the head.

Council housing was a device invented in order to meet a perceived danger that poor people might find themselves without a decent roof over their heads, but council tenancies nowadays are by no means limited to people who could be regarded as 'needy' in any ordinary sense. When in 1982 Copeland District Council, in Cumbria, sent an official to ask tenants why they had got into arrears with rent payments, one family explained that the problem had been the cost of a second annual holiday they had taken in Algeria to make up for the fact that it had rained on their first holiday in Malta.

What of the private landlords, meanwhile? As council rents sank in real terms, the figures that private landlords wanted to charge in order to get an economic return on their investment made them look like sharks by comparison – so rents remained controlled, to protect tenants from 'exploitation'. If a landlord cannot make a profit by renting, his obvious alternative is to get rid of his tenants and retrieve his capital by selling to owner-occupiers. This created a real danger of wholesale evictions; so, to rent control was added security of tenure: a tenant once in place cannot legally be given notice. Under the 1974 Rent Act, the 'fair rent' for a house or flat is determined by a local government official by criteria which are left mysterious (Rent Officers are expressly directed to ignore the factors of supply and demand), and a sitting tenant not merely is guaranteed a home for life but has the right to pass on his tenancy to his child and, in some cases, his grandchild. When a private letting does become available (perhaps because the existence of a sitting tenant in another part of the house makes it virtually unsaleable, and the owner might as well get some return from his property), it has become common for a prospective tenant to agree a rent with the landlord, move in, and go straight round to the Rent Office to get the figure just agreed declared 'unfair'. Again, the practice of invoking State power in order to force private rents below what landlords are willing to accept is not confined to tenants in desperate financial straits. In March, 1980, no less a figure than the Attorney-General of the United Kingdom engaged in legal battle with the landlady of his comfortable *pied-à-terre* in the suburb of Wimbledon in order to get the (remarkably modest-sounding) rent of £25 a week reduced to £17.

About 1970 a schoolteacher friend of mine inherited a small house containing a sitting tenant; she found that, year by year, the rent she was legally allowed to charge fell slightly short of the cost of repairs she was legally required to make; such cases are perfectly normal. Notice what has happened in such a situation. Nominally, ownership of the house remains with the private individual, but this is a legal fiction: in reality, the right to decide how to use the house – ownership in the real sense – has been appropriated by the State, and what my friend inherited was in effect a liability to a special, irregular kind of tax. Nor is this 'tax' always payable exclusively in cash. Some tenants make their landlords' lives hell; if the landlord tries to protect his interests, he may find himself reported to the local authority with a view to proceedings for harassment under the Protection from Eviction Act, 1977. Because landlords now have little motive to keep their houses in good repair, detailed regulations lay down their duties in this respect; for the retired men or widows who have traditionally made an income for themselves by investing a nest-egg in houses for rent, it is no fun at all to be faced with an order giving them eight weeks to, for instance, 'form the rebate of a door by a planted stop (25mm x 38mm size) fixed with 38mm No. 8 countersunk screws spaced 75mm from the end of each member and at intermediate points not more than 600mm apart' – on pain of possible imprisonment.

The result of all this, predictably enough, is that private tenancies have almost disappeared. Where private landlords do still try to run their properties as a business, they commonly aim to let to ambitious young bachelors or well-heeled foreign visitors, who are sure to move on before long – just the kind of people who could afford good accommodation easily in an uncontrolled market. Existing landlords who can get vacant possession sell their property for owner-occupation. Anyone with liquid capital who invested it in houses for rent, unless he could bring them within one of the categories exempt from the law (such as holiday lettings), would be scarcely sane.

This might not matter to would-be tenants, if council housing had succeeded in replacing the private landlord's function of supplying accommodation of the types and quantities needed in different places. But local authorities build the wrong kinds of housing, in the wrong places. For a small-scale example I do not need to look further than the village where I live. Our housing authority recently carried out an extensive building programme which has given us exclusively one-bedroom houses for the elderly, while larger houses for couples with children have all been segregated in another village separated from us by several miles of hilly and winding road. Simultaneously, another arm of local government has closed the school in the other village and transferred its pupils to our newer and larger school. (This, in an area where few families run cars and fewer mothers have driving licences.) A case like this seems laughable – but not to the people involved: many couples in my area are seriously affected by not being able to live near Gran and pop round on a casual basis to ask her to look after their children for an hour or two.

Other failures in the public housing programme have been on a grander scale. The switch from houses to blocks of flats in the postwar period represented a decision made by the State in defiance of consumer preferences. (In 1952, when the *Architects' Journal* proposed to solve Liverpool's housing problem by building a two-mile ring of twenty-storey blocks surrounding the city centre, a local newspaper polled people on the waiting list for council accommodation and found that 96 per cent of them wanted houses rather than flats; but Conservative and Labour councillors alike became convinced of the virtues of high-density housing, despite the fact that it is dearer to build, and national government offered local authorities higher subsidies for flats than for houses.) A major demographic change in modern Britain has been the great increase in the proportion of young one- and two-person households, but this is often ignored by council housing programmes which continue to cater mainly for traditional families and the old.

As long as I can remember, there has been a 'housing problem' in Britain. Because of the cheapness of council housing once one gets into it, local authorities have to impose rationing schemes which cannot possibly be sensitive to all the human factors which are actually relevant in an individual case. A woman desperate to get away from a husband who bullies her and her children (while keeping within the law) will get no house from the council, since she is 'voluntarily' joining the queue at the bottom. Yet, at least since the beginning of the 1970s if not longer, there has been a substantial excess of houses over households in the country as a whole; in 1977 the Department of the Environment commissioned a survey which showed that more than three per cent of the national housing stock was standing empty. Many of those empty houses were privately owned, and had been rented before extensions to rent control made this uneconomic; many others were owned by local authorities and were deliberately kept vacant in order not to interfere with 'development' schemes which might, or might not, one day come to pass (a council has little motive to worry about forfeiting rental income, since it can always take more through the rates).

For those on the left of politics, the private landlord has become a stock bogey figure. A 1973 Fabian Society pamphlet argued that 'To socialists, and even to many who would merely like to see "capitalism with a human face", the ownership of one man's home by another has always been repugnant.' Nick Bosanquet, in a critique of the liberal movement published in 1983, condemned 'a system based on private landlords [as] essentially archaic'. But these reactions, though widely shared, seem to be purely ideological. They are not accompanied by any rational argument suggesting that private renting harms people's interests in practice (and in fact private renting remains the norm, and seems to work quite well, in many other Western countries that lack rent-control laws). These ideological attitudes are perhaps reinforced by horror stories about the 'Rachmanism' of the early 1960s, which consisted of buying up houses that were cheap because they had sitting tenants, and 'winkling' the tenants out by techniques of harassment against which the law then gave less protection than it does now. Some of the less thoughtful sort of socialists speak as if Rachman were the archetype of the private landlord – whereas he and his kind were landlords for as short a time as they could manage! Far from being an evil against which rent control provides a necessary bulwark, 'Rachmanism' was a product of rent control: it is only when the presence of a tenant is enough to destroy the capital value of a house that 'winkling' has a purpose.

By the 1980s it is surely very clear to anyone who is prepared to let everyday experience weigh in the balance against ideology that rent control has been a disaster. Even people on the socialist side of politics have in many cases come to accept this. Another Fabian Society publication which came out in the same year as the pamphlet quoted above took a more down-to-earth line:

> . . . the decline of the private landlord has brought, and is still bringing, acute misery to many families. . . . For the poor and the underprivileged, the unmarried mother and her child, the immigrant and the large family the decline of the private landlord is not a cause for ideological satisfaction, rather a grim reality.

In 1983 Anne Sofer, an SDP member of the Greater London Council, was moved to nostalgia by reading Ron Barnes's autobiography of Hackney working-class life in the 1930s: 'Gran informed Mum that there was a flat going on her landing . . . so into Craven Buildings they went. Later, however, my parents moved away from the flats to . . . a . . . house, with a beautiful large garden'; but 'Gran missed her chats with the women when she was on her way to market of a morning,' so 'within six weeks she was back in her old flat in the Buildings.' As a councillor, Ms Sofer had had many cases of constituents wanting to move from one council housing unit to another for reasons more pressing than Mr Barnes's Gran: frail parents to be nursed, grandchildren to be looked after so that daughter-in-law could go out to work, and so forth – but she had invariably failed to solve her constituents' problems.

> These days [she mused] it would have taken Gran years to get the transfer out and a transfer back would have been a near impossibility. And an army of estate officers, social workers, doctors, councillors, and probably by the end geriatric advisers, would have been enlisted on her behalf and the file of letters relating to her transfer application would be an inch thick.
>
> What . . . is the meaning of a phrase like 'living in a free society' for the people who feel as trapped and as little able to take charge of their own lives as some of my constituents do?

In the Second World War very many important goods were rationed; people could not get as much of them as they wanted, and what they could get was often of poor quality. Forty years later, food rationing and clothes rationing are distant memories. Food and clothes are provided by the market mechanism of voluntary exchanges between private producers, retailers, and consumers; and consumers get the quantity and quality they want, when they want it. Rented accommodation, by contrast, is provided as a public service by the State, and consumers by and large cannot get what they want. Under the market system, certainly, there are tensions between producers and consumers – consumers would always prefer things to be a bit cheaper and the quality a bit better, producers would like to get a bit more money for rather less expenditure of resources. But these tensions are marginal: if the ideal is a little beyond a consumer's means he can settle for a second-best. In the field of housing it is often plain impossible for a would-be consumer to get even approximately what he wants, because money cannot buy it.

Nor are the ill-effects of rent control confined to frustrated tenants and would-be tenants. Far from it. One of the factors often commented on in connexion with Britain's miserable industrial performance in recent decades has been the extreme reluctance of workers in dying industries to move to areas where new opportunities are opening up. Even when suitable jobs are available, workers have often preferred to use all the political pressure at their disposal to force government to subsidize loss-making industries out of taxation, and governments of both parties have often yielded to the pressure. People who ought to know better put this down to laziness, or to the excessively generous levels of State unemployment benefit. Norman Tebbit, then Minister for Employment, made his famously callous suggestion that workers ought to get 'on their bikes'. In March 1980 an editorial in the *Spectator*, usually an intelligently liberal magazine, commented that 'The great reluctance of unemployed people to move to where there is work is powerful evidence that life on the dole is tolerably good.' It is nothing of the kind. For a family man installed in a good council house, the right to remain in that house may be his most valuable single asset: if he moved elsewhere he would have to go to the bottom of another council's waiting-list. The *Spectator* was in effect complaining because people who have lost their source of income are reluctant to throw away their capital too. But, while this reluctance to move is perfectly understandable, at the same time it acts as a strong brake on the nation's industrial regeneration. State action in the field of rented accommodation is hurting all of us, including those who are neither landlords nor tenants.

A market is a system by which the preferences of consumers determine what uses the productive resources of society will be put to. Rent control has failed, as any State intervention in the operations of a market is likely to fail, because it has uncoupled decisions about use of resources from the pressure of consumers' wants. If there were no laws limiting freedom of contract between landlords and tenants, then a strong desire by many individuals to rent accommodation, reflected in willingness to devote a relatively high proportion of their income to rent, would make the letting of houses a relatively attractive proposition, so that those who owned spare accommodation would be inclined to let it out, and those who owned liquid capital which could be invested in the construction of houses for rent would be likely to choose this way of investing it. As it is, no degree of willingness by would-be tenants to pay for more rented accommodation translates into a motive for a private person to become a landlord. By introducing laws designed to protect the interests of the dwindling class of tenants *already in place* and not wishing to move elsewhere, the State has gravely injured the interests of *would-be* tenants by depriving them of the power to influence the behaviour of private owners of resources that could be used to provide them with accommodation.

(Having blamed rent control for creating unemployment, I should add that it is of course not the only or even principal cause of our high current level of unemployment. Modern job-security laws are another potent factor and these are very analogous to rent-control laws, being intended to protect the interests of employees but in practice greatly damaging the interests of people who *would like to become* employees. Any manager of a small business in the 1980s will tell you that a prime consideration when developing the business is to avoid changes which would mean taking on extra staff, because the costs of getting rid of them again if things go badly are now so great. It is noteworthy that although the Thatcher administrations since 1979 have introduced several purely economic liberal measures, such as reduction of inflation and abolition of exchange controls, grossly illiberal aspects of the legal framework within which economic life occurs have been left virtually untouched.)

While the State has deprived would-be tenants of the power to influence the behaviour of potential private landlords, through the institution of council housing it has given them the possibility of influencing the provision of accommodation via the political process rather than the machinery of the market. But this is a very crude and unsatisfactory alternative, because it gives consumers no way of registering the strength of their *relative* preferences for alternative uses of resources. Liberals sometimes talk as if the State simply squanders resources on projects that offer no real benefits to anyone at all; perhaps this does something happen, but I believe it is a mistake to dwell on it – surely most State enterprises do yield some benefits. The real problem is that the State often chooses to satisfy minor wants rather than acute needs (and satisfies them inefficiently). When a commodity is provided by the machinery of the market, consumers have to decide not merely whether they want it but whether they want it *enough* to forgo alternative uses for their income. If the supply of a commodity is determined politically, on the other hand, citizens who want the commodity have little reason to hold back from using their political clout to demand it, because the State provides such a large range of goods and services to so many people that the resources freed by failure to supply a given commodity are quite unlikely to be used in ways that benefit the same people. Perhaps I am very keen to see the State subsidize a theatre, or a whole class of theatres across the country. If I and the other people who feel as I do about the value of drama had to keep the theatre solvent ourselves, the cost in terms of other kinds of consumption forgone would be so great that we would, regretfully, stand back and let them close. But if the State does not spend the money in this way, most likely it will be spent on something that we keen theatre-goers happen not to be very interested in: so it makes sense for us to press for State subsidies to the theatre, or whatever else we care about.

Thus decisions about how to allocate resources, if made politically, are made not in terms of the relative strengths of consumers' wants but in terms of the relative skill of different interest groups at manipulating the political system. Public life becomes a sea of individuals and groups all constantly asking, with various degrees of urbanity or shrillness, for more resources. Only a finite quantity of resources are available, so decisions get made almost accidentally, in terms of which pressure-group can best publicize its case, who knows how to get access to the relevant decision-makers, which minister is felt to deserve a success, and the like – all of which has very little connexion with satisfying people's real needs. Richard Crossman's Cabinet diaries show how, as Paul Johnson wrote in a review, 'Labour governments [and, surely, not only Labour governments] burden themselves with too much legislation, and too much intervention in the economy, ever to do anything properly. Even the most important cabinet papers are often unread, people do not turn up to meetings, minutes are doctored. . . . ' 'Now I realize,' wrote Crossman, 'how rarely great issues are discussed in cabinet as issues of principle and how one moves normally through a series of *ad hoc* decisions on narrow issues.' If this is true of highly-paid, full-time national government ministers, how much more must it be true of local government councillors who are likely to be less able and certainly have much less time to devote to their public role. Running an economy is a job so massively complex that, as Adam Smith put it in *The Wealth of Nations*, 'no human wisdom or knowledge could ever be sufficient.' We need to leave it to the market because its system of transmitting information and motivation via prices is subtler than any human alternative. (The experience of trying to run an economy purely by the command system is described sarcastically by a Soviet author, D. Antonov: 'to draft an accurate and fully integrated plan for material supply just for the Ukraine for one year requires the labour of the entire world's population for ten million years.')

In the Second World War it was different. For the time being it really did not matter too much if other things went wrong, provided that the one central task of conquering the Axis went right; and this job, while of course not simple, was sufficiently limited and well-defined to be grasped and planned by human minds. But 'planning for peace' is nothing like planning for war: there is no one goal to be achieved.

One result of the nature of modern public life is that, since members of the middle class tend to be much more skilled than manual workers at the political arts of persuasion and publicity, it often emerges that the Welfare State in practice acts to transfer resources from poorer to richer, which makes something of a mockery of its ostensible purpose. Julian Le Grand has shown that in 1972 members of the professional, employer, and managerial classes had almost half as much again spent on them by the NHS (per person reporting ill) as semi-skilled and unskilled manual workers. Poorer people tend to start work and thus begin paying National Insurance contributions younger than members of the middle class, yet the latter get more benefits because they tend to live longer. Indeed, according to the Nobel-prizewinning economist George Stigler, it is a general truth, both confirmable by observation and predictable on theoretical grounds, that 'Public expenditures are made for the primary benefit of the middle classes,' while being financed by taxes paid largely by the poor and the very rich.

Likewise, socialism is often justified in terms of providing a counterbalance to the allegedly overwhelming power of large corporations over individuals' lives, but the reality is the opposite: large firms can afford to develop expertise in manipulating the political system, while individuals cannot. If there is a conflict between road haulage or air transport interests who want a new motorway or a new airport, and private citizens who live where the motorway or airport would be sited, it is very difficult for the private individuals, however strong their feelings, to make the same impact on the decision-making process as the transport industries can easily do. (In a pure market economy, on the other hand, the private individuals do not need to make an impact; if they are unwilling to accept the price the transport interests are prepared to offer for their land, the motorway or airport cannot be built.)

In a market system, producers are forced constantly to study and adapt to the wants of consumers, as expressed in their spending decisions. The forests of tower-blocks which disfigure our cities could not have been created in a market system. If housing were produced purely by private enterprise, then some landlords might have tried building at much higher densities than were previously normal, but if life in such accommodation proved as unpleasant as (to most people) it apparently is, they would have discovered before many years were out that they could get tenants only at very low rents, which would have pushed them back towards building in a more traditional fashion. (No doubt there are a minority of people who find high-rise living entirely acceptable and would prefer to use their spending power in other ways, and these would naturally gravitate towards the low rents of the smaller number of tower blocks that did get built. The market system, because it responds to the separate spending 'votes' of millions of consumers rather than to decisions by a few officials, can provide relatively easily for a diversity of consumer preferences – the market, as it were, offers consumers proportional representation rather than a winner-takes-all form of control over production.)

The politicians and officials who authorized the tower blocks must have been aware that some tenants would have preferred other kinds of accommodation; but they had no strong motive forcing them to worry about that fact. It was easy for them to pooh-pooh the protests that they heard as ignorant laymen's reaction against novelty, which would soon vanish as people got used to the new kind of life. Fashion in architectural thought seems to have made those responsible for municipal housing deaf to tenants' views for a very long time. If housing were provided by private landlords, they would have thrown fashion overboard the moment they became aware that it contradicted consumers' preferences; it would have been economic suicide to do otherwise. But probably no national politician or local councillor or council official has ever become poorer through choosing to build unpopular kinds of housing – a councillor is quite unlikely even to be voted out of office for such a reason, because accommodation is only one of the many commodities provided by local government, and democracy gives the voter no way to discriminate between the activities his delegate has performed well and those he has messed up.

One virtue of the market is that it enables individuals as consumers to exert control over production decisions, so that resources are diverted to those uses where they can yield most real benefit. Another virtue is that it maximizes the *quantity* of benefit derived from each resource, and minimizes waste. By treating each resource as the private property of some individual, it gives that individual a motive to husband the resource so that it yields most good.

The point can be illustrated by a trivial example. In my university department, two electric typewriters are housed in neighbouring rooms. One is in the departmental secretary's office; legally she is not its owner, but in practice it is controlled by her and no one else touches it without her permission. The machine next door is available for any member of the teaching staff to use. The secretary's typewriter is beautifully looked after; it has given many years of good service, and if any problem arises its 'owner' has it seen to without delay. The 'public' machine, by contrast, is mistreated badly. Users rarely replace the dustcover, and sometimes even leave the motor running overnight; the typeheads fill with dirt, faults are left to cure themselves, the work done by the machine deteriorates, and fairly soon it will be a write-off. Taking good care of an electric typewriter requires a certain amount of effort – it is quicker not to bother to replace the dustcover after use, for instance. To the secretary, it is worth making this effort because it is repaid in terms of easier and more satisfying work with the machine in future. But many of the individual users of the 'public' machine no doubt calculate, consciously or unconsciously, that it is pointless for them to do their share of looking after the machine, since they cannot force other users to be equally careful; so the machine is neglected.

This example is on a very small scale, but what is true on a small scale is true in the large. Consider, for instance, how stocks of some species of fish have been virtually eliminated by overfishing in the North Sea and elsewhere. Fish in the sea are a public resource, so no one fishing enterprise has a motive to restrain its catches. It cannot prevent others taking the fish which it does not, so for each enterprise it is rational to take as much as it can while stocks last. If it were technically feasible, a liberal would prefer the world's oceans to be divided up into privately-owned sectors separated by underwater fences impermeable to fish; then it would be in the interests of each owner to take each year only as many fish as enabled the stock to keep up its numbers.

Conversion of public to private resources looks superficially like a deprivation. Even if the individuals who do not acquire property rights in the privatized resource are compensated for loss of public access to it, it still seems as if something is being taken from the many and given to the few. But this overlooks the fact that owners (of resources on a larger scale than an electric typewriter) can only gain from their property by selling its products. If all the live herring in the world belonged to one or another of a few hundred 'sealords' who managed their shoals so as to preserve or increase their value over the long term, herrings would be cheap today. As it is, for years anyone was free to catch herring anywhere on the high seas, and herrings came close to extinction. As Adam Smith put it in his *Theory of Moral Sentiments:*

> It is to no purpose, that the proud and unfeeling landlord views his extensive fields, and without a thought for the wants of his brethren, in imagination consumes himself the whole harvest that grows upon them. . . . The capacity of his stomach bears no proportion to the immensity of his desires. . . . [The rich] consume little more than the poor, and in spite of their natural selfishness and rapacity, though they mean only their own conveniency . . . they divide with the poor the produce of all their improvements.

The market has the virtue of directing each resource in society to the use which will yield most benefit to consumers. Replacement of the market by the command system of social organization is objectionable because it robs consumers of their power to influence producers, and because it leads to wasteful, destructive uses of society's resources. Perhaps worst of all, though, it creates a class of people with a direct interest in further increasing State power and in misusing the resources which come under the control of the State: namely, State employees.

Any employee of the State has an interest in the growth of State power, because it improves his own career prospects. If this seems unduly cynical, consider how totally uninterested those who staff the Welfare State have been in the idea of replacing it by a negative income tax. The only serious argument that might be offered in favour of the Welfare State is that it is designed to redistribute income from richer to poorer, which equalitarians regard as a desirable goal. In fact it scarcely does this; in many cases it does the opposite. But, even if it did, there would be a far cheaper and fairer way to achieve the same goal. Milton Friedman, the University of Chicago economist who is probably the best-known contemporary advocate of classical, Adam-Smith-style liberalism, frequently points to the desirability in this respect of replacing the complex structure of State-produced benefits in kind with a simple extension to the income tax system whereby, just as those whose incomes exceed a certain level pay out a proportion in tax, so those whose incomes fall below a given minimum would receive cash benefits which they could use to buy themselves the necessities of life which they cannot afford from their own resources. It is absurd, as Friedman sees it, for the belief that poor people need State help in order to get a decent level of medical attention or schooling to be taken as implying that the State ought itself to operate hospitals and schools. If private enterprise can use resources to achieve a given goal more efficiently than State agencies (and the truth of *this* is by now scarcely controversial), then surely the best solution must be for the State to give poor people the wherewithal to buy private medicine and schooling? Not only would they get more overall that way, but there would be no question of wasting public benefits on individuals who could perfectly well afford them from their own pocket.

One argument against the negative income tax idea is that it would give the poor too much freedom. The criticism would commonly be wrapped up in vaguer language, but in blunt terms the objection is that poor people would squander negative tax payments on fags and booze rather than using them to pay for medical insurance. There is quite a lot to be said in answer to this and I shall return to the issue later, but let me point out now that it represents a staggering degree of paternalism. Someone who makes the objection presumably believes that he himself knows roughly how to apportion income sensibly between basic necessities and pleasant luxuries, but he apparently regards the poor as a group of childlike sub-men who cannot be entrusted with comparable responsibility for themselves. Supporters of the Welfare State have commonly also been supporters of the policy of granting independence to African and other colonies, in many of which the inhabitants have been exposed to modern political and technological arrangements for only a few decades at most. I find it bizarre that people can insist that Africans have every right to run their own lives, but at the same time deny that right to their own countrymen.

However, State employees ignore the negative income tax idea for a different reason: it would put a number of them out of a job, and worsen the working conditions of very many of them. Hospitals, for instance, would need to be staffed whether they were operated by the State or by private enterprise, but private enterprise uses human resources – like any other resources – efficiently; a private enterprise hospital may have as many doctors and nurses working in it as an NHS hospital, but it is likely to manage with fewer administrators, and the administrators it does have will be expected to earn their keep. In that eight-year period quoted on p. 34 when NHS hospital productivity fell by 11 per cent despite a staff increase of 28 per cent, the increase in *administrative and clerical* staff was 51 per cent. This is the sort of thing that is virtually impossible under private enterprise: staff cost money, so a private hospital system that allowed itself to become so top-heavy would have to increase its charges so much, relative to competitors, that it could not possibly survive.

If people employed by the State in responsible positions were sincerely and intelligently concerned to maximize the welfare of the ostensible beneficiaries of their services, they ought to be clamouring for the organizations they serve to be privatized and for the system of State benefits in kind to be replaced by a negative income tax. In reality, they invariably oppose any such moves with fervour. (An example is the proposal floated a few years ago to replace the direct public provision of schooling, in an experimental region of Kent, with provision of vouchers that parents could use to pay for schooling in either State or private schools. This, it was repeatedly said by spokesmen for the State schooling service, would lead to 'chaos' of an unspecified kind.)

All producers naturally tend to exaggerate consumers' need for their products and the price they are worth. When private-enterprise producers do this it is called advertising. Sometimes consumers are taken in by an exaggerated advertising claim; but they learn by their mistakes, and they can always choose not to buy. When people engaged in producing a State service set out to create extra demand for their wares and better terms of service, on the other hand, the people they need to convince are not individual purchasers but legislators and others who have the power to spend other people's money rather than their own. Obviously, then, it is far easier for people working in the public service than it is for their equivalents in private enterprise to improve their career prospects by creating unnecessary jobs and providing lavish facilities for themselves (which they honestly believe to be necessary in the public interest – we are all very good at self-deception). In their own 'advertising campaigns', State employees often make claims that would lead to trouble if they were put forward by a profit-making organization. According to police statistics, the number of burglaries shot up by 54 per cent in the decade 1970-1980, helping to justify the huge increase in the number of policemen mentioned on p. 48. In 1981, however, it emerged from independently-gathered statistics that this increase was an artefact of police techniques for recording crime; in reality the incidence of burglary was constant over the ten years. (Because the police are a State service, there is no question of prosecuting them for making false 'advertising claims'.) The almost inexorable growth of State power cannot be blamed on some conspiracy between a few individuals to reduce the British people to the status of serfs; it has a lot to do with the fact that employees of the State all have a special interest in the growth of their own little corner of State activity.

The operation of this principle in the Civil Service is remarkably illustrated in Leslie Chapman's book *Your Disobedient Servant*. In 1967 Mr Chapman was appointed regional director for the Southern Region of the Ministry of Works (now the Property Services Agency), and inaugurated a programme of seeking economies in the Region's activities (without changing any of its output). He found massive scope for savings, both in equipment and personnel.

> Less grass needed to be cut. . . . Lawn standards were pointless for grass which stretched between store sheds and was criss-crossed by overhead pipes and cables. There was no useful purpose in heating gigantic stores the size of aircraft hangars to normal office temperatures when the contents would be quite safe at lower temperatures. . . . There was no need to conserve and maintain eighty or so cranes and lifting devices when experience over a long period showed that only half a dozen were needed. . . .

An extensive chauffeur-driven car service was provided for staff, almost all of whom could drive; and so it went on.

In the light of his surveys, Mr Chapman was able to reduce overall regional expenditure by about 35 per cent with no fall in output of work. Directors of other regions refused to believe that similar saving would be possible in their regions (though sample surveys quickly refuted this). Ministers in two governments took up Mr Chapman's ideas and ordered similar policies to be applied nationally; the Civil Service failed to carry out these orders, and in due course Mr Chapman found his position in the Civil Service becoming so untenable that he took early retirement.

What is distinctive about a 'Welfare' State is that it provides the citizen with goods and services whose production and distribution can without difficulty be controlled by private market interactions. There is a core of State activities which are necessarily performed by the State because the market is inherently incapable of providing them. The two obvious examples are defence of the realm, and a judicial system which enforces private contracts and punishes force and fraud. More generally, there are the range of what economists call 'public goods' (some economists prefer the term 'collective goods'). A 'public good', to an economist, is not something that is as a matter of fact provided publicly, but rather something that, if provided at all, cannot be provided exclusively to those who choose to pay for it – which makes it difficult or impossible to provide it through the mechanism of the market. The example commonly cited is the lighthouse: there is no way to stop sailors who have not subscribed to a private-enterprise lighthouse service from seeing its beams and acting on their warning, so it would seem to be impossible to run private-enterprise lighthouses profitably. (As it happens, the example is less straightforward than it seems: private enterprise did play an important role in the development of British lighthouses. But we need not go into this question here.) Defence might be regarded as a particularly central example of a public good.

Liberals accept that States are needed to produce public goods, and also to limit the production of 'public bads' such as air pollution. (These 'bads' are symmetrical with public goods in the sense that it is not possible to protect particular individuals from them if those individuals choose not to accept an arrangement by which they are compensated for exposure to them.) It is the fact that public goods cannot be withheld from non-payers that justifies coercive taxation. But liberals would add that the categories of public good and bad must be defined narrowly, since the extension of State power needed to produce extra public goods or control extra public bads is itself a major public bad – as Milton Friedman puts it, 'Every government measure bears, as it were, a smokestack on its back.'

When State action is justifiable, furthermore, it ought to leave as much decision-making as possible in private hands. A liberal will prefer to limit pollution by means of a tax which makes the polluter pay the true social cost of his emissions and leaves him to choose whether a given pollution-creating activity is worth paying this cost, rather than by allowing the State to impose an absolute ban on some categories of pollution and allow others to occur freely, irrespective of commercial considerations. Environmentalists and others hostile to commerce sometimes talk as if public bads were absolute evils, which ought to be eradicated totally; but that is silly. To quote Milton Friedman again, 'We could have zero pollution from automobiles, for example, by simply abolishing all automobiles. That would also make the kind of agricultural and industrial productivity we now enjoy impossible, and so condemn most of us to a drastically lower standard of living, perhaps many even to death.' As in every department of life, we have to strike a balance between advantages and costs: the optimum solution is not zero pollution, nor the very large amount of pollution that would occur if everyone were allowed to pollute freely, but the intermediate amount that would occur if each polluter paid the social cost of his emissions. State action *may* cause the total quantum of pollution to be closer to this optimum than it would otherwise be, but there is no guarantee of this. As Friedman points out, 'Generally, it is no easier for government to identify the specific persons who are hurt and benefited than for market participants. . . . Attempts to use government to correct market failure have often simply substituted government failure for market failure.'

Enthusiasts for State growth tend to discover and exaggerate public-good aspects in almost everything, and to assume that governments face no difficulties in correcting 'market failures'. State financing of education, for instance, is very commonly defended on the ground that education benefits not only the recipient but also the rest of society, in ways that have nothing to do with the educated person's market value to an employer. Even Milton Friedman has defended State finance for schooling on the ground that 'The education of my child contributes to your welfare by promoting a stable and democratic society.' Yet the willingness of parents to scrimp and save from taxed income in order to pay for their children to be privately educated suggests that education is seen as a great enough 'private good' that it will be bought in ample measure without State intervention. A good is not straightforwardly purely public or purely private; most goods have both public and private aspects, and liberals demand that the public aspects must predominate before State intervention can be justified. In fact, the claim that education yields a public benefit is invariably made in very vague terms. I studied many fascinating things in schools and universities, but the things I have learned which affect my behaviour *as a citizen* (as opposed to my performance as a salaried university teacher, or my individual ability to solve problems specific to me and my family) are overwhelmingly things I have read in newspapers or learned in the 'University of Life'. E.G. West has pointed out that advocates of State-financed education, from Macaulay in 1847 to the writers of the Robbins Report on Higher Education in 1963, have treated it as axiomatic that education reduces crime, yet statistics show that juvenile delinquency is increased by raising the school-leaving age and that the experience of going to work is a major factor in reducing crime. Even Nick Bosanquet, in his attack on the new liberalism quoted on p. 64, now accepts that the public-good argument for state-financed education has been 'conclusively' refuted.

(Fred Hirsch has given the public/private good problem a novel twist by arguing that, in affluent, crowded societies like ours, private goods are frequently identical with public bads. Thus, to acquire a second home in the idyllic Welsh countryside is to make that countryside a bit less idyllic. In such conditions, Hirsch suggests, market competition comes to resemble a crowd all trying to see over each other's heads by standing on tiptoe. Clearly, if the State is needed to control public bads it should control the special class of public bad identified by Hirsch along with the rest; perhaps there should be a special tax on rural second homes. But I cannot see that Hirsch makes a case against the view that 'positional goods' such as access to rural tranquillity, like any other goods, are better distributed by the market than by command.)

Defence, the judiciary, and the financing of public goods, were for Adam Smith the three proper fields of State activity. Many contemporary liberals – though, as we shall see in later chapters, certainly not all – would concede one or two other functions.

Some liberals would argue that the State ought to control monopolies. To the economist a monopoly is objectionable because lack of competition allows prices to be raised above the level at which they cause the optimum quantity of a product to be supplied. If one tailoring firm had a monopoly in the supply of clothes, people would have fewer and less well-made clothes than they now have, and resources that could have been used to make clothes would be diverted to uses in which they benefited consumers less. (Also, the owners of the monopoly would be extremely rich, but that is not a relevant point: we criticize aspects of social organization for the harm they do to some people, not for the good they do to others.) Of course, a clothing monopoly could not survive unless the State actively enforced it as it does the postal monopoly. If prices were raised to take advantage of the monopoly situation, it would be profitable for other producers to enter the market and undercut the monopolist's prices.

There are a few goods, however, which are arguably 'natural monopolies'. The subscribers to a telephone service, for instance, want not just to belong to a network but *to belong to a network to which all other subscribers belong too*. As in the case of 'public goods', the liberal will be anxious to define 'natural monopolies' as narrowly as possible; thus he might point out that a monopoly of *telephone service* is not a monopoly of *communications* – if a private monopolist of telephone service tried to exploit his position by large price rises, consumers could react by writing more letters and making fewer phone calls. That said, there is a respectable liberal argument for State control of pricing or State ownership in the case of genuine natural monopolies (though Milton Friedman argues that both of these alternatives are in practice even worse than uncontrolled private monopoly).

Some non-liberal economists have argued that private monopoly in modern economies extends far beyond the handful of areas which appear to be natural monopolies for special technical reasons. Even if this were so, it would scarcely be a ground (as the economists in question suggest) for extending State intervention. The most plausible explanation for monopoly in such cases would be monopoly-promoting behaviour by the State, which should be abandoned. The UK and other modern States make life unnaturally easy in many ways for private companies that have attained dominant positions in the market. For instance, starting a new business which might compete with the big boys is a gamble, but heavy taxation, and the quite astonishing burden of paperwork which the State inflicts on all businesses and which represents a far greater proportional cost to a small business than to a large one, tip the odds attached to the gamble heavily against the potential entrant to a market. (If the business fails, the State does not shower the unsuccessful proprietor with money in order to balance the odds.) Despite this, research by John Jewkes has shown that monopoly just does not occur on the scale that non-liberal economists have suggested: the top is still a slippery place.

Friedman, and many other contemporary liberals, would add to Adam Smith's agenda for State action the duty of guarding the interests of individuals who cannot provide for themselves, such as children and lunatics. Most children are provided for by their parents; but if a child has unusually cruel or feckless parents, or is an orphan, he cannot fend for himself and Friedman would argue that the State should look after him rather than leaving this task to private charity. Again, however, any liberal would want to draw a tight boundary round the class of people who are regarded as non-participants in the market system because of youth or infirmity. One of the liberal's objections to the Welfare State is that it effectively broadens this category to include masses of ordinary able-bodied adults in command of their mental faculties. Liberals tend not to see it as any proper function of the State to raise people's income just because they are relatively poor.

As we have seen, if this *is* to be done then the liberal method would be Milton Friedman's device of a negative income tax, rather than an array of benefits in kind. But Milton Friedman is a very moderate liberal, and many of his important works (such as *Capitalism and Freedom*, 1962) were published at a period when welfare-state ideology was much more ingrained in the public mind than it is now, so that there were limits to what he could propose if he hoped to be taken seriously. Younger liberals are less inclined to accept the legitimacy of a general policy of State redistribution of income. Some would concede State provision of a very basic 'floor' of subsistence for the few unfortunates who cannot manage to keep body and soul together by their own participation in the market, on the ground that relief of extreme poverty is a 'public good'. It hurts us to see beggars and starving people in our environment (or perhaps even to know that they exist, unseen); but an individual who chooses not to make donations to poverty-relieving charities still gets the benefit of being spared this distress, provided others do contribute, so all must pay for the relief of poverty as all must pay for lighthouses. Others would argue that, as it were, Britain in the 1980s is not India – degrading, extreme poverty of the kind whose relief could arguably be seen as a public good would be vanishingly rare in a modern society like ours even if there were no State provision, and private charity would be more than adequate to cope with what did occur. Furthermore, Robert Sugden has done research on patterns of giving to charities which suggests that what donors aim to 'buy' in making donations is not so much (for instance) relief of poverty, as *the knowledge that they personally are helping to relieve poverty*. The truer this is, the less substance there is in the 'public good' justification of State welfare activities.

Private charity has the virtue of being self-limiting: when the State takes responsibility for relief of poverty, it creates a set of people who have an interest in exaggerating the problem and setting the 'poverty-line' ever higher. Surely we are all familiar with the contradiction that members of the State salariat repeatedly talk as if the country contained an army of people in desperately penurious straits, while from one's personal experience one would be hard put to identify anyone so poor as to be an appropriate object of charity? (Town-dwellers perhaps resolve the paradox by supposing that the really poor people are out of sight in other parts of town; but I live in a rural community where people of all income-levels know each other – and where *average* income is quite low by current English standards – and here too such people can scarcely be found. We have a local charitable fund established long ago, when times were harder, and its income has to be used to pay for pensioners' colour-television licences and the like, for want of any more pressing use.)

Probably most contemporary liberals would reject the concept of a progressive income tax, which redistributes across the whole range of incomes. If a 'floor' of subsistence is provided it ought to be financed, like other State activities, from taxation which either falls equally on all citizens, like the

annual membership fee of a club, or perhaps which is levied at a
flat rate on all expenditures on consumer goods and services, on
the ground that a person's total consumption measures his gain
from membership of his society. (Furthermore many liberals
would question the right of people who receive State benefits to
vote. Democracy is not an end in itself, but a means to the end of
good government; to give governments the opportunity of
winning votes by paying public money to voters is likely to
ensure very bad government.) Since State activities in a liberal
society are few, taxation is low, so that questions about the
precise system of taxation lose their urgency. But it is worth
examining why liberals reject the idea of redistribution from
richer to poorer, since, obviously, this concept lies at the heart
of Welfare State ideology.

   In the first place, even if morality were thought to require
either equality of incomes, or at least some closer
approximation to equality than the market yields, there is no
way that State action could achieve that result. In a society in
which most decisions are made politically rather than in the
market, individuals do not stop striving to better their lot; they
simply redirect their efforts towards the new source of benefits.
If increased money incomes are robbed of their value to the
individual by steeply progressive taxation, then people will
strive to secure other kinds of benefit – money is only a device
for getting real goods, after all. Our State provides extensive
subsidies for the arts – picture galleries, opera, and so forth.
These are not in the economist's sense 'public goods' (there is
no *technical* difficulty in charging for admission), and it seems
implausible that most of the poor people on whose behalf the
Welfare State is supposed to spend perceive a strong need for
these things; but the upper-middle-class types who know how
to influence the State like them, so the State gives them the
opportunity of visits to the opera subsidized heavily by ordinary
blokes out in the sticks who prefer relaxing in front of video
recorders which they have to buy themselves out of taxed
income. Good working conditions are tax-free, so Leslie
Chapman found little enthusiasm among his Civil Service
colleagues for economies such as 'reduc[ing] the acreage of
ornamental gardens round a building. . . . To attract recruits,

my colleagues argued, it was necessary to show splendid surroundings and well-furnished buildings impeccably maintained. No one ever demonstrated that anyone was ever recruited for these reasons but . . . it helped to make life very pleasant for those already in.' I speak of what I know; my own profession of university teaching is a good example of the privilege produced by the Welfare State. University teachers do highly fulfilling work, usually in very pleasant surroundings, with, for many of us, one or two trips each year to attend academic gatherings in attractive overseas destinations. Many of us strive honestly to give the taxpayers value for money, but I cannot believe that more than a small fraction of us would retain our jobs if university education were financed voluntarily by the beneficiaries and by charitable endowments.

Inequality is inevitable, whether in a market or a command system. The difference is that, in a market system, the individual's urge to a better life is harnessed to the satisfaction of others' wants; in a command system one person's success is bought at others' expense. To put the point very personally: the Welfare State, looked at objectively rather than through rose-tinted ideological spectacles, is largely an enormously costly device for subsidizing people like me, with our 'civilized', middle-class tastes. I cannot believe that people like me are a proper object of public charity.

To a committed socialist, this may simply show that the current British political system is a perversion of true socialism, that the so-called Welfare State has been hi-jacked by the 'ruling class' and needs to be repossessed and returned to the service of its rightful beneficiaries. To that I would reply in words of David Friedman: 'In the ideal socialist state . . . People who make decisions will show no slightest bias towards their own interests. There will be no way for a clever man to bend the institutions to serve his own ends. And the rivers will run uphill.'

Material inequality will occur under any political system. But it is by no means clear that income-differentials in a market system tend to be larger than those produced in a command system. Looking round the contemporary world, I have the impression that the opposite is the case, and this is surely not surprising. The totality of power in a command society is finite, so skilled operators can commandeer almost all of it and divert so much of the national income to themselves that little is left for the rest. A market system is open-ended, it stimulates the constant creation of novel income-generating activities and thus gives everybody the best chance of finding some lucrative outlet for their diverse talents. There is an immense amount of socialist mythology about existing inequalities. People sometimes speak as if the limited market economy of modern Britain produced massive money differentials; but, according to *Inland Revenue Statistics*, 1983, the top one per cent of the population currently receives 5.2 per cent of national personal income *before* tax. Surely, many will see this as a surprisingly small rather than a surprisingly large differential?

Liberals go further, though, and argue not merely that inequality is inevitable but that there is no moral justification for redistribution. In a free market, if one individual's contributions to society are ten times as lucrative as another's, then the first individual has given ten times as much value and is entitled to ten times the return. The State has no resources of its own; it can make the poor less poor only by making the rich less rich, and liberals tend to feel that progressive taxation is not merely inexpedient (because, for instance, it reduces the incentive for possessors of highly-valuable skills to work long hours), but actually immoral: it is a device by which society exploits its more prosperous members by taking their productive contributions and then depriving them of their fair return.

Particularly objectionable from a liberal point of view are taxes on capital, such as capital-gains tax or death duties, since these are blatantly unrelated to any notion of payment in exchange for services rendered. Collectivists often justify capital taxes by suggesting that even a self-made man cannot be seen as having created his wealth independently: we are all dependent in all aspects of our lives on the society we inhabit, so our society has every right to decide how to dispose ultimately of the accumulations of wealth which rich men are allowed to use temporarily. But this is a bad argument from a good premiss. Of course society is an interdependent web; but the fact that a successful businessman may overestimate his individual responsibility for his achievement does not imply that he leaves unpaid debts behind him. Insofar as he drew on contributions from other individuals, he presumably paid those individuals the market rate for what they provided; as for the State's contributions – a peaceable working environment, a network of roads linking him with suppliers and customers, and whatever else the State provided – he paid his share of the costs of these through taxes on income and consumption (much more than his share, if income tax was progressive). No doubt he benefited too from intangible contributions of friendship and respect from neighbours and acquaintances; but he repaid these in similar intangible coin, or he would not have received them for long. There are no debts to society left outstanding.

And, even if there were, there would be no way to repay them in cash. Society is an abstraction, it has no bank accounts. States like to identify themselves with the societies they rule, but that is intolerably presumptuous of them – most elements of English society were not put there by the State. A State is just one of many human organizations within a society, special in some ways, but not entitled to quasi-mystical reverence. The organization called the United Kingdom does quite a good job of providing Britons with security and conflict-resolution services, just as the organization called Marks & Spencers does a good job of providing us with underwear. We are not tempted to confuse the Marks & Spencer organization with the immensely rich and complex web of interpersonal relationships, institutions, and patterns of behaviour which we call 'British society', and we ought not to make the same mistake in the case of the State. The reason why the United Kingdom inherits large portions of people's wealth when they die, whereas Marks & Spencers inherits nothing even from the most regular wearer of St Michael Y-Fronts, is not because the UK is owed the money but because the UK has a police force and, ultimately, an army, and Marks & Spencers has nothing of the kind.

(Furthermore, in modern Britain capital taxes are insignificant in terms of the proportion of State revenues they yield; their *only* important function is to destroy accumulations of private wealth. People who dislike the institution of private property argue that the notion of private entitlements to resources is ultimately arbitrary and morally unfounded. Liberals reply that all resources must necessarily be controlled by *some* individual human or human organization – the particular organization called the State has no special moral entitlement to wealth it has not created, and it is best from everyone's point of view for ownership of resources to be divided between many individuals and organizations rather than concentrated in one. To talk of 'society' controlling resources is strictly meaningless: societies are not the kind of things that can take decisions or act.)

Basic disagreements about morality are hard to resolve, because of lack of common ground on which to build agreement. We all know that socialists reject the morality of private property and market determination of incomes, pointing out that it is a matter of luck whether individuals begin life with natural talent, supportive parents, and/or an inheritance of material wealth, all of which are very relevant to the question of how much they can later earn in the market. They often say also that the worth, in moral terms, of an individual's contribution to society cannot be accurately measured by his or her money earnings. To this the liberal replies that there is no other measure: we could not possibly agree on how incomes should be distributed if we seriously set out to decide in terms of moral worthiness. But it remains open to the socialist to argue that complete equality is the *moral* ideal, even if expedience dictates some divergences from the ideal in practice.

However, although that point of view is perhaps logically unassailable, it is easy to show that the great majority of those who advocate it are in practice grossly hypocritical. The relevant point here is that State redistribution is almost entirely internal – only some loose change is distributed as 'foreign aid' overseas, and few calls are heard for massive diversions of State resources from the British Welfare State to overseas beneficiaries. Morally speaking this is incomprehensible. In the Third World there is plenty of really horrifying, degrading poverty, of a kind unknown in Britain. If prosperous

Englishmen have a moral duty to forgo their own earnings in order to benefit impoverished strangers, then the morality can hardly be affected by the question of whether the strangers live in Hastings or Falkirk rather than Dacca or Dar-es-Salaam. Morally speaking, what is relevant is only the degree of poverty; if socialists were serious about equality they should be saying to less-prosperous Britons 'Don't be so selfish; by international standards you are rich,' and bleeding all of us white to pump resources into the Third World. Of course this does not happen; indeed, people on the left of politics often favour policies which severely *increase* international income-differentials, for instance the erection of trade barriers which prevent consumers here trading freely with poor producers overseas and force them instead to maintain the incomes of relatively well-paid British producers. None of this is explicable in moral terms, but morals have nothing to do with it. 'Compassion' is a useful piece of cant for politicians to win elections with, but what really determines how the Welfare State distributes welfare is the fact that Britons have British votes and foreigners do not. Welfare benefits are bribes which help the State to maintain its power; there is nothing 'compassionate' about giving away other people's money.

Perhaps the reader is one of the small minority who gives a significant proportion of his own income to overseas charities and sincerely wishes that the State would force everyone to do likewise. To that rare and excellent person, the liberal would reply: first, that moral principles accepted by such a tiny proportion of the population ought not to be enforced on all (many people think it is wrong to drink alcohol, but that does not give them the right to enforce Prohibition on the rest); and, secondly, that while private charity is admirable, using British taxpayers' funds to make 'aid' payments to overseas States does impoverished foreigners little good (indeed, as the LSE economist Peter Bauer – now Lord Bauer – has frequently demonstrated, it does them a great deal of harm). The best real long-term hope for the Third World is not aid but free trade, which supports individual foreigners' attempts to develop ways of earning their own living.

It puzzles me to know how socialists think poorer Britons

would suffer if State redistribution and welfare programmes were abolished. Perhaps they think that the rich man who now has two Rolls-Royces would have four, and so on, leaving no resources free to satisfy poor people's basic needs. But conspicuous consumption is *encouraged* by redistributive tax policies (a point to which we shall return in Chapter 6). We would expect rich people to want to consume less, not more, under a liberal system which allows them to save and pass on their wealth to their children without losing most of it in tax. And anyway there are so many more relatively-poor than relatively-rich individuals in any society that the consumption of the latter cannot hope to squeeze out that of the former; far more fortunes are made selling cheap goods to the mass market than selling hand-crafted luxuries to the few. The real objection to the free market, I believe, is a paternalist conviction that poor people would not spend their money sensibly if their middle-class betters did not make their spending decisions for them. What evidence is there for an assumption of such breathtaking arrogance?

Take the case of schooling – arguably a favourable example for the socialist, because free-market schooling involves adults forgoing current consumption not for their own long-term benefit but for that of their children. If poorer people are indeed as feckless as supporters of the Welfare State appear to assume, perhaps one of their most likely failings would be to neglect their children's education. Yet what are the facts about schooling in England before the 1870 Education Act? In 1813 the philosopher James Mill wrote that, within a fifty-mile radius of London ('which is far from the most instructed and virtuous part of the kingdom,' as he added in an aside to his fellow Scots), 'there is hardly a village that has not something of a school; and not many children of either sex who are not taught more or less, reading and writing. We have met with families in which, for weeks together, not an article of sustenance but potatoes had been used; yet for every child the hard-earned sum was provided to send them to school.' In 1813 the growing prosperity of the Victorian period lay in the future; as the century wore on, there occurred what E.G. West has described as a private-school 'explosion'. By 1858, according to the

Newcastle Commission on Popular Education which conducted an exhaustive statistical survey, virtually no child was failing to receive schooling, with the average length of schooling being 5.7 years. The ratio of children in school to the entire population was 1 in 7.7 – more than in Prussia, where schooling was compulsory. The commission found that parents who were themselves uneducated were remarkably good judges of teachers; within a few weeks of a good man being appointed to a previously unsuccessful school it would be full to overflowing with new pupils.

What we regard as a proper amount of education for a child has increased since the mid-nineteenth century. But so have working-class incomes. In 1962, total current expenditure on British education was less than the tax collected on tobacco (a tax which is paid by poor and rich alike – the most bloated capitalist does not smoke two cigars at once). Is it suggested that the descendants of the parents who sent their children to private schools while living exclusively on potatoes have become so degenerate that they would grudge lesser proportions of their own far more lavish incomes? I cannot believe it; but, if they really are so degraded, what can have degraded them if it is not the Welfare State's endlessly-repeated lesson that 'Nanny will sort out the big things in life for you; you just get on with enjoying yourself on the pocket money that Nanny allows you'?

If parents were left completely free to buy whatever education they chose for their children, no doubt occasional parents would make very odd decisions which others might not see as being in the child's best interests. But then the State does that, too, without being able to plead poverty as an excuse; recall the case of Claire Tomalin's son, discussed on pp. 36-7.

What is likely is that the patterns of activity which emerged in a liberal society would differ quite a lot from the patterns of activity promoted by a command system. Command systems always tend to favour what is orthodox, what is seen as morally uplifting or in accordance with traditional values, rather than what is experimental, offbeat, 'underground' or louche. Partly, no doubt, this is because people who attain positions of responsibility in a political structure tend to be po-faced men with traditional tastes, and partly it is because traditional values are perceived as supporting State power while 'underground' movements may threaten it. But the consequence is that, although the world of business is often seen as hostile to iconoclastic, experimental styles of living, in reality just the reverse is the case. Probably many men in the record industry find the various waves of modern music as unpleasant as I do, but if it is what the kids want then to a businessman his personal tastes are irrelevant – he produces the discs, because there is a market for them. In a thoroughgoing command economy such as those of Eastern Europe, on the other hand, pop music is scarcely obtainable. The State asserts by implication that its tastes are the real, 'proper' tastes, and conflicting tastes (however real for those who hold them) are somehow improper and do not need to be taken into account.

Samuel Brittan, assistant editor of the *Financial Times* and a leading British advocate of classical liberalism, put it as follows in his book *Capitalism and the Permissive Society* (1973):

> The values of competitive capitalism have a great deal in common with . . . contemporary radical attitudes. Above all they share a similar stress on allowing people to do . . . what they feel inclined to do rather than conform to the wishes of authority, custom or convention. Under a competitive system, the businessman will make money by catering for whatever it is that people wish to do – by providing pop records, or nude shows, or candyfloss. He will not make anything by providing what the establishment thinks is good for them. An individual citizen is free to maximise his income by using his abilities (and his capital if he has any) to cater for public tastes. But he does not have to. He can go for the easiest or most congenial job, or the one with the most leisure; or, like most of us, he can find some compromise. . . . In any case his life-style is his own.

It is ironic that so many partisans of this or that brand of 'alternative society' believe that in some vague way socialism is on their side. The reality is that thoroughgoing socialism would be likely to kill almost all of their various attempts to create the good life stone dead. However, as Brittan goes on to say, ' "competitive capitalism" is not a partisan slogan. When it comes to the test of practical application, it has at least as many opponents among Conservatives as among Labour supporters, and among businessmen as among trade unionists.' Ten years later I think Brittan would have to concede that there are now a few more genuine liberals in the Conservative Party than there are in the ranks of Labour. (In the Federation of Conservative Students, the hard-line liberal faction are coming to be known as the 'libbies', and they are starting to spread out from universities into the constituencies rather as hard-line socialists penetrated the Labour Party in the 1970s.) Nevertheless, Brittan's point remains broadly true now, as it was in Adam Smith's day: businessmen and the propertied classes are no more natural supporters of a genuinely free society than any other group. Markets force them to cater to others' free choices, often much against their own instincts.

This, then, is the case for the market. It was made by Adam Smith two centuries ago; only a few years ago it was seen as a quaint hangover from the days before democracy turned the State into Everyman's servant rather than his master. Writing in the *Times* in March 1976, Harry Johnson described the current view of Smith among professional economists as 'out of date and incompetent in the elementary theory of his subject'. For many years just one institution in Britain was concerned to publicize the case for the market, namely the Institute of Economic Affairs, a small, privately-financed organization run by Arthur Seldon and Ralph Harris (now Lord Harris of High Cross) which since 1957 has issued a steady stream of pamphlets and books discussing market solutions to various problems. For much of its existence the IEA was derided by orthodox thinkers.

Recently the IEA had won widespread recognition as one of the most valuable of the country's intellectual resources, and it has been joined by similar, newer organizations such as the Adam Smith Institute. By September 1978 the *Times* recognized the resurgence of the liberalism which Smith preached as 'the most interesting intellectual movement of our times'. 'The British socialist state,' it predicted, 'is doomed to disappear because it is felt by too many people to be a hateful way to run their affairs. . . . It is now the writers of the left establishment that have the appearance of being retreads, bouncing along with synthetic rubber stretched over the tired canvas.' In 1980 Milton Friedman's popularization of Smith's market principles, *Free to Choose*, captured widespread attention as a BBC television series.

(Milton Friedman is probably best known for his theory of monetarism. He has argued, on the basis of historical data, that inflation is caused solely by State actions affecting money-supply. Monetarism is only tangentially relevant to the liberal political movement. It is primarily an empirical claim about economic cause and effect rather than a prescription for policy; many liberals do not accept it as true; and it is not clear that liberalism need necessarily entail special hostility to inflation, although most liberals are in fact hostile to it. From the liberal point of view, Friedman's importance lies less in the new theories he has created than in his ability patiently and skilfully to restate the old ideas of classical liberalism, and to show how they are fully as relevant in modern conditions as they were when first invented.)

Meanwhile, as we shall see, the logic of liberal thought is being extended from the strictly 'economic' domain to areas of life not previously seen as having any connexion with economics; and, inside and outside the field of traditional economics, liberal principles are being pressed to logical conclusions which Adam Smith never dreamed of.

4/Economists of Love and Power

There is much more to life than buying and selling – thank goodness. No matter how intellectually convincing the economic arguments for a free market may be, they leave many people unmoved. They seem to treat human beings as cold, calculating automata swayed only by thoughts of money and money's worth. Economists reply that they make no assumptions about people invariably setting out to maximize their money incomes; often, an individual may prefer more leisure and less money rather than *vice versa*. And even when someone sets out to gain money this is not necessarily because he wants to spend it on selfish consumption; it may be for altruistic motives, as when someone tries to raise money to pay for better schooling for his child, or contributes heavily to charity. Nevertheless, the sceptic responds, the liberal's world-view overlooks large areas of our lives which are not economic *at all* – where decisions about getting and spending, goods and costs just do not arise. Furthermore these are some of the most important areas of our lives. A politics founded on economic theory implies a hopelessly blinkered, one-dimensional vision of the human condition.

If 'economics' means only what economics traditionally has meant, then surely this is a valid point. But one aspect of the liberal intellectual revolution has been the development of new styles of economic thinking. A New Economics has emerged, which does not contradict classical, Smithian liberal economics but treats it as a special case, relevant just to those particular aspects of human behaviour which are commonly mediated by money. For the new economists, their subject is not about one special category of human activity; it is a method of thinking about *any* activity. There is economics wherever there is choice. The choices that consumers make when they decide how to spend their money, or the choices made by enterprisers when they decide how to invest their capital, are an attractive category of choices to study because money makes economic behaviour measurable and economic theories testable. But the same principles that are easy to observe when money is involved are equally relevant to all other kinds of choice, and hence to all human action.

For some, this may render the dependence of political liberalism on economic theory more palatable. Others, admittedly, may find that the new economists' picture of human behaviour confirms their worst fears about the bleak inhumanity of the liberal view of Man. (To which the new economists would no doubt reply that they are not setting out to paint a pretty picture of our species, but an accurate one.)

The key figure in the 'New Economics' is Gary Becker, a colleague of Milton Friedman at the University of Chicago. Becker first made a name for himself with his book *Human Capital* (1964), which applied the tools of economic thinking to the study of how individuals invest in education in order to increase their lifetime earning potential. For Becker – as, indeed, for liberal economists in general – it is a naive error to think of 'capital' as meaning merely holdings of money, or of property that can be sold for money (with the corollary that the members of society can be divided into a group who possess significant quantities of capital, and another, larger group who have virtually none). Capital, fundamentally, is whatever can be made to yield an income. Land is an important form of capital (as everyone agrees) not directly because it can be sold, but because it can be rented out to people who have a use for it, or used directly by the owner in some way that will generate income. It is precisely because land yields an income in this way that it can be sold, and the price it fetches is a measure of people's beliefs about its income-yielding potential. All this is uncontroversial. But then, equally, the knowledge and skills locked up in a person's head must be regarded as a part (and a very important part) of his 'capital'. These things differ from land or money in that, once acquired, they cannot be exchanged (I can teach you, but this does not cause me to lose my abilities; I cannot hand over my brain to you). But they have the essential feature of capital: they yield future income. Whether someone works as an employee or for himself, he lives off his particular skills, abilities, and knowledge, some perhaps inborn but much acquired through formal or informal education and training. Becker quotes Benjamin Franklin: 'An investment in knowledge pays the best interest.' From this point of view, it no longer makes sense to divide society into 'capitalists' and 'workers'. Everyone is both: we all deploy the human or physical resources at our disposal in order to produce a certain level and style of life for ourselves and for those we care about.

The idea that mental attributes are capital is not original to Becker, but he is probably the first to have applied to it the sophisticated mathematical techniques of modern economic theory. Becker's pages are not easy for the layman; they bristle with graphs and algebraic equations. He uses these to explain why various observable facts about education, income, and employment are predictable, given the standard axioms of economics. For instance, unemployment is regularly higher among unskilled than skilled workers (not only in periods when new technology is increasing the demand for skilled labour), because the skills of skilled workers commonly embody an investment by their employers which the employers cannot afford lightly to discard. The greater an individual's natural ability, the more it pays him to improve that ability by investing in education (a finding which is not made irrelevant by State provision of 'free' education, because an important cost of education is the income that *could have* been earned if the individual chose to work rather than study). Most of the points in *Human Capital* represent novel explanations of reasonably familiar facts, but some conclusions are more controversial. For instance, the finding just mentioned suggests that it is contradictory for people sympathetic towards socialist ideals to regard State support for higher education as a 'good thing', as they tend to: unless they are prepared to make higher education not merely available but actually compulsory for the entire population, people who regard equality as an important goal might do better to outlaw higher education rather than encourage it. (This conclusion might be resisted by the large proportion of such people who make their own living from the higher-education industry.)

Human Capital extended the concept of 'capital' to non-commercial assets, but continued to discuss 'income' chiefly in terms of money earnings. In subsequent writings, though, Becker began to take seriously the fact that the concept of 'income' is in principle no more tied to cash than capital is. Economists in the twentieth century have often let the convenience of their calculations blind them to a fact of which the eighteenth- and nineteenth-century British founders of economic theory were perfectly well aware: individuals seek money incomes not because they want money for its own sake, nor even because they want the goods that money buys for their sakes, but because they want the intangible, often emotional benefits that goods can be used to produce, and to avoid the disbenefits that goods can be used to dispel. I buy a car, not because I want to call a lump of painted metal my own but because I can use it to solve my transport problems. I buy food not because owning it makes me happy but because I can use it to avoid the misery of hunger. The distinction between 'work' and 'leisure' is a myth: even when we are not doing the things for which an employer pays us, we are 'working' to produce satisfactions for ourselves and for others. A household is not a retreat from work but a little factory, and 'income' in the money sense is simply one of the raw materials it uses.

Another of those raw materials is time, which is a highly relevant factor in the production of many human satisfactions: 'A boat moored to the dock all season, the daily newspaper tossed out without being unfolded, or a quick lunch gulped down between appointments contributes . . . less utility than would a leisurely . . . use of each of these items.' The cost of anything, to an economist, is what one has to give up in order to get it; as incomes have risen sharply in modern history, time spent on non-revenue-earning activities has become correspondingly dearer. People often notice that, in a rich country like the USA, individuals are wasteful with material goods but behave grudgingly with their time, rushing from one activity to another and being unwilling to let time slip by unregarded – despite the fact that the standard working week is shorter for Americans than for inhabitants of more traditional societies, so that one might on the face of it expect Americans to be easy-going about time. For Becker, this contrast suggests no difference in tastes between Americans and others: the relative price of time to things is higher for Americans, so they are more economical with time and less with things (just as someone who finds that bread is getting dearer and rice cheaper will satisfy his appetite using more rice and less bread). Likewise, people sometimes justify progressive taxation by arguing that wealthy individuals show by their behaviour that an extra pound is worth less in real terms to them than it would be to a poor person; it is often suggested that advertising creates pseudo-wants whose satisfaction gives rich people no real fulfilment. For Becker this inference is unwarranted:

> It has been alleged that wealthy households reveal their relatively low evaluation of their money by 'frivolous' expenditures on 'inessential' convenience items, but these expenditures may also be interpreted as an efficient substitution away from their relatively scarce resource, time. . . . Such behavior indicates nothing about the absolute direction of change in the marginal utility of money income.

(Incidentally, though Becker does not say so, some liberals would point out that if taxation policy is to be decided in terms of the relative utility of money, and if an extra pound really is worth less to the man who earns £100,000 a year than it is to the man who earns £5,000, then this constitutes an argument not for progressive taxation but for its opposite. If a rich man and a poor man each earn an extra pound by their activities in the market then both are entitled to an equal increment of satisfaction in return for those activities. On the assumptions stated, this would imply taxing the poor man at a higher rate than the rich man, and perhaps establishing a 'supplementary benefit' system to top up the incomes of the very rich from State funds. These implications may suggest that there is something wrong with the premises.)

In a household, satisfactions are produced by teamwork. Some of Becker's most fascinating writings discuss the economics of marriage and family life. Marriage is itself a market, of a kind. At any time there are so many men and so many women of marriageable age, each of whom has various preferences as between members of the opposite sex, but marriage of any man to a given woman implies that he is unavailable for marriage to other women (and *vice versa*), just as use of a particular physical resource by a given producer or consumer implies that it is unavailable to others who could have used it. Becker argues that, given certain fairly plausible assumptions about the goals people have in marrying and the nature of the information available to them when searching for a mate, economics predicts that marriage-partners will be similar with respect to most traits, but *different* with respect to those traits which are 'substitutable', such as ability to earn money. (Earning-power is 'substitutable' because a high-earning partner can hand money over to a low-earning or non-earning partner, whereas a partner high in intelligence, for instance, cannot hand over a portion of his intelligence to his spouse.) Empirical research confirms the prediction: married couples are highly correlated in terms of features such as IQ, but high-income men tend to marry low-income women.

This latter differential is greater than can be explained by the fact that the *average* man earns more than the average woman. But issues of financial equality between the sexes are quite relevant to marriage: a move to increase women's earning-power relative to that of men tends to reduce the gains from marriage, and should therefore lead to fewer marriages and more divorces.

(As we have broached the subject of women's liberation, it is relevant to mention a further unobvious economic consequence of enforced economic equality between the sexes pointed out by another New Economist, Ivy Papps. Since an employer in a competitive economy cannot pay his labour force more than the value of its marginal product, legally-enforced increases in women's wages must be offset in the long run by (open or hidden) decreases in the wages of men doing the same work. In a society like ours, women work disproportionately in low-wage employment, and more middle-class than working-class wives work. Both of these facts imply that a law such as the Sex Discrimination Act represents a transfer of earning power from poor to rich households: low-earning men are more likely than high-earning men to be in competition with female colleagues and therefore to lose income to them, and their losses are less likely to be offset by their wives' gains. Ms Papps suggests that this may explain why the Women's Liberation Movement is often welcomed by educated men and women, who are likely to profit from it, and greeted with hostility by less educated men and women who are likely to lose by it.)

Becker's theory of marriage predicts (to simplify strenuously) that the gains from marriage rise with income, so that wealthier people should marry earlier and be less likely to divorce than poorer people. Although these predictions conflict with popular belief, American statistics tend to confirm them.

What, the reader may ask, about love? An economist might be forgiven for leaving love out of his equations; but Becker does not take that easy option – he cannot, since it is crucial for him to stress that the 'income' from marriage is much more than the flow of tangible goods and services consumed. As a result, parts of his analysis read bizarrely indeed to anyone accustomed to the fairly arid subject-matter of traditional economics.

> If . . . M_1 and F_2 were in love and had mutual and full caring, the optimal sorting would become M_1F_2, M_2F_1, and M_3F_3 because the incomes resulting from this sorting, $m_{12} = f_{21} = k > 6$ . . . can block the sorting along the diagonal. . . . The difference between k and 6 measures the output of love produced by M_1 and F_2.

After several pages of this sort of thing, Becker concludes 'I have shown . . . that the marriage market is more likely to pair a person with someone he cares about than with an otherwise similar person that he does not care about.' Well, some of us knew that without the help of mathematical economics. But that is unduly snide; Becker's analysis of love and caring yields not only results which are blindingly obvious but also other results which are subtle and unexpected.

Thus, people who would like to see society organized more on the basis of 'mutual aid' and less on that of individualistic competition sometimes point out that, within the family, mutual aid does seem to work rather well. Not only does the head of the household distribute his resources fairly unselfishly (which is not too surprising, given that he made a voluntary choice to take on family commitments), but children also tend not to engage in really savage competition for welfare against one another or their parents, though their family membership is quite involuntary. Becker shows that this is expected, *irrespective of how selfish the children may be*: a result he calls the 'rotten kid theorem' implies that provided the family contains *one* person who cares enough about the others to transfer resources to them, it actually pays all the others to behave *as if* they cared about one another even if they do not.

> . . . sufficient 'love' by one member guarantees that all members act as if they loved other members as much as themselves. As it were, the amount of 'love' required in a family is economized: sufficient 'love' by one member leads all other members by 'an invisible hand' to act as if they too loved everyone.

The reader may retort that this analysis implies considerable naivety about the degree of selfishness commonly exhibited in practice by brothers and sisters. I, too, have risked life and limb in resolving inter-sibling fights over Dinky toys; but it seems to me that these phenomena are not as damaging to Becker's thesis as they look. His predictions assume understanding by family members of the economic situation they are in, and of course very young children are likely to lack this understanding. What his theorem implies is that children of a loving parent should behave less egotistically as they learn more about the dynamics of family relationships, and this, surely, is true?

Becker's approach has implications for altruism outside the family also. One of his central assumptions is that we should not postulate major differences of temperament or taste between different groups of people, if their differences in behaviour can be explained instead as rational responses to different economic circumstances by people whose temperament and tastes are broadly similar.

An immediate consequence is that the idea that a command economy might be governed by a group of intellectuals who are not only relatively skilled at social planning but also relatively high-minded and disinterested is a delusion:

> . . . persons only choose to follow scholarly or other intellectual or artistic pursuits if they expect the benefits,

both monetary and psychic, to exceed those available in alternative occupations. Since the criterion is the same as in the choice of more commonplace occupations, there is no obvious reason why intellectuals would be less concerned with personal rewards, more concerned with social well-being, or more intrinsically honest than others.

Another consequence has to do with the charitable behaviour of different classes in society. Private charity is an important phenomenon for liberals; in a free society charity alone takes the place of the Welfare State in providing a safety-net to preserve the most unfortunate members of society from misery and starvation. Socialists, and socialist-inclined anarchists such as Kropotkin, have often suggested that people living in humble circumstances do a good deal of spontaneous helping one another out, whereas the middle classes are more inclined to 'keep themselves to themselves'. The suggestion is that money makes people selfish, and that this moral debasement of the relatively rich provides another justification for progressive or even punitive taxation. I have to say that I am sceptical about the alleged facts: my personal observations by no means confirm that poorer people do more for others than richer people. But, assuming that the facts are as stated, Becker's approach offers an explanation which does not suggest any moral difference between income-groups. Henri Lepage, the leading contemporary advocate of liberal thought in France, has explained the implications of Becker's ideas in the following terms. Suppose that altruistic activities serve to contribute to an individual's self-respect and/or the esteem in which others hold him. Like any other economic good, these satisfactions can be produced from different inputs having different costs; some other respect-generating activities, for instance, may well be less time-consuming than charitable work. In that case, people for whom time is relatively expensive will naturally tend to substitute some of these other activities for altruism in the production of esteem, and 'this explains why it is usually in very poor societies or among the working class that phenomena of social solidarity are most marked; that does not correspond to a difference in human nature, but simply to the fact that in these cases such activities are the most efficient means of achieving the desired goal.'

This is all very well, but it hardly comforts the reader who fears the arrival of a society in which the only safety-net for failure is charity by people who are ever less inclined to be charitable as they get ever richer. However, the analysis suggests that the rich will begrudge only those kinds of charitable activity which use up their own time. One kind of charitable activity is very economical of time, namely giving money. Richer people can (and do) give more money to charities than poorer people (indeed, Becker even claims that as people get richer they give higher *proportions* of their income to charity, though this is denied by other writers). Because of the advantages of the division of labour, gifts of money – though they may *look* less morally admirable – are in practice a more efficient way of achieving charitable purposes than gifts of time.

Becker's economic theories touch on a wealth of other social phenomena, such as crime, fertility-rates, fashion, advertising, most of which there is no room to discuss here. Let us just take an interesting example. Why does any society have customs and traditions, he asks in an article written jointly with his Chicago colleague George Stigler, who specializes in applying the New Economics to information and knowledge considered as a good. Because deciding how to behave is itself a costly activity, requiring time-consuming 'research' into the implications of alternatives if each decision is made independently, on its own merits. It is much 'cheaper' to follow set rules. Of course, sometimes it will pay in the long run to ignore the traditional rule and work out one's own solution to a question about how to act, but that option is rational only if the greater long-run returns from the autonomous action outweigh its greater initial cost. So, naturally, young people – who have longer to amortize their decision costs – are more innovative and less respectful of tradition than the old. At a fundamental level their preferences are no different, but the same fundamental preferences imply different patterns of behaviour in different circumstances.

It should be said that there are clear limitations to Becker's approach. In particular, his assumption that fundamental preferences are constant is no more than a convenient axiom; it is not something he has discovered (or, perhaps, could discover) by observation. As he puts it himself, 'Since economists generally have had little to contribute, especially in recent times, to the understanding of how preferences are formed, preferences are assumed not to change substantially over time, nor to be very different between wealthy and poor persons, or even between persons in different societies and cultures.' In less skilled hands, this axiom is made to yield somewhat absurd conclusions. Brian Micklethwait, a leading light of the London-based Libertarian Alliance, argues in all seriousness that the proliferation since the 1960s of sex shops, pornographic magazines, and the like does not correspond to a change in taste, morality, or law but merely to the rising cost of time: modern men and women must, as it were, use artificial aids to squeeze the maximum of sexual pleasure from expensive minutes spent in bed. We shall see in Chapter 6 that, for another important group of liberal economists, change in consumer preference is itself fundamental to an understanding of society, rather than something to be explained away. Nevertheless, many of the findings of the New Economics are unaffected by that proviso.

A specially topical aspect of the New Economics is its analysis of racial prejudice and discrimination. Becker has written a good deal on these matters; but perhaps even more interesting is the work of the economist Thomas Sowell of the University of California at Los Angeles, whose books – particularly the recent *Knowledge and Decisions* – in some ways stand in between the outlook of the Chicago school and that of the 'Austrians' to be discussed in Chapter 6.

Sowell is interested in the policy of 'reverse discrimination', under which the United States is setting out to compensate certain racial minorities for centuries of adverse treatment by encouraging or even legally enforcing openly preferential treatment for members of those minorities. For instance, an employer may be required to employ a certain proportion of blacks or persons of Spanish descent in his workforce even if this means choosing them in preference to better-qualified people who are not members of these minorities. At present reverse discrimination (often called, euphemistically, 'affirmative action') is a very widespread phenomenon in American society. The ethnic groups to which reverse discrimination applies are determined by a quango, the Equal Employment Opportunity Commission; remarkably, they include 'Orientals', a group which – as this term is understood in the USA – enjoy higher incomes and more favoured jobs than the average American.

Sowell comments on reverse discrimination, first, that insofar as it is aimed at a real problem that problem is very largely created by State and State-encouraged action. For instance, high unemployment among American blacks, whose family backgrounds tend to provide them initially with fewer marketable skills than whites, is caused by institutional arrangements that have artificially eliminated the supply of low-paid work that would give them the experience to move on to better things.

> Historically, lower skill levels did not prevent black males from having labor force participation rates higher than that of white males for every U.S. Census from 1890 through 1930. Since then, the general growth of wage fixing arrangements – minimum wage laws, labor unions, civil service pay scales, etc. – has reversed that and made more and more blacks 'unemployable', despite their rising levels of education and skill, absolutely and relative to whites. . . . The alternative explanation of high black teenage unemployment by 'racism' collides with two very hard facts: (1) black teenage unemployment in the 1940s and early 1950s was only a fraction of what it was in the 1960s and 1970s (and was no different from *white* teenage unemployment during the earlier period), despite the obvious fact that there was certainly no *less* racism . . . and (2) unemployment rates among blacks in their mid 20s drop sharply to a fraction of what it was in their teens, even though the workers have not changed color as they aged, but only become more experienced.

But Sowell goes on to argue that it may in any case be a myth that the groups favoured by reverse discrimination are in fact economically underprivileged in American society (even leaving aside the 'Orientals', who are known to be better off than the average American). For instance, statistics used by the government agencies overseeing reverse discrimination regularly ignore crucial demographic facts. Employers are often required to prove non-discrimination by employing quotas of various minorities which match the proportion of those groups in the population as a whole, but this

> disregards huge differences in age distribution among American ethnic groups, due to differences in the number of children per family. . . . The high-level positions on which 'affirmative action' attention is especially focused are positions normally held by persons with many years of experience and/or education – which is to say, persons more likely to be in their 40s than in their 20s. The purely demographic disparities among groups in these age brackets can be extreme. Half of all Jewish-Americans are forty-five years old or older, while only 12 per cent of Puerto Ricans are that old. Even a totally nondiscriminatory society would have gross 'underrepresentation' of Puerto Ricans in the kinds of jobs held by people of that age.

In a liberal society, employers have a concrete motive for ignoring racial prejudices: they do not pay. If there is widespread unwillingness to employ members of a given group, then the wages that such people can command will be relatively low; an employer who flouts the prejudice by employing them will increase his profits, and competition between employers will erode the wage-differential. It may be, of course, that prejudice is so strong that an employer who blatantly hires disfavoured persons will lose customers. In that case a liberal would argue that it is morally wrong to penalize the employer for the attitudes of his customers; but it remains true that the employer will be motivated to take on disfavoured workers wherever he can 'get away with it' – behind the scenes even if he cannot risk it at the reception desk. (The history of South Africa illustrates this point graphically. The pressure for economic *apartheid* has come consistently from white trade-unionists: the slogan of the white miners in the Rand rebellion of 1922 was 'Workers of the World Unite and Fight for a White South Africa.' Pressure for elimination of economic barriers against non-whites has regularly come from the representatives of financial capital, whose profits are damaged by the system.)

One of the effects of American reverse-discrimination policies, Sowell points out, is to remove the economic motive not to discriminate, or even to create an opposite economic motive. 'The general unattainability of many quotas means that penalties fall equally on discriminatory employers and nondiscriminatory employers. . . . Moreover, the ease with which a discrimination case can be made makes minorities and women more dangerous employees to have, in terms of future prospects of law suits if their subsequent pay, promotions, or other benefits do not match those of other employees or the expectations of administrative agencies.' Someone with a taste for racial discrimination loses nothing by indulging it, if he is forbidden to take commercial advantage of the lower supply-to-demand ratio for the labour of the disfavoured group, and could not hope to comply with the legal quota requirements even if he were more fair-minded; and discrimination avoids storing up possible trouble in the future. So he may as well discriminate. So he does.

When commentators such as the *Daily Telegraph*'s 'Peter Simple' discuss racial issues in terms like these, one cringes: the danger of glib arrogance riding roughshod over real, severe human problems seems so great. It is difficult to maintain this attitude to Thomas Sowell, after turning over a copy of *Knowledge and Decisions* and noticing that, apart from being a distinguished academic economist, and one who backs up his general arguments with a wealth of references to detailed research findings, Sowell is also (as appears from his photograph on the dust jacket) a black man. Sowell has a personal reason for the passion with which he denounces the institutional barriers now being created to the advancement of American minority groups – barriers which are not confined to employment but extend into many other areas of society.

Is 'reverse discrimination' simply a well-meaning mistake, then, which does nobody any real good? By no means. As Sowell points out, one class of people gain greatly from current policies: namely, those who staff and service the many agencies which supervise these policies, workers in the 'race relations industry'. Many, perhaps most of them are not members of the allegedly disadvantaged minorities.

The 'affirmative action' policy . . . had enormous impact on the agencies administering such policies. For example, within a period of three years the EEOC's [Equal Employment Opportunities Commission's] staff of lawyers increased tenfold. The impact on minority employment has been found to be relatively minor. Blacks have rejected preferential treatment 64 percent to 27 percent. Four-fifths of women also reject it. Indeed, no racial, regional, sex, income or educational group studied by the Gallup Poll favors preferential treatment. Yet the drive of the administering agencies . . . has been enough to continue [these] policies. . . .

The inclusion of 'Orientals' among the groups entitled to reverse discrimination is quite rational from the point of view of the true beneficiaries of the policy. The career structure within the race relations industry is improved by bringing more racial groups within its purview, so that if (as is the case in the USA) race relations workers themselves determine which groups count for reverse discrimination purposes we would expect them to err on the side of generosity – to themselves.

The domain of racial discrimination is not unusual in these respects, and Sowell does not suggest that it is:

The growth of administrative agencies is not merely the growth of an arm of government performing assigned tasks. It is the growth of a sector with its own political initiatives . . . constantly pushing for an expansion of its activities and benefits . . . programs whose costs exceed their benefits may not only continue but expand . . . it is understandable that between 1950 and 1970 [US] government payments to farmers increased tenfold, even though the number of farms were reduced about 50 percent, that heavily criticized programs like Urban Renewal had their appropriations tripled in less than a decade, or that expenditures on elementary and secondary education have risen exponentially while both the numbers and performances of [pupils] have been declining.

(If the domain of racial discrimination is 'special', it is because of the quasi-religious deference with which orthodox beliefs in that domain are treated. Dissent is heresy, to be eliminated ruthlessly. Dan Aronoff has written about the 'viciousness with which some of [Sowell's] opponents attack him. His arguments have rarely been addressed by his opponents, but his person is constantly being attacked.' Aronoff tells of his own experiences discussing Sowell's work with academics concerned with community relations – workers in the race relations industry, in other words. 'Their responses range from "Uncle Tom" and similar abusive expressions to more sober rejections . . . one scholar told me he couldn't stomach an approach which didn't impute social outcomes to intentional actions. When I cited statistical evidence, he said that "people are not numbers". When I described some of the conclusions of economic theory, he said: "the real world is more complicated than textbooks".' People make a good living out of race relations; a threat to that living is no occasion for the niceties of rational thought.)

If members of the State salariat are able to influence their own (tangible or intangible) income through their behaviour at work, then they too are economic agents and their activities can be explored and explained using the tools of market economics. The 'Virginia School', a group of scholars based mainly in the State of Virginia, does just this. As Gordon Tullock, one of the leading 'Virginians', has put it, thinking about 'bureaucrats' (civil servants and quasi-civil-servants) has lagged a couple of centuries behind thinking about business. In the Middle Ages and later, merchants were seen as carrying out a social duty; their attempts to maximize profits were perceived as immoral failures to limit themselves to asking the 'just' price for their merchandise, though people said little about how 'just prices' could be determined, and what was said made little sense. Adam Smith changed our view of businessmen: the only 'just price' for anything is the price that emerges from free bargaining between suppliers and purchasers who can be regarded as acting purely selfishly *in their behaviour towards one another* (irrespective of how selfish or otherwise they may be in the rest of their lives). This selfishness is not anti-social: it promotes the welfare of members of society more efficiently

than businessmen could do if they *tried* to act philanthropically.
In the case of public servants, on the other hand, it is still
common to assume that self-interest is irrelevant to their
decisions.

> Most of the existing literature . . . assumes that, when an
> activity is delegated to a bureaucrat, he will either carry out
> the rules and regulations or will make decisions in the public
> interest regardless of whether it benefits him or not. We do
> not make this assumption about businessmen. We do not
> make it about customers in the market. I see no reason why
> we should make it about bureaucrats. . . . The theory of
> bureaucracy should be based upon the assumption that
> bureaucrats are as self-seeking as businessmen, and it should
> concern itself with the design of constraints which will make
> the bureaucrats' self-interest identical with the interests of
> society.

Tullock is not just nihilistically attacking all bureaucracy as
bad. Indeed, the Virginia School is much more willing than
many other groups discussed in this book to recognize that
States produce valuable services, and to accept that in many
cases only States can produce those services. The Virginians'
point is far subtler: like businessmen, bureaucrats' behaviour
too yields, via an 'invisible hand', a pattern of production and
consumption that none of the participants individually plan or
anticipate. This pattern tends to be much less well geared to the
real welfare of citizens than the pattern produced by business,
but there are concrete devices that can improve it.

We usually assume for simplicity that an owner of financial
capital aims to maximize his money profits. Of course that is
over-simple. For instance, some men start publishing firms
knowing that they could make more money in other lines,
because literary activity yields an intangible 'income' which for
some people can outweigh a large shortfall in money income.
But the assumption that businessmen care only about the
measurable factor, money, is like a physicist's assumption that
an inclined plane is perfectly smooth – he knows the assumption
is wrong, but it is close enough to the truth to be worth making
for the sake of calculation. In this spirit, what factor can we treat

the bureaucrat as aiming to maximize? We get a good approximation to reality, the Virginians suggest, if we suppose the bureaucrat aims to maximize the *size of his bureau*.

William Niskanen develops the economic implications of the size-maximizing principle in his book *Bureaucracy and Representative Government* (1971). (Niskanen is an economist who spent much of his career working in Washington for the US civil service, vainly attempting to improve its efficiency.) Intuitively, I find the assumption very plausible: it matches my own experience of work in a university department. In Virginian terms this is a 'bureau': it operates mainly on a regular grant of money which is related tenuously, at most, to voluntary payments made by 'customers' in exchange for its services. Discussions in departmental meetings frequently revolve round the issue of how we can maximize our allocation of university funds and keep our full complement of staff or, preferably, increase it – just as discussions at university level often concern attempts to maintain or increase our university's funding *vis-à-vis* other universities or other types of public expenditure. We very often discuss how to present and publicize our activities to make them seem, to those who control funds, to deserve continued or increased support. Questions of whether our ways of spending public money *actually* do the public more good than alternative possible uses are rarely raised; people feel embarrassed if, occasionally, they are. It is not that we are exceptionally selfish, deceitful people – there would be no way for us to judge such questions if we were particularly concerned to do so. Here are our research projects, which we engage in because we believe them to be worthwhile, and here are our graduate students, good chaps all, seeking footholds on the academic career-ladder: how can we weigh what we know and love even against the dimly-understood activities of the Biology or the Drama department, let alone against the myriad uses to which the funds could be put if they did not enter our university? We cannot; so we push for expansion of our little empire, and so does every other bureau and sub-bureau in the land.

What pattern does the 'invisible hand' produce from this? According to economic theory, that depends on the degree of competition between bureaux providing equivalent services, and – since knowledge affects bargaining power – on the distribution of knowledge between bureaux and their paymasters. In many cases, a bureau is a monopolist with, effectively, a single customer: the North Yorkshire Constabulary is the only supplier of police services in North Yorkshire, and its services are bought by the ratepayers of North Yorkshire acting collectively. In such circumstances, it is predicted that the provision of police services will fail to coincide with the social optimum that would emerge from a competitive market with many sellers and many buyers, unless two utterly unrealistic conditions are met: namely, that the single customer knows everything there is to know about the costs of providing various levels of service, and that the single seller (the police force itself) knows nothing at all beyond the funding actually received for the service being currently provided.

In reality, of course, the providers of the service are the experts, and those who pay for it are relatively ignorant about the costs of alternatives. Reality is much closer to the opposite extreme of knowledge distribution, under which the police are fully aware of the economics of their work and the public know only what they are actually paying for what they are actually getting. At that extreme, the bureau is predicted to grow, past the socially-optimal point, to the point at which the customer is indifferent as between buying the service at that price and not having it at all: every street would have a couple of genial bobbies helping old ladies to cross safely, but paying for them all would bleed us so white that it would be a toss-up whether we preferred to manage without any police.

(Here I treat the ratepayers of the county as making the decision about how much police service to buy. If the decision is out of their hands; then the relevant costs are not the costs to the ratepayers but the costs to whoever makes the decision. These costs might be much lower, in which case the police force would tend to grow far larger still.)

Of course knowledge is never as unequally distributed as this. Members of a bureau will always tend to know more about the relative costs of different levels of service than the customers know, but the customer will have at least some knowledge. Members of the bureau can improve their bargaining position by striving to minimize customer knowledge. (When the Thatcher government began to impose spending limits on local authorities, it was widely reported that social services departments were choosing to sacrifice relatively vital activities and leaving behind-the-scenes fat untrimmed, which is a good way of making the necessary costs of a service appear higher to outsiders than they are. In 1983 a law lecturer in a British university published a statement claiming that his and his colleagues' workloads were shockingly low, and his Vice-Chancellor reacted by threatening him with dismissal, with little consideration for niceties about academic freedom or the scholar's duty to pursue the truth wherever it may lead. Tullock quotes a number of American examples of the same phenomenon.) Conversely, competition between bureaux providing equivalent services is a good way to increase customer awareness of necessary costs, and there can be a useful degree of 'competition' in this sense even when bureaux enjoy local monopolies: it would be hard for the North Yorkshire Constabulary to pretend that a given level of security costs £X million if the Cumbria Constabulary is managing to provide the same level of security at half the price. (Happily for me, universities come off particularly well in this respect: one would predict far less over-funding of universities, whose products are very substitutable for one another, than of, say, the armed forces, which enjoy something much closer to a perfect monopoly.)

There is a temptation to see the modern State as something which has developed a life of its own, constantly seeking to aggrandize itself at the expense of its subjects. Of course, in a literal sense States are not alive. It is, principally, this urge of individual bureaucrats to enlarge their separate bureaux which makes the State *behave* as if it were alive and greedy to swallow up its subjects' freedom. While there is general agreement among the population that the State's sphere of activity is restricted to particular services which only a State can provide – that is, while there is no 'consumer demand' for other services from the State – the natural expansionism of bureaucracy may be held in check. Once citizens in general come to accept the Welfare State axiom that *any* type of good may appropriately be provided by the State, there ceases to be any necessary limit to State aggrandizement short of the point at which it consumes so much of the national product that the citizens are no better off than they would be in conditions of lawless anarchy.

Appropriate institutional arrangements can limit the excessive growth of bureaux; but only the political process can provide these arrangements, and economics applies to political behaviour, too. The Virginia School analyses the actions both of voters and of politicians in economic terms.

There is of course a famous traditional school of thought which analyses politics in terms of economics. According to Marxism a person's political standpoint is determined by his role in the productive process, whether as provider of capital, renter of land, or seller of labour. We have seen that the distinction between 'capitalist' and 'worker' is much less clearcut than people supposed until recently; but, even accepting that distinction, the Virginia School is unimpressed by Marxist theories of the economic determination of politics, based as they are on classes rather than individuals. Marx implies that, on occasions when an individual's self-interest conflicts with the wider interest of the class to which he belongs, he subordinates the former to the latter; according to the Virginians, that rarely happens in real life. 'The phenomenon of textile unions and textile firms combining to bring political pressure for the prohibition of Japanese imports is much more familiar in the current American scene than any general . . . political activity of labor, capital, or landed interests,' as James Buchanan and Gordon Tullock pointed out in one of the earliest Virginia School texts.

Normally, we expect an individual to vote for a policy, or for the package of policies offered by a candidate or a party, if he believes that on balance he personally stands to gain from the policy or policies (making due allowance, naturally, for uncertainties about whether political promises will be translated into action). In most Western countries (Switzerland is an exception) citizens normally choose large bundles of policies on an all-or-nothing basis by voting for a party, rather than voting for individual policies case by case, and this creates the seemingly paradoxical situation that voters can actually damage their collective interests by acting rationally. As an artificially simple example, suppose there is a community containing just nine voters. Some policy which would impose £1 of costs on each voter is greatly desired by voter A – it would increase his personal welfare by £7, though doing nothing for the others. A needs only four of the other voters to get this policy passed by a majority; and he can do this, if it is bundled up in a package with four other comparably-expensive policies which other individual voters have a similar special interest in – the whole package will give each of the five voters £7 of welfare in exchange for only £5 of total costs. Yet, from the point of view of the total society, each policy is being bought for £9 and is doing only £7 worth of good. In its miniature way, this is surely a very familiar picture of how special-interest politics nowadays puts together 'constituencies' of various groups, each of whom is near-fanatically keen on some idiosyncratic cause. In real life it is not often possible in practice to check whether the social costs of such horse-trading exceed the gains, but it comes as little surprise to learn that, mathematically, they easily may.

Virginia School members ask how democracy can be prevented from producing such negative outcomes. Perhaps because they have a tendency to relish algebraic manipulation, their answers are in terms of rejigged voting rules – the paradox of society choosing to pay £9 in order to gain £7 would be eliminated by a rule requiring changes of policy to receive 60 per cent or 70 per cent agreement rather than merely '50 per cent plus one', and Buchanan and Tullock suggest on mathematical grounds that a desirable constitution would impose a higher threshold of assent to a proposed collective action 'the more closely this action amounts to the creation and confiscation of human and property rights'. (Voters can rationally choose to adopt a constitution that prohibits many *individual* policy-changes which they would rationally favour, because from each individual voter's point of view the constitution may prohibit more unfavourable possibilities than favourable ones. Like other liberals, Americans of the Virginia

School tend to look askance at the reluctance of the British political tradition to impose constitutional limits on the sovereignty of Parliament.)

An alternative to the more-than-majority voting rule which the Virginians do not explore, although it is arguably more practical (though yet more alien to British traditions), would be to unbundle policies, and move to a Swiss system of 'direct democracy' by frequent referendums. And many liberals would take it for granted that, if any action amounts to the confiscation of human or property rights, an acceptable constitution should disallow it however large the majority in favour – but we have seen that the Virginians are relatively pragmatic about individual freedom; they seem unconcerned about imposing any kind of costs on individuals so long as the gains to (other) individuals outweigh them.

Bureaucrats seek to maximize the size of their bureaux, and voters their personal gains from public policy. Politicians, obviously, aim to maximize the number of votes they receive, and they can do this by seeking out policies which meet with voters' approval, just as businessmen try to design products that will sell to customers. (James Buchanan has pointed out that Keynes's recipe for using demand-management to emancipate society from the rigours of classical economic discipline was doomed to failure: it rested on the naively false assumption that politicians, being 'civilized' men, would be fully as willing to push the tiller in an electorally-unpopular direction, when the recipe required that, as they were to pull it in a vote-winning direction when this was economically appropriate.) A party making large 'monopoly gains' by being first in the field to offer voters a newly-popular 'product', say reduction of inflation, will find competitors moving in to capture a share of its 'market'.

These things may seem no more than cynical ways of expressing banal truths, but if the economic approach to politics is taken seriously it yields results which are not obvious or trivial. For instance, would we expect the number of parties in a political system to affect the degree of difference between their policies? Intuitively it is not obvious that we would: one can imagine a two-party system being highly polarized, with its opposing parties further apart than any pair of parties in a three-party system. But now consider a more obviously 'economic' problem: how does the operator of an ice-cream stall maximize his sales on a crowded beach? If he is first in the field, presumably he takes up his position in the middle of the beach. If a second ice-cream seller arrives, his best location is right next to the first man: that way he has a fair chance of getting half the customers, but if he stations himself anywhere else then he will be further away than the first man from more than half of the bathers. Only when a third salesman arrives does it pay him or his predecessors to space themselves out. Now return to politics, and notice how the virtual two-party system of the 1950s and 1960s was marked by 'Butskellite' consensus, whereas we nowadays have three major parties (counting the Alliance as one) and several further significant groups, and the contrast between Conservative and Labour is far greater than before.

Some people regard this view of politics as just too cynical to entertain. At a conference organized by the Institute of Economic Affairs in 1978, Jo Grimond – a very liberal Liberal, and the last British politician one would suspect of choosing his policies on 'profit-maximizing' grounds – insisted that the economic view of politics does not work. 'A lot of [political decisions], I think, could come only from personal beliefs. Many Members of Parliament don't want power' – and he quoted the example of a rather eccentric extreme left-wing former Labour MP.

Of course, if some politicians do not set out to gain power and do not get it, this does not hurt the economic analysis; individuals differ in the extent to which they act on principle rather than in terms of self-interest, and an economist is as willing to recognize the existence of politicians who put principles before popularity and remain firmly on the back benches as he is to recognize the existence of businessmen who insist on offering consumers what they think the customers ought to want and rapidly go out of business. But there is more to Grimond's point than that. Politicians do trim, but even the successful ones are often not *merely* trimmers – they compromise their principles but, arguably, do not abandon them wholesale.

Understandably, because sincerity is part of what consumers want. Someone who buys a front-loading washing machine does not care whether its makers used to produce the top-loading kind, but a politician known to swing like a weathercock is an unattractive candidate. *If* successful politicians are sometimes even sincerer than can be explained by their need to be perceived by voters as such, then the economist's explanation is that, when the very considerable personal costs of achieving political success (the wear and tear of electioneering, the mind-numbing boredom of constituency work, and so forth) are subtracted from the other rewards attached to that success, the balance is so low that the career appeals only to those who can derive large intangible rewards from promoting causes they care about.

The point is worth bearing in mind, when parliamentarians complain about their poor pay, archaic working conditions, and the like. The country whose public life is most highly principled is to my mind unquestionably Switzerland; there are many reasons for this, but one relevant point is that members of the Swiss parliament receive no salary.

For people who prefer to live in a world of romantic make-believe, the New Economics can seem fairly merciless in the way it strips the mystique from aspects of life both public and private. All it does, however, is to take seriously the idea that society is everywhere staffed by people whose behaviour is governed by the same mixture of selfishness tempered by redeeming flashes of decency which two thousand years of the Christian tradition have taught each of us to recognize in ourselves. It is up to us so to arrange the institutions of society that the general good is promoted, not hindered, by the nature of fallen Man.

5/Professions Versus the Individual

Liberals oppose the authority principle wherever they find it. 'Government', the State, is never the sole repository of authority in a society. In previous ages, the church was a rival to the State as a source of authority in European societies; in Roman Catholic countries, for many people, it still is. In late-twentieth-century England the established church no longer plays this role, and in recent decades the Church of England has been a follower rather than leader of secular trends, jumping belatedly and without dignity onto fashionable bandwagons. But its mantle of authority has been assumed by other groups. Doctors, it is often said, are the twentieth-century priests. More generally, the learned professions have elevated themselves to a greater or lesser extent into sources of authority over various domains of life; like the authority exercised by the church in earlier periods, the authority of the professions is partly dependent on State backing and partly autonomous.

The rise in status of the professions might be seen as part of a general movement in society which has increasingly tended to rob consumers of their sovereignty over production and transferred it to organizations claiming to represent productive workers. A professional organization such as the General Medical Council or the Law Society is, after all, a genteel sort of trade union which has been very successful in negotiating closed-shop agreements. To quote Eliot Freidson's widely-respected study of the medical profession, 'so far as the terms of work go, professions differ from trade unions only in their sanctimoniousness'. But the learned professions deserve to be considered separately, because their mode of exercising authority is in a sense specially insidious. When a manual workers' union sets out to achieve a closed shop or some other bargaining point, there is little mystery about its motives: a better standard of living for its members and/or its leaders. The professions involve a mystique; professional organizations invariably claim that their function is to serve the public by maintaining high standards of performance, a claim which few ordinary trade unions would dream of making. The learned professions, by definition, involve complex intellectual skills which outsiders find hard to evaluate, and it is suggested that these groups of workers must therefore police themselves and weed out unsuitable practitioners in order to protect the public from substandard work which they could not guard themselves against on the basis of their own knowledge – particularly since the consequence of poor work in domains such as medicine or law can be more catastrophic than an unwise choice of sofa or food-mixer.

There is a measure of truth in this; but only a measure. Many other trades involve complex skills difficult for the layman to assess, yet they are not controlled by guilds possessing authority comparable to that of professional organizations. If the electrician who rewires my house, or the mechanic who overhauls my car, do their work really badly, the consequences may be even more final than those which ensue from poor legal advice; and I personally find it far easier to check the advice I get from a solicitor than to monitor an electrician's or a mechanic's work. Yet anyone is free to set up as an electrician or a mechanic; there are quite a lot of people about who are working as car mechanics with no formal qualifications. Even so, one does not seem to hear of more people being electrocuted by incorrectly-installed wiring or killed by wrongly-fitted brakes than one hears of people getting into serious messes through poor legal advice. Nor do people seem to have much trouble choosing better rather than worse mechanics or electricians when several are available; word gets round when a superior practitioner sets up in business locally, and people like me who find cars mysterious listen to friends who are obviously better judges of mechanics' aptitudes, just as, perhaps, some of my friends listen to my comments on good and bad solicitors.

Surely, it is not mainly because of the complexity of their skills that doctors and lawyers belong to powerful professional organizations and electricians and mechanics do not. It is because doctors and lawyers are drawn from the middle class, attracted the deference which within recent memory was granted automatically to anyone with a certain kind of accent and clothing, and have been able to apply their intellectual talents to political manoeuvring as well as to the acquisition of their professional expertise. Mechanics and electricians speak in unpolished tones and dress like the manual workers they are, and their talents, being practical rather than intellectual, give them little advantage in political dealings. No doubt the professions would always have been somewhat more lucrative, because intellectual abilities are scarcer than practical abilities; but, the more life comes to depend on political rather than straightforwardly commercial relationships, the stronger the relative position of the learned professions becomes. Some decades ago professional men were people who were commissioned to do jobs of work like any other tradesman. Nowadays they determine much of the fabric of the layman's life, irrespective of his own wishes.

In one chapter I cannot offer a comprehensive survey of the professionalization of modern life. Instead, I shall look at two examples drawn from opposite extremes of the spectrum of professional occupations, and show how both have succeeded in exerting very comparable malign influences over individual members of society. What is true of two such different examples, I suggest, is very likely to be true across the professional board.

My first example is the profession of architecture and town planning. (Technically these are counted as two distinct professions, but in real terms they are different specializations within the overall activity of designing the built environment, and practitioners of both branches are influenced by the same body of ideas and theories.)

As we saw in earlier chapters, the activities of members of this profession since the war have had many unhappy consequences. A friend whose job it is to know such things tells me that if you ask older inhabitants of an urban area what one aspect of modern life they most dislike, they tend to have little hesitation in identifying 'redevelopment'. Admittedly, we cannot know what the results would have been like in practice if architectural fashions in the postwar decades had been very different from what they actually were, but on the face of it this does seem to be a case where professionalization of an activity has not succeeded in producing good service to the public. And architecture is an interesting case, because the arguments for treating it as a profession seem rather weak. Bad architecture does not have the thoroughly lethal consequences which can arise from bad medical practice (there are State building regulations, enforced by inspectors, which control safety aspects of building techniques, so the architect cannot claim that his professional expertise is what safeguards us against the roof falling in). In legal matters many otherwise competent adults really are close to children, having no idea what their situation is before the expert explains it, but architectural practice deals with the design of places where we live and work day-in, day-out, and ordinary people certainly have views about what they find satisfactory and what they dislike in this domain. Agreed, they may not be able to envisage possible new designs; but they can and do make judgments about existing buildings.

It might seem that the architecture side of the architecture-and-town-planning trade could quite adequately be controlled by the market mechanism of consumer preference, so that the ostensible purposes of professional status are irrelevant to it. (Town planning is a special case: its very existence as an activity presupposes that decisions within its domain are made by organs of State rather than via the market.) Early in the twentieth century architecture was not yet a profession, and it was controversial whether it ought to become one. Seventy eminent architects and artists addressed a memorial to the Royal Institute of British Architects complaining that professionalization was 'opposed to the interests of architecture as a fine art,' that 'the profession of architecture is an absurdity.' A few decades later architecture was professionalized by virtually any criterion. The Architects' Registration Act of 1938 made it illegal for anyone not in membership of the RIBA to call himself an 'architect': the producers' cartel had succeeded in invoking State power to enforce its dominant position in the market for building design.

Like any other cartel, the RIBA enforces practices which are much more easily understood in terms of protecting the interests of the members and the organization than in terms of protecting the public. Its scale of minimum fees is only the most obvious example (unsurprisingly, it does not set *maximum* fees). Or consider the rules on competitions. Clients commissioning important buildings often want to improve their chances of getting a good design by throwing it open to competition, but they are not allowed to select the entry they prefer: RIBA rules require that judging must be in the profession's rather than the client's hands, and that the client must commit himself beforehand to build the design which the judges choose.

(The one ultimate measure of professionalization which has eluded the RIBA is a legal ban on non-members *practising* architecture; when Derek Senior wrote his layman's guide to the profession, *Your Architect*, he mentioned that most private houses were still not architect-designed, while commenting wistfully that 'more than one Minister of the Crown has suggested that to buy a house which has not been designed by an architect . . . is like engaging an unqualified surgeon to remove your appendix.' In this respect, not just in connexion with architecture but more generally, Britain remains relatively faithful to its liberal past. I am still free to accept your commission for an appendectomy, so long as I do not pretend to be a qualified surgeon. In the USA, for instance, it is illegal for someone without official medical qualifications even to prescribe a simple folk remedy as an unpaid act of friendship; and State licensing of commercial trades stretches to laughable extremes – in the American State where I spent several years, barbers were licensed.)

Derek Senior's book just referred to, which was published in 1964 under the aegis of the RIBA, is quite revealing about architectural attitudes. Senior was not himself an architect, and the Foreword by the RIBA President warned that 'neither I nor any other architect will accept all that Derek Senior says by way of criticism or proposes by way of remedy for the faults he sees.' Yet, to a reader who does not come to Senior's book with the prior assumption that British architects are a highly superior body of men, his treatment seems almost sycophantic. Again and again Senior suggests that the mere client should not presume to try to impose his will on his architect – even though, unfortunately, 'there are still a few architectural lackeys who will obsequiously indulge a benighted client's every whim. . . . ' Most architects would not stoop so low; indeed they no longer see themselves as acting on behalf of the nominal 'client' merely because he is providing the cash. 'The architect . . . regards his client as the agent of the building's users'; 'He can legitimately claim that the public's interest in the visual quality of its everyday environment will be best served by allowing his own trained judgment to override the prejudices of an aesthetically untutored client – and in the long run the client himself is likely to prove grateful for his firmness . . . his duty as an artist is to offer the users of buildings a visual experience of the highest order that they may be (*or, given the opportunity, may become*) capable of appreciating' (my italics).

The profession has succeeded quite well in persuading clients to accept this subordinate position, and it has been helped in this by the fact that the growing State domination of economic activities means that private clients have increasingly been replaced by official bodies which spend other people's money rather than their own. 'Councillors with strong anti-modernist prejudices [i.e. who are reluctant to condemn their voters to life in stacks of concrete shoe-boxes] may exercise their right to blow off steam, but more often than not they do so in the form "I think it stinks, but if the architect says it's beautiful . . . " If they do press their objections, the majority can be relied upon to act on the principle that there is no sense in keeping a dog and barking yourself.' (There are various grounds on which one may reasonably dislike the phenomenon of privately-held capital, but it is worth noting that few private clients say to their architect 'I think it stinks, but here is my cheque for £X million so that you can get it built.')

Of course there is a nugget of sense in the architect's attitude to the client, as Senior portrays it. The client is not the only person affected by the appearance of a building: beautiful architecture is a 'public good', ugly architecture a 'public bad'. That might be a reason to give the public at large some say in the design of buildings. But in practice architects' insistence that *clients* should not be the judges of good architecture means that *architects themselves* take over this function; and it is not clear why they see themselves as better equipped to act as proxies for the general public than their clients are.

In two very important ways they are worse equipped. Architects' clients represent a wide spectrum of the population, and if one of them is aesthetically eccentric in one direction another will have the opposite eccentricity, whereas architects belong to a small, tightly-knit intellectual community who are all exposed to the same tides of aesthetic fashion at the same time. More important, architects have a clear interest in making a reputation for themselves by producing remarkable, aesthetically extreme buildings, while the public (and architects' clients) may often prefer buildings in unobtrusive good taste. Now that the austerely brutal 'modernism' which dominated architectural thinking for much of the twentieth century has come to be very widely rejected even by architects themselves, it is becoming obvious how the professionalization of architecture has served in practice to impose on masses of laymen who dislike it a style of building and even a style of urban life that happened to seem good to a few influential but idiosyncratic men at a particular point in history. As Bruce Allsopp wrote in 1974, 'The supreme fallacy of modern architectural thought is that if the architect designs what he knows, by his own introverted standards of pure architecture, to be best, the public *ought* to grow to like it. Why the hell should they?'

The swing of fashion has thrown architects much more on the defensive than they were twenty years ago, but their attitude of superiority to lay taste is far from dead yet. In 1982 a competition was held for an extension to the National Gallery in Trafalgar Square. One entry, by Richard Rogers (co-architect of the Pompidou Centre in Paris), exemplified just the kind of 'progressive' style that the man in the street often finds fairly thoroughly repellent – as Gavin Stamp described it, 'exposed construction, exposed services, exposed staircase pods . . . [a] composition of rods, shafts and staircases [completed by] a tower with a revolving top'. Owen Luder, then President of the RIBA, despite the neutrality that might be thought appropriate to his position went on record as hoping that the judges would 'have the courage' to choose the Rogers entry, which 'is the work of a man who has said, "That is what I think the answer is, and sod you." '

David Watkin, in his book *Morality and Architecture*, brings out very clearly the way in which architects (not only in the twentieth century – but very strikingly in the twentieth century) have elevated their personal tastes and foibles into moral imperatives which the rest of society are obliged to accept. In our century the chief source of architectural fashion has been Germany, home of the Bauhaus whose leader Walter Gropius wrote in 1935 that 'the ethical necessity of the New Architecture can no longer be called in doubt.' Twentieth-century architectural theorists, according to Watkin, have commonly been what Sir Karl Popper has called 'historicists' – believers, like Marx, in an inexorable trend of social development which it is either impossible or immoral to resist. (The impossible/immoral ambiguity is strongly present in Marx's thought also.)

The Swiss-American Sigfried Giedion's *Space, Time and Architecture* (1941), described by Gropius as 'the standard work on the development of modern architecture' and republished in many editions and many languages, announced that 'in spite of the seeming confusion there is nevertheless a true, if hidden, unity, a secret synthesis, in our present civilization. . . . The contemporary movement is not a "style" in the nineteenth-century meaning. . . . It is an approach to the life that slumbers unconsciously within all of us.' In the work of twentieth-century architects, according to Giedion, 'past, present and future merge together as the indivisible wholeness of human destiny.' When Giedion descends from these windy abstractions to identify specific components of the modern cultural imperative, as Watkin points out, 'we come sharply down to earth and discover that they are no more than his own tastes and fancies: " . . . the undulation of the wall, . . . the open ground-plan". . . . who can pretend that a preference for an undulating rather than a straight wall represents some permanent and unchallengeable reality?'

For architectural 'historicists', tradition is totally irrelevant: the aim is architectural revolution, not evolution. Sometimes this attitude has been expressed with extreme fanaticism, as for instance in 1919 by Bruno Taut: 'our (traditional) concepts, "space", "homeland", "style"! To hell with them . . . ! Destroy them, break them up! Nothing shall remain! Break up your academies, spew out the old fogies . . . Blast! Blast!' (Two years after publishing these ravings in his magazine *Dawn*, Taut was appointed Director of Municipal Construction for the city of Magdeburg, and later went on to direct some of the most important housing developments of Weimar Germany.) Such attitudes took longer to develop in Britain, but, when James Stirling (currently perhaps the leading 'modernist' architect in Britain) was a student at the Liverpool School of Architecture in the late 1940s, the intellectual atmosphere there left him 'with a deep conviction of the moral rightness of the new architecture'. By 1961 a *Progressive Architecture Manifesto* was published in Oxford which announced that 'In the event of war breaking out . . . we ask you to bomb as many historic buildings as possible. Most of these buildings are at present either museums or houses of prayer and are not usually inhabited. Loss of life will be minimal and your bombs will save future generations. Do not be sentimental.' Of course we know that (presumably) youthful follies like this are often tempered in practice by seniors' caution, but they serve to make very clear which way the weathercock of fashion is pointing.

In any case, extremes of anti-traditional folly were often *not* avoided. Nothing done in Britain in the 1960s quite matches the achievement of the People's Republic of China in totally razing the monumental city walls of Peking; but Watkin points out that Sir Leslie Martin produced a scheme for the 'development' of Whitehall that was taken quite seriously by government (although eventually dropped in 1965), which would have involved 'the elimination of numerous buildings of interest throughout a vast area both in and near Whitehall from the smallest shop to the largest public building'. Many lesser acts of unnecessary vandalism did in fact take place. In a 1967 article, 'Architects' Approach to Architecture', Sir Leslie explained that architects had come to understand 'that there had to be some kind of complete and systematic re-examination of human needs and that, as a result of this, not only the form of buildings, but the total environment would be changed.' Watkin comments: 'The so-called "human needs" are defined arbitrarily, arrogantly, and with a complete disregard for the importance of tradition as a guide to the architect.' Leading architects have made the most bizarre pronouncements about human needs; an influential book by the world-famous Swiss architect Le Corbusier, after defining architecture as 'a question of morality', goes on to specify among other things that a bathroom must always contain 'gymnastic appliances' and that each bedroom must have a dressing-room attached: 'Never undress in your bedroom. It is not a clean thing to do.'

Twentieth-century architects have derived their morality from collectivist political movements. Mies van der Rohe, in a 1924 article on 'Architecture and the Will of the Age', derived prescriptions for modern architecture from the observation that 'The individual is losing significance: his destiny is no longer what interests us. The decisive achievements in all fields are impersonal. . . . ' Sir James Richards, a chief advocate of modernist architecture in Britain, wrote in 1940 that if anyone dared to criticize modern architects this would be because 'they forget that they are looking at people as individuals, whereas it is people as Society that architecture has to cater for.' What was needed in the twentieth century, for Richards, was not building produced by individual architects and bearing the stamp of their personal styles, but impersonal 'anonymous folk architecture'. To the obvious objection that folk architecture already existed in the shape of the semis and bungalows being produced in the thousands by speculative builders in suburbs up and down the country, Richards responded in ideological terms that the products of private-enterprise speculative building did not count, since they '*form no part of a socio-cultural whole*'. Ideological blinkers have blinded the profession to important twentieth-century housing achievements. Despite repeated claims by collectivist-minded architects, town planners, and politicians that they give a high priority to providing decent housing for the masses, Martin Pawley has pointed out that one of the most impressive actual achievements in this area, in West Germany after the devastation of the Second World War, is never mentioned:

Between 1946 and 1950 2.5 million homes were constructed, for the most part in small contracts spread all over the country, by small builders with small resources lacking essential materials. This performance is over twice as impressive as that of Britain. . . . The authentic achievements of 1946 to 1950 are almost all anonymous: the cumulative triumph of myriad entrepreneurial operations carried out in obscurity. For that reason, while architects and planners pay homage to Garden Cities and Unités, whose actual contribution to the problem of homelessness has been minimal, the German post-war housing effort barely receives statistical acknowledgment.

A key figure in the politicization of architectural thought was Nikolaus (later Sir Nikolaus) Pevsner, a German who emigrated to England in the 1930s. Pevsner's *Enquiry into Industrial Art in England* (1937) declared that 'a style of our age must be an unexclusive style, and its merits must be collective merits not distinguishing one individual or class.' In his highly influential *Pioneers of the Modern Movement* (1936) Pevsner condemned all European architecture from 1760 to 1860 on the ground that, because 'it is based on individual inventiveness, a genuine universal style could not therefore spring from it.' Perhaps it is easier for us than it was for Pevsner's readers in the 1930s to appreciate that condemnations of individual taste or individual style as immoral and contrary to the spirit of the age merely serve (since any architecture must reflect *some* style, *some* taste, and the calendar is not going to jump from the wall and announce what type of architecture it requires) to clear the ground for the architect to impose his own views as self-appointed spokesman for 'the people' – anyone who queries the architect's will is only an 'individual'. The original edition of *Pioneers of the Modern Movement* announced that 'this new style of the twentieth century . . . because it is a genuine style as opposed to a passing fashion, is totalitarian.' In later editions Pevsner prudently replaced 'totalitarian' by 'universal', but his writings manifest a truly totalitarian desire to allow no tiny detail of the environment to be controlled by consumer preference rather than by his all-embracing social ideology. He was offended by the pictures used by Cadbury's to ornament their chocolate boxes, which he felt should be discarded in favour of pictures 'in harmony with [Cadbury's] clean, simple and bright factory buildings' . . . 'The approach adopted by some of [Cadbury's artists] to the designing of a box for a given commercial article was certainly not the right one. Neither a circus scene nor a still life of fruit has a natural and easily understandable relation to chocolate.' Although Pevsner had come to England to escape Nazi authoritarianism, he found it difficult to accept that the liberal British tradition which allowed a foreign Jewish refugee to make a successful career here simultaneously allowed architects' clients to specify the traditional building styles they preferred, with scant regard for the authoritative opinions of professionals. Discussing the architecture of London in 1957 he commented: 'In no other capital known to me would it be possible to see major buildings still going up which are so hopelessly out of touch with the [twentieth century] . . . reactionary beyond belief . . . inscrutable to a visitor from abroad. . . . '

Pevsner was entitled to his strongly negative opinion of Victorian architecture, but he was not satisfied with condemning its aesthetics. For him, rotten architecture sprang from a rotten social system. In 1943 he wrote that 'It is the things of the spirit in which the Victorian age lacked vigour and courage. [Surely a remarkable verdict?] Standards in architecture were the first to go . . . the iron-master and mill-owner . . . felt no longer bound by one particular accepted taste. . . . The new manufacturer had no manners, and he was a convinced individualist. If, for whatever reasons, he liked a style in architecture, then there was nothing to prevent him from having his way and getting a house or a factory or an office building or a club in that style.'

One problem with Pevsner's picture of (as Watkin puts it) 'crude middle-class patrons, captains of industry with coarse clothes, bad manners, and loud accents, roaming offensively about Victorian England, throwing their money about commissioning bog-oak chairs and Butterfield churches,' is that it is factually false. Paul Thompson has shown that the influential patrons of High Victorian architecture were not the new middle class but the old aristocracy: 'It is difficult to think of a single building commissioned by a manufacturer which was crucial to the development of the High Victorian style.' But in any case, is it not intolerably arrogant to condemn a whole large class of people as having 'no manners', with the unspoken implication that once things are left to the architectural profession civility will infallibly be maintained? I wonder how frequently Victorian manufacturers responded to polite comments on their building plans in terms like 'Sod you.'

(Strangely, for much of the last twenty years of his life before he died in 1983 Pevsner was Chairman and later President of the Victorian Society. Perhaps the Will of the Age had changed.)

Although the professionalization of architecture is defended as leading to better service to the public, its practical consequence has often been to give a free rein to theories which treat people as objects rather than subjects. Despite architects' professed concern with the welfare of the Common Man, the victims of brutal modernist architecture are predominantly working-class people who in late twentieth-century Britain have to accept the housing provided for them. As Bruce Allsopp wrote, 'It is astonishing with what savagery planners and architects are trying to obliterate working-class cultural and social patterns.' Members of the middle class can afford to opt out of modernism in their own surroundings and to 'gentrify' the areas of unpretentious terrace housing for Victorian artisans which city planners have not got round to 'redeveloping'.

There is a sinister alliance between architectural and military thought. We have already seen Maxwell Fry commenting approvingly on air-raids; Martin Pawley describes how 'Every morning during the "blitz" winter of 1940/41 planners scanned and photographed the vistas opened by each successive night of bombing – before burning midnight oil at drawing boards and typewriters drafting the outlines of new cities and social orders.' Le Corbusier's influential enthusiasm for apartment blocks raised from the ground on *pilotis* or massive stilts was originally motivated by the idea that poison gas barrages could flow harmlessly underneath the buildings and pure air be sucked in higher up; his belief in achieving a given density of habitation by building a few *superbloques* widely scattered across parkland, rather than continuous low-rise dwellings, was justified in terms of dispersing the targets for bombers (the *superbloques* themselves were to be shielded with a heavy roof-layer of concrete). According to Martin Pawley, the birth of the New Towns idea in 1938 had as much to do with strategic considerations of safety against air-raids as with public health or aesthetic considerations, and the strategic issue remained important until the development of nuclear weapons made any degree of decentralization irrelevant.

Perhaps the most far-reaching scheme of town-planning ever proposed was put forward in the USA in 1947, apparently in all seriousness rather than as a science-fiction fantasy, by the 'President's Advisory Commission on Universal Military Training'. In order to minimize the potential damage from an atomic bomb strike, the entire current pattern of settlement in the USA was to be replaced by a system under which, as Pawley recounts it, 'the whole of the United States was to be divided into units twenty-five miles square, an industrial complex was to be located at the centre of each unit while the sides would house the working population in long strips at a linear destiny of 160 dwellings per mile.' Pawley quotes a 1950 book on town-planning which suggested that this scheme showed how 'the essential qualities which render a city less vulnerable to attack from the air . . . are the same qualities we desire in a decent environment in peace.' As Pawley comments, 'To the true devotee of the Garden City even the total destruction of the traditional matrix of civilization was not too high a price to pay for "a decent environment." '

Twentieth-century architecture is an example of the professionalization of a calling that only marginally has the characteristics which are used to justify professional status. For our other example let us turn to what is generally accepted as the clearest case of an occupation meriting that status: medicine.

Many people might agree that society would do well to force architects to be more responsive to consumer demand while still feeling that it is thoroughly desirable for doctors to enjoy the autonomy, the freedom from pressures both commercial and political, which is what professional status implies. Houses and offices are things everyone has everyday experience of, so a client can tell his architect broadly what he wants even though he cannot fill in all the technical details. When the average person contracts a serious disease, on the other hand, he is unlikely to have much personal experience of it, and still less will he be knowledgeable about the range of drugs, surgical operations, or other means available to cure it. Furthermore, even the worst architecture will only blight the quality of its users' lives while they live or work in or around it, while bad medical practice can end the client's life. In this situation, many laymen have felt, it is thoroughly desirable to be able to use the services of a body of workers who have constructed for themselves regulatory and disciplinary systems which function to maintain and raise standards of knowledge and practice that laymen cannot assess – an occupationally-specialized State within the State. Allowing medicine to come as fully under the thumb of the ordinary State as most other groups seems unwise; even to people otherwise optimistic about State intervention it is obvious that politicians are not specially qualified to make medical judgments. This is one reason why the medical profession in Britain and elsewhere has been extremely successful in its own natural wish to gain and preserve the maximum control over its activities and freedom from outside interference.

But it is only one reason. We shall see, below, that the mystique of medical knowledge is exaggerated. Indeed, it is remarkable how willing laymen were for many decades to accept the profession's picture of all qualified doctors as paragons of wisdom and expertise, considering that immediately before entering the profession the same people were medical students, who have always been a by-word even as students go for irresponsibility, riotous behaviour, and exam-passing by dint of feverish last-minute burning of midnight oil. I suggested at the beginning of the chapter that gaining professional status depends on the political skill and negotiating power of a given group; surely, the fact that doctors have succeeded very well in achieving this goal has a lot to do with the fact that they deal with us when we are helpless and frightened – which obviously puts them in a strong position for bargaining.

However they have managed it, it is undeniable that the modern medical profession has achieved great power.

According to the very sober, un-radical commentator Rudolf Klein, 'The history of the British health service is the history of political power, Ministers, Civil Servants, Parliament accommodating [themselves] to professional power. . . . Many policy options . . . have been removed from the agenda of policy discussion because the political costs of overcoming professional resistance are judged to be excessive.' The profession has a high regard for itself, often seeming to see itself not merely as one learned and respectable trade among others but – in a way parallelled, probably, only among lawyers – as *the* pre-eminent or only repository of 'real', important knowledge in society. Anecdotal evidence of such attitudes abounds. I think, for instance, of a highly-educated academic acquaintance who was engaged to study linguistic problems of communication between doctors and patients on behalf of the General Medical Council and found that the Council had difficulty settling on an appropriate job-title. The (to her) obvious suggestion of 'Research Associate' was brushed aside, since obviously no-one lacking a medical qualification could be described as doing 'research'.

All this might not matter, if medical pretensions were justified by medical achievements. Clearly, a liberal is not likely to complain about the fact that one lucky group in society has managed to make itself relatively independent of State intervention. But, after many decades during which the medical profession was generally seen as perhaps a bit conservative and a bit smug but essentially worthy of respect, since about 1970 it has come to be widely recognized that the modern medical establishment is a very mixed blessing indeed. A number of commentators argue that the harm done by the medical profession nowadays is very great and perhaps even outweighs the good, and commonly this development is blamed on the way that twentieth-century medicine has grown into an autonomous structure of authority, largely unresponsive to consumers' feelings.

The charges made against modern medicine are that it diverts massive resources towards activities which are regarded as glamorous within the profession and advance the careers of those who engage in them, but which at best achieve only trivial improvements in the public's expectation or quality of life; and, worse than this, that the developments in medical practice which are encouraged by the ethos of the profession often tend to dehumanize patients, and not infrequently brutalize them in ways which would incur universal shocked condemnation if they were not protected by the aura of sanctity that attaches to the concept of medicine. Some critics suggest that the authority of medicine has now grown so great as to 'medicalize' people's whole attitude to life, so that a healthy person is nowadays induced in various ways to think of his health not as a natural state to be taken for granted but as a temporary phenomenon enjoyed by courtesy of the profession; and Irving Zola even argues that medicine is replacing religion and law as the chief institution of social control. Zola's thesis seems to me overblown and contrived, and the concept of 'medicalization of life' is a subjective, debatable notion. But the other charges are relatively objective and well supported; and it is very widely agreed also that the concrete benefits produced by twentieth-century medical advances have been far smaller than the rhetoric of the profession suggests, so that any harm it does is correspondingly less excusable.

One problem in assessing recent critiques of the medical profession is that many (though not all) of them relate chiefly to medicine in America, and the worst aspects of modern medicine seem to have proceeded a good deal further on balance in the USA than in Britain. This is a quantitative rather than a qualitative difference, and there are many respects in which the British medical situation is as bad as the American. However, it is worth pausing briefly to consider why British doctors have less influence over the nature of laymen's lives than doctors in the USA. Though it may seem paradoxical for an opponent of the Welfare State to admit it, there is no doubt that the existence in Britain of the National Health Service is highly relevant.

The USA has no State organization similar to the NHS; but that does not mean that producers of medical services are controlled by consumers via ordinary market mechanisms, like producers of food or clothes. What the USA has is a very powerful producers' cartel, the American Medical Association. Milton Friedman has identified the AMA as perhaps the strongest trade union in America; writing from a very different political perspective, Jeffrey Berlant suggests that Friedman understates the case. Like any trade union, the AMA is active in promoting its members' financial interests, often in ways that run directly counter to the consumer's interest (as when it acts to restrict the number of places in medical schools in order to reduce the supply and hence maintain the price of medical services). The monopoly position enjoyed by the profession means also that, like architects in Britain, American doctors can devote far more effort and resources to activities which they themselves find fulfilling and which are highly esteemed by fellow-professionals, irrespective of the wishes of the public, than they would be able to do if they had to convince patients that their services offered better value than alternatives.

For instance, most consumers of medical services prefer not to go into hospitals unless they have to, for all kinds of good reasons apart from expense. On the other hand, as John Bradshaw has suggested, 'In a hospital the doctor's a god, he can keep the patient at a distance, take X-ray pictures of him, stick needles into him, operate on him. . . . To go out into the community, to get mud on your shoes, dirt on your nice clean white coat – this doesn't appeal to most doctors, no matter what it might achieve for their patients.' Accordingly, in America much more than in Britain, medicine nowadays is hospital-centred, and home visits by GPs are a thing of the past.

Of course, the State plays a role in maintaining the position of the American medical profession, but its role is tool rather than master: the strong position of the AMA depends on the fact that it has secured legislation giving it a tight legal monopoly on the supply of medical services. In Britain the NHS, despite its real failings, has to a limited extent served as a means by which the State exerts a countervailing force against the tendency of the profession to monopolize power in the domain of health, so that the British doctor still faces less temptation than his American counterpart to advance his career through ego-tripping, inhumane technical brilliance rather than boringly but decently serving the ordinary public. Rudolf Klein shows that, before Lloyd George's National Health Insurance scheme of 1911, the average British doctor was 'the poor relation among professional men', often working under contract for Friendly Societies, Works Clubs, and the like to look after the health of their members, and subject to a fair amount of competition from people lacking medical qualifications. Friendly Societies and Clubs were highly cost-conscious: they forced the doctors who worked for them to stick to cheap basic medicine rather than expensive sophistication. According to Klein, the 1911 scheme was 'a giant step forward in the emancipation of the medical profession from lay control', since it made doctors answerable in much of their work to a State which was more willing than budget-conscious local voluntary societies to allow the profession to set its own standards. The NHS was another large step in the same direction, but even that retained the machinery – unparallelled in the USA – of consumer complaints to partly-lay local Executive Councils, as 'a salvage operation designed to save something from the wreck of lay control over medical services'.

Keeping medicine cheap may not sound too attractive to a reader convinced by the large claims that are made about the triumphs of sophisticated modern medicine. But what is the basis for those claims? In England and Wales, life expectancy rose between the 1850s and the mid-to-late 1950s, and has remained more or less unchanged since then (in the 1960s life expectancy began to *fall* in the USA and many other Western countries, though not in Britain). It is uncontroversial that most of the rise resulted from rising standards of nutrition, housing, and sanitation, which were made possible by higher incomes and had little or nothing to do with medicine. The last part of the rise in life expectancy can be attributed to the discovery of antibiotics and certain other key drugs; most of these discoveries were made by pharmaceutical companies rather than by the medical profession. We have to go to a doctor to get them, but that is because medicine has secured a monopoly over their prescription; the useful ones are not many, nor are the indications for their use very subtle. According to Ivan Illich, 'some experienced clinicians believe that less than two dozen basic drugs are all that will ever be desirable for 99 per cent of the total population; others, that up to four dozen items are optimal for 98 per cent. . . . The new tricks that have frequent application are so simple that the last generation of grandmothers would have learned them long ago had they not been browbeaten into incompetency by medical mystification.' Illich points out that in Mexico, where he lives, many drugs are freely available over the counter which are on prescription-only in more 'medicalized' countries. (If we prescribed our own antibiotics in the light of advertising claims, personal recommendations, and so forth, no doubt we would often be less than perfectly judicious in our choice; but it has been proved that the prescriptions of doctors, too, are in practice swayed more by commercial advertising than by the disinterested professional medical literature.)

The fact that ninety-nine per cent of the population only ever need a few novel drugs or health procedures that could be mastered by laymen will seem irrelevant to someone who thinks he might be among the one per cent who can be cured by a piece of sophisticated medical expertise and will not be cured without it. Such cases do exist, and for the people involved modern medicine is a boon. But this benefit is offset – according to some critics, far more than offset – by the large part of modern medicine whose only consequence for patients is to offer a small prolongation of life at the cost of great suffering (though from the professional point of view it can often be highly career-enhancing work).

Reading some of the medical critics, one is reminded of how American generals in Vietnam used to see 'light at the end of the tunnel' when throwing more and more resources into an unwinnable war. In the case of medicine the war now is against mortality itself. Remarkably, sixty per cent of all money spent on health in the USA is spent on care in the last year of life. As Ian Kennedy put it in his Reith Lectures, 'Heroic forms of intervention, in which the only hero is the patient, become the order of the day,' and one condition after another is violently annihilated in the battleground of the patient's body even though the patient is very unlikely to survive long anyway. Illich notes that 'In terminal cancer, there is no difference in life expectancy between those who end in the home and those who die in hospital [and] by staying at home they avoid the exile, loneliness, and indignities which, in all but exceptional hospitals, await them.' However, the profession's enthusiasm for the hospital has been granted such a free rein that, for the contemporary American, 'Death without medical presence becomes synonymous with romantic pigheadedness, privilege, or disaster.' Kennedy quotes the late Senator Hubert Humphrey as having described the experience of the chemotherapy used to treat the cancer which killed him as 'chemical death'. Discussing the procedure of cardiac catheterization sometimes used on heart patients (though, incidentally, Dr Maurice Pappworth has described it as a procedure 'of absolutely no value in diagnosis or treatment'), Drs J.W. Harthorne and B. Castleman wrote in the *New England Journal of Medicine* of the 'abject terror' it induces in some patients, and the fact that 'sudden death due to psychological stress alone may ensue'. In other words the patients die of terror. The religious and science-fiction writer C.S. Lewis published a novel in 1945 in which evil was symbolized by a scientific experiment in which a human head was kept alive and conscious separately from its body. There is now an operation called 'hemicorporectomy', sometimes carried out in cases of cancer in the lower half of the body, which involves cutting the patient in half at the waist and keeping the upper half alive separately; some of these half-people have been kept alive for years.

Occasionally a child is born with a defect in the immune system which protects us from infections. Normally such babies soon die; but, now, some of them can be kept alive in perfectly sterile conditions. I have seen a photograph of such a child on a country walk with his parents. Father trundles a trolley from which airlines stretch out to a little glass-helmeted, space-suited figure, an alien on his own planet. The plastic glove through which he clutches his mother's hand is the closest he can expect to come to human contact, ever.

If you or I were ill and were told that our only hope of postponing extinction were some horrific procedure leading to a period of more or less distant approximation to healthy life, we might find it hard to summon the strength of will to refuse and to opt for a relatively natural death, particularly if our will had been sapped by a long illness – and particularly if medical careerists were dealing with us on the assumption that they were the best judges of our interests. Inside a hospital, it becomes psychologically very difficult for a patient to assert himself *vis-à-vis* the nurses, let alone the consultants. (In any case, it is a fairly grey area of English law whether adults even have the right to refuse treatments which medical orthodoxy deems necessary for survival.) But thinking about the issue abstractly, while we are in good health, is it not plausible to say that it would be better for everyone if these 'heroic' techniques had not been developed, so that the terrible question of whether to opt for them in particular cases did not arise? After all, we must all die some time.

And they would not have been developed, surely, if medicine had not become an autonomous profession free of consumer control. A rich patient in a pure market system of health care might well choose to buy himself a lease of life through one of these procedures, if it were available, but the fact that they are available stems from the ability of the profession to indulge its own taste for frontier-breaking high-tech research. If the use of resources flowing into medicine were determined by consumer demand then it would almost all be used for current consumption of established health procedures and little would be available to invest in abstruse research. As things are, however (until, quite recently, public distrust of the profession became so great as to begin to penetrate the profession's defences against lay opinion), when doctors have discussed retrenchment of their activities it has been not in terms of giving up the high-tech end of medicine but of shuffling off unglamorous routine cases onto lower-level workers.

In 1952 a distinguished Guy's surgeon, Sir William Ogilvie, characterized the shift in professional orientation away from cultivating practical clinical experience towards experimental research as 'something new and sinister', liable to destroy people's faith that doctors 'are the servants of the patients whom we have undertaken to care for'. That shift became very complete. Fifteen years later, the (British) doctor Maurice Pappworth described how physicians seeking promotion were finding that appointment boards 'have come to regard a grain of research experience as worth a ton of clinical experience'.

Pappworth's book *Human Guinea Pigs* shows how it has become common in modern medicine for hospital patients to be used, without their knowledge or consent, in medical experiments which sometimes involve procedures that are both horrific and dangerous, for programmes of research that are unrelated to the patients' maladies and often seem to have little purpose other than swelling the experimenter's list of trivial research publications. '[S]ome doctors . . . regard hospital patients as somehow part of their possessions, as material conveniently available for their personal use in the furtherance of science.' In the early 1950s it seemed to be well established that a wave of blindness in infants had been caused by a vogue for treating premature infants with high oxygen concentrations, but three American doctors decided to check this by deliberately giving such treatment to thirty-six premature infants; eight of them duly became irreversibly blind in both eyes. Pappworth assembles many comparable cases from the published literature. But he points out that

> for obvious reasons, the worst experiments go unrecorded. . . . One such case concerns a London hospital where an experimental physician wished to practice the technique of lumbar aortography. . . . The subjects chosen . . . were eight patients who had been admitted with gastric ulcers. . . . The procedure was carried out in the X-ray department and the patients were obviously under the impression that it was part of the business of taking X-rays of their stomachs. As a direct result of the experimental procedure three out of these eight patients died.

(Illich comments on how Pappworth was attacked for 'undermining the trust lay people have in doctors, and for publishing in a paperback what could "ethically" be told only in literature written for doctors.')

Some of the phenomena discussed above are extreme and perhaps rare (though there is nothing rare by now about the conversion of inevitable death into an occasion for displays of medical virtuosity). But these things are only the tip of an iceberg. Much more generally, the charge runs, the medical profession persuades us that we need its services when, left to ourselves, we would take health for granted, or persuades us that we can benefit from sophisticated procedures when simpler and less invasive treatment is all that is worthwhile. Because the mystique of professional authority conceals from us that medics are traders hawking their wares like any others, in our fear we are far more trusting than we would be of ordinary commercial advertising. Officially our doctor is our 'medical adviser', but the social reality is more accurately reflected by the language used by the ladies of my village who describe themselves picturesquely as 'under' this or that doctor. Except in extreme cases, what conditions count as illness is ultimately a subjective decision; Eliot Freidson quotes abundant hard evidence that the profession sees the boundaries of illness as far wider than laymen do, and is systematically biassed towards action when the likely benefits of action and inaction are at best evenly balanced. (This is undoubtedly less true of GPs in Britain than it is of most doctors, because the capitation-fee system gives them no economic motive to overtreat; but, even in countries where fees are based on treatment, the bias probably has as much to do with subtle psychological tendencies to overvalue one's own expertise as with crude money considerations.)

In one famous study, successive teams of doctors were asked to judge which of a group of children needed tonsillectomies; each team, including the last, recommended almost half the children it saw for the operation, yet the children examined by each team were those *not* selected for the operation by the preceding teams. Increasingly, people who have heart attacks are put into intensive coronary care units, despite the fact that statistics have shown that survival rates in such units are rather less than at home. (This latter finding is usually explained by reference to the frightening atmosphere of dehumanized technology in such units. To a cardiac specialist this factor may not seem to count: just as a historian may describe the seventeenth century as 'not my period', so for a cardiologist the psyche is not his organ.) Again and again it has turned out that some orthodox, sometimes highly invasive, medical technique is either useless or even (as in the case of the low-fibre diet prescribed for diverticular disease of the colon until about 1970) positively harmful for the condition it purports to treat, to say nothing of deleterious 'side-effects' which have often proved quite central for patients. No intellectual discipline can avoid mistakes, but the professionalization of medicine makes it slow to react to such findings, and unwilling to acknowledge its fallibility. To quote Brian Inglis, writing in the *Spectator* in 1980:

> Following a [television] programme which had shown a particularly horrendous breast cancer operation, a surgeon was allowed time to criticise the programme: and he denounced it as dishonest, on the ground that the operation is not now employed. This was simply untrue; extended radical mastectomy has been widely used here, and although the fact that it is ineffective as well as mutilating has been clear from the mortality statistics for some years, there are still surgeons who subject patients to it.

Ian Kennedy points out that medical paternalism has even led to women having breasts removed without consultation.

What the profession is finally coming to recognize, now we have all rumbled the fact that it is not about to come up with penicillin-like 'magic bullets' that cure cancer or heart disease once they have appeared, is that preventing disease through healthy patterns of everyday living offers far more scope for improving our lives than searches for new techniques of cure. It is natural that the profession has neglected this side of the health picture: they have little role to play in it. Even that wartime *Picture Post* recognized that the way forward in health needed to lie in prevention rather than cure, and it forecast that the foundation of a National Health Service would encourage this. It did not, because the NHS was staffed by people who shared the same professional outlook as any other doctors. As John Bradshaw points out, the medical profession is now conceding that the low-fibre diet which industrial food technology has made available is a major health hazard. The virtues of a high-fibre diet 'have been extolled for many years,' but those who argued for it were 'stigmatized by the orthodox medical profession as unscientific food cranks'. In the 1950s and 1960s an American called Adelle Davis synthesized a vast mass of nutritional research into a series of popular books showing how common health problems could be avoided or dramatically alleviated by the simple use of various vitamin supplements to rectify cases when an ordinary diet failed to supply some particular individual need. Her book *Let's Get Well* contains well over two thousand references to the scientific literature. The medical profession appeared to have little enthusiasm for her work, and when my wife spent a few days in hospital in 1976 it seemed to be regarded as quite a concession that she was 'allowed' to take her bottles of vitamin capsules in with her.

Things are changing. There are signs that the profession is beginning to recognize that it has to treat whole men rather than diseased organs, and to acknowledge the value of prevention and the limits of its own abilities. But it is easy to exaggerate this change of heart. Ian Kennedy's Reith Lectures contained a number of questionable points of view (I find it odd that both he and Ivan Illich choose a socialist standpoint from which to launch their critiques, since in practice collectivist approaches to social organization tend to be much friendlier than individualist approaches to professional pretensions), but it seems undeniable that they were a serious contribution to a matter of grave public concern. However, the Professor of Medical Microbiology at the Welsh National School of Medicine reviewed them in the *Times Literary Supplement* in terms which may be inferred from his closing sentence: 'An institution which runs a television comedy series about the SS is capable of anything.' (In the preface to the paperback version of the lectures, Kennedy quotes reactions from the medical press: 'ludicrous'; 'ill-conducted public rant'.)

Of course I am not saying that we would be better off with no doctors. The medical profession does a lot of good as well as a lot of harm. So does the car-manufacturing industry; but we do not encourage Ford, Vauxhall, and British Leyland to group themselves into a cartel, to clothe themselves in a mystique of professionalism including royal patronage and a self-denying ordinance against advertising by individual manufacturers, and to persuade the public 'not to worry about which car is best for you – your local motor dealer is trained to make these decisions in your interest, trust him and buy what he offers you.' (Nor do we feel obliged to greet our neighbour with a respectful 'Good morning, Motor Dealer Smith', on the ground that plain 'Mr' is an inadequate honorific, while regarding sellers of alternative transport like bicycles as seedy backstreet shysters.)

Like any other producer group, orthodox medicine can continue to provide the consumer with good products and value for money only if it is constantly forced to win its spurs anew in the marketplace. It is wrong for the State to place its weight behind one particular authoritative structure of health care, whether by public payment of its practitioners' fees or by grants of legal monopoly. *If* it is right for the health needs of the population to be funded from taxes, this should be done by giving people who cannot afford what they want money and leaving them to decide how to spend it. In a free health market, it might be that practitioners boasting the qualification issued by Guy's or Bart's would retain a reputation as good people to use, or they might become known for sharing an obsession with granny-torture, and be seen as a poor buy in comparison with some alternative corps of health workers with their own qualification who are trained to cure what can be cured safely and to allow hopeless cases to die decently. Medical qualifications, like any other degrees or certificates, would be useful shorthand ways for consumers to check what type of training a worker had received or what kind of exams he had passed; but no particular qualifications would have any special 'official' status.

Let me emphasize that I have personally known many doctors who seem very decent, wise men who genuinely place their patients' interests before their personal convenience. What I am saying is that such attitudes exist despite rather than because of professionalization. Nobody suggests that changes in the way an occupation is organized will turn decent men into monsters; but they can cause marginal changes in workers' attitudes (or cause a different type of workforce to be recruited), and the changes encouraged by professionalization are changes in the wrong direction.

Thus far the medicine I have discussed has been medicine aiming successfully or unsuccessfully at the cure of conditions that are fairly unambiguously identifiable as ailments. For some liberals, however, the most serious charge against modern medicine is that it includes one large and influential branch which is no more concerned with 'illness' than the Spanish

Inquisition was, and which uses methods that are no less objectionable in a free society: namely, psychiatry. Freidson has pointed out that it is characteristic of the professions in general that when a citizen enters their domain he is expected to play the role 'of a house pet, or a child, dependent on the benevolence and knowledgeability of the adult caretaker'. Psychiatry is unique among the consulting professions in that adults are forced into its domain against their will.

On the face of things it is very mysterious how we ought to interpret the fact that some adults exhibit behaviour which seems strikingly deviant and irrational by the standards taken for granted by the majority. In the twentieth century the orthodox interpretation has been that madness is an illness, alongside 'flu, TB, or cancer, and treatable by the same kinds of activity that medicine uses for illnesses of more 'ordinary' categories. What is more, there is a widespread feeling that to deny the reality of 'mental illness' is callous, inhumanely reactionary.

One powerful historical reason for this, I believe, is the First World War controversies over 'shell-shock'. Young men who broke down in face of the unimaginable daily horrors of trench warfare and wandered away from the front were commonly shot as deserters. Medical men often argued that these people were suffering from psychiatric disorders induced by their experiences which ought to exempt them from punishment for their actions, but the conservative military mind frequently refused to entertain this defence. Once the bloody chauvinism of the war had subsided, it seemed plain to decent men that the psychiatrists were right and the Blimps wrong: surely those young men ought not to have been shot in cold blood by their comrades. From a liberal point of view, however, this is not the only possible conclusion. Indeed the young men should not have been shot, but it was not their minds that needed mending. What was wrong was that States had created a situation in which people were expected to tolerate horrors that it is not natural to encounter or endure. Without belittling the bravery of the many who did soldier on unflinchingly, when one reads about conditions in Flanders one is tempted to say that it was the non-deserters who were 'mad' – except that the word is never

applied to behaviour which is practised by a majority and
approved by the holders of power.

The leading liberal critic of psychiatry is Thomas Szasz, a
Hungarian now in his sixties who emigrated to the USA at the
age of eighteen and since 1956 has been Professor of Psychiatry
at the State University of New York. (His surname,
incidentally, is less difficult than it looks: it is pronounced
'sahss' and means 'Saxon'.) In a series of books and articles
Szasz argues an uncompromising view: there is no such thing as
mental 'illness'. In his own vivid metaphor, asking a member of
the medical profession to 'cure' the deviant behaviour that we
call madness (or neurosis, or schizophrenia, or psychosis . . .) is
like calling for a television engineer to adjust the unsatisfactory
programme one is viewing. (It says something about
professional authoritarianism that the publication in 1961 of
Szasz's *Myth of Mental Illness*, which whether it is ultimately
correct or misguided is certainly intelligently and
knowledgeably written, led to an – unsuccessful – attempt by
the Commissioner of the New York State Department of
Mental Hygiene to have Szasz removed from his academic
post.)

Szasz does not deny that people who are mad and wish to
become sane can be helped and that this kind of service could be
a genuine expertise, though I have the impression that he
envisages a legitimate psychiatry as being more akin to the work
of a priest than to that of a doctor. (Szasz might not put it that
way; he is strongly opposed to Christianity, which he regards as
an ideology for slaves.) But what chiefly concerns him is not the
question whether madness might be successfully treated
voluntarily but the fact that at present its treatment involves
massive and grievous invasions of citizens' liberties – invasions
which are almost never justifiable in terms of principles that we
would recognize as overriding civil rights when madness was
not in question. We go along with them only because psychiatry
wraps itself in the aura of superhuman wisdom and altruism
that professionalized medicine has succeeded in constructing
for itself, and thereby induces States to grant it a measure of
control over people that would scarcely be conceded to any
other group.

Large numbers of people are kept in lunatic asylums (Szasz quotes figures of a quarter of a million admissions a year in the USA), which are commonly very unpleasant places to be. The great majority are not there voluntarily (Szasz gives evidence that the small minority of admissions which are called 'voluntary' often in practice involve deception of the patient, and this is also true in Britain). People on the outside, when they give the matter a moment's thought, tend to tell themselves comfortably that 'madmen have to be locked up because they are dangerous to themselves and others.' But, as Szasz points out, 'Drunken drivers are dangerous both to themselves and to others. They injure and kill many more people than, for example, persons with paranoid delusions of persecution. Yet, people labeled paranoid are readily commitable, while drunken drivers are not.'

Szasz does not explore the question of why driving under the influence of alcohol is treated as a crime rather than a reason for committing the offender to an asylum (a 'punishment' far greater than a fine or loss of driving licence, though it is not called a punishment). But it is plausible to say that the class of people who drive after drinking includes too many individuals possessing significant power in our society for their behaviour to be classified as madness. In general, it is clear that psychiatric coercion is exercised predominantly against politically weak members of society: 'It is a fact that the vast majority of committed patients are members of the lower classes. Upper-class persons are virtually immune from this sort of social restraint.' One might suppose that this is because 'mental illness' is much commoner among the poor (either because a good standard of living preserves sanity, or because sanity is needed to secure prosperity). But there is more to it than that. A standard British work, D. Henderson and R.D. Gillespie's *A Textbook of Psychiatry* (seventh edition, 1950), comments that 'Certification is . . . undesirable where the patient occupies an important public position, e.g., director of a company, partnership, etc.' Perhaps these authors took themselves to be making an innocent suggestion that when people can afford to arrange for their own medical needs it is unnecessary to impose arrangements on them. But that is not what they said, and it would not make sense: the justification for involuntary certification is supposed to be that (whether they can afford it or not) mad people will not choose medical attention which they need. It would be odd for a surgical textbook to specify that appendectomy is undesirable for a patient holding an important public position. However, unlike appendicitis but like imprisonment, 'mental illness' carries a social stigma, and psychiatrists are more willing to impose that stigma on powerless members of society than on their middle-class peers.

A remarkably revealing source of information about attitudes in the psychiatric profession is the psychiatric section of hearings by a 1961 US Senate Subcommittee on Constitutional Rights, which forced the profession to confront the issue of involuntary certification explicitly. (According to Szasz the issue receives strikingly little attention in the psychiatric literature.) The psychiatrists who testified before the Subcommittee repeatedly pressed for greater powers to coerce patients into asylums without legal formalities (which give the patient the possibility of resisting): 'psychiatry now seeks to modify legal procedures [so as to] facilitate and not hinder prompt access to treatment by all citizens who need it. . . . ' Yet, even without these helpful reforms, Szasz quotes case after case of individuals forcibly detained and invasively treated in asylums for years on the flimsiest of grounds – sometimes, it would seem, pure administrative convenience. (Szasz's examples are American, but the British picture has been very similar.)

Again and again the witnesses before the Subcommittee betrayed the fact that they saw psychiatric coercion as justified by behaviour whose 'deviance' was blatantly dependent on an arbitrary standard of normality. One ornament of the profession argued that psychiatric hospitals should not all be of the 'open' type: 'If a man brings his daughter to me from California, because she is in manifest danger of falling into vice or in some way disgracing herself, he doesn't expect me to let her loose in my hometown for that same thing to happen.' Mores have changed in twenty years, and it is hard now to think back to a time when sleeping around showed that a girl was insane and needed locking up. (The same psychiatrist protested that he was as keen on patients' civil liberties as anyone else: 'I haven't seen anyone restrained [i.e. straitjacketed] for some time, and now with the drugs, there is rarely need for it.')

Once people are allowed to be deprived of their civil rights because they express opinions and behave in way that appear irrational although they do not interfere with others' rights, then there seems to be no principled bar against treating straightforward intellectual nonconformity as a crime – or as worse than a crime: crimes incur maximum sentences while psychiatric coercion is open-ended, and the most serious criminal offenders are never subjected to lobotomy or electro-convulsive 'therapy'. In the fourteenth century, someone who sincerely believed and insisted that constitutional democracy as we know it was desirable and feasible and that it was immoral for a king to rule without a democratic mandate would surely have been recognized as a madman. But we do not need to go as far as the Middle Ages to see madness depending on the eye of the beholder. In 1952 H.A. Overstreet, a psychologist who rarely failed to support the 'enlightened' causes of his day, wrote:

> A man . . . may be angrily against racial equality, public [i.e. local authority] housing, the TVA, financial and technical aid to backward countries, organized labor, and the preaching of social rather than salvational religion. . . . Such people may appear 'normal' in the sense that they are able to hold a job and otherwise maintain their status as members of society; but they are, we now recognize, well along the road toward mental illness.

The transparency of this technique of redefining political opinions one disagrees with as a symptom of illness is surely remarkable. (Or do I say that only because I score fairly high on Overstreet's scale myself?)

The 1950s were a conformist time, and in the 1960s Western societies became more tolerant of 'deviance' of various kinds. But, if the threat of psychiatry diminished for a while, more recently it seems to have been on the increase. Peter Schrag and Diane Divoky have described how it has become routine for American schools to use drugs to control unruly children: their estimate in 1975 was that between half and one million schoolchildren were being drugged in this way, mostly with Ritalin (a psychoactive drug whose known 'side-effects' include retardation of physical growth and in some children terrifying hallucinations). Children are required to take this drug every schoolday often for years on end, the parents being blackmailed into consent by threats that the child may otherwise be kept back a year, transferred to a special school, or the like. This treatment is justified by a diagnosis of 'minimal brain dysfunction' ('MBD'), an entirely hypothetical psychiatric disorder: the word 'minimal' refers to the fact that *no* evidence of brain damage or disease is observable other than the unruly behaviour which causes it to be postulated. What American school psychiatrists call an 'MBD child' is in plain English a rowdy child who finds school boring (many schools are).

In Britain, the Mental Health (Amendment) Act, 1982 – though in some ways more liberal than the law it replaced – contains no provision for mental patients to get access to a court of law to call their detention or treatment into question. (This was eliminated from the draft legislation through what one barrister described as 'a rearguard action by the Royal College of Psychiatrists, which . . . succeeded in banishing any non-medical component from the review of treatment decisions'.) And for the first time in English law it lays down clearly that the consent of a mental patient to treatment is not required.

All this is not to suggest that the phenomenon called 'mental illness' does not cover some real and very large human problems. Our asylums are not filled with people whose 'deviance' is limited to holding political views in advance of their time. But, Szasz says, learning to live as a member of a human society is a fearfully difficult, emotionally-demanding business, and particular circumstances often make it far more demanding for some individuals than for others. It is no matter for wonder that some individuals develop mentally in very strange directions indeed, but none of us *finishes* learning, and each of us must learn for himself or herself. How many of us can look inside ourselves honestly and find no irrational, unresolved mental conflicts? The State in a free society enforces laws preventing individuals encroaching on one another's freedom, but it has no right to go further and forcibly mould the behaviour of individuals who are not interfering with the freedom of others into an officially-approved pattern. It is not for a State to decide whether the behaviour and morality usual in Midwest America circa 1950 is superior or inferior to, say, those of the Trobriand Islands circa 1850, or to some new cultural pattern yet to be evolved; individuals must work out through free interactions with one another how life should best be lived. If someone in our society wanders through the streets naked or with a bag on his head, or fails to keep reasonably clean, then Szasz would be very glad to see him *offered* advice and help (perhaps including drugs) that might enable him to achieve a less tormented life; but he must not be *forced*. It won't do to say that coercion is justified because the mental path that the unfortunate man has taken itself hinders his recognition that he needs help; a Protestant could say the same about joining the Roman Catholic church.

If a 'madman' interferes with the liberty of someone else, then he should be punished like anyone else. For Szasz, the *reductio ad absurdum* of the theory of madness as illness is the spectacle of courts of law trying to decide whether some offender is legally 'responsible for his crime' or not, and requiring psychiatric 'expert witnesses' to apply tests of responsibility which the psychiatrists themselves often admit make little sense in their own terms. When we hear the details of the crimes of mass murderers like Peter Sutcliffe or Donald Nilsen, what can it mean for us to go on and ask whether they were 'sane' when they committed them? If we hold that someone who commits a serious offence because of insanity should be detained 'at Her Majesty's pleasure' because it is too dangerous to let him loose before he is deemed unlikely to repeat the offence, then *any* person who commits that offence should be given an open-ended sentence for the same reason. Conversely, if we feel that a 'sane' murderer or child-molester is entitled to the mercy of a fixed date of release, then the psychiatric profession has no moral right to withhold that mercy from anyone. As things stand, for Szasz psychiatry is an area of grievous tyranny within nominally free societies, and many psychiatrists are guilty of 'crimes against humanity'. They are so-called doctors whose job is to harm rather than to heal.

We saw it happen in Nazi Germany, and we hanged many of the doctors. We see it happen in the Soviet Union, and we denounce the doctors with righteous indignation. But when will we see that the same things are happening in the so-called free societies? . . . Or is the very possibility of perceiving many of our leading psychiatrists and psychiatric institutions in this way precluded by the fact that they represent the officially 'correct' views and practices?

Clearly, Szasz pulls no punches; sometimes he risks alienating the reader by overstating his case. At one point, for instance, he argues that the notion that certain people are not responsible for their actions because of 'insanity' is an unusual aberration of the twentieth-century West: 'It was unknown in ancient Greece.' This is simply false – see Plato's *Laws* (IX 864D). Szasz does admit that some conditions diagnosed as 'mental illness' might indeed turn out eventually to be caused by physical malfunctions of the nervous system, in which case they would count as real 'illnesses' in his terms too. He argues that the possibility of this *future* discovery is no justification for regarding the conditions as illnesses *now*, and that in most cases the ascription of irrational behaviour to brain disease is as fancifully circular as American school psychiatrists' 'MBD'; but it seems regrettable that Szasz did not even confront the issue, so far as I know, before writing the preface to the 1974 British edition of *Law, Liberty, and Psychiatry*.

But sometimes you have to shout to be heard. We know that decent average citizens are quite capable of constructing rationalizations for themselves that enable them to live comfortably with a Dachau at the end of their street. Szasz has made a case which I do not believe the profession of 'psychiatry' can answer.

All professions (even psychiatry, I am sure) contain some body of valuable expertise. But expertise, like any other resource, ought to be a commodity available for purchase by individuals who decide that they need it, not a means of social control. Nowadays – to quote Eliot Freidson one last time – 'expertise is more and more in danger of being used as a mask for privilege and power rather than, as it claims, as a mode of advancing the public interest.' And, since paper 'qualifications' are used as the device by which admission to professional and other positions of social privilege is regulated, society is increasingly infected by what Ronald Dore has called the 'diploma disease'. It ceases to matter what a man is or does – what matters is which certificates he has persuaded some diploma-issuing authority to grant him. As Dore shows, this disease is less advanced in Britain than perhaps any other country in the world (it is particularly severe in the primitive nations of Africa and Asia), but we are catching up fast. In the decade and a half that my own career has lasted I have watched the occupation of university teaching taking great strides away from the concept of imparting knowledge that learners wish to acquire because it seems to them interesting or useful, towards the concept of making employment for colleagues by creating qualifications that States can be persuaded to regard as prerequisites for admission to privileged social positions. Lacking the bodies of ethical principles that have evolved within old-established professions such as medicine and law, the academic world often seems from the inside to be entirely cynical about this process: what matters is whether a qualification can be sold, not whether those who grant it believe that it improves its holder's performance in the position to which it admits him. Yet academics, too, present to the outside world an impressive appearance of dignified, disinterested learning. So I hope it does not seem unduly arrogant of me to suggest that other groups, while no doubt more principled than us, may not always be entirely what they seem.

6/Entrepreneurs as Explorers

The economic tradition founded by Adam Smith two hundred years ago was developed very largely by other Britons, and it remained the dominant framework of economic thought in the English-speaking world simply because in practice language-barriers are powerful hindrances to the flow of ideas. However, this 'mainstream' has always suffered from serious defects as an account of how economic systems function. We saw in Chapter 4 that members of the Chicago and Virginia Schools are nowadays arguing that economic principles apply much more widely than just to the production and consumption of goods that are sold for money. But the deficiency I am referring to now is separate: even with respect to economic life in the narrow traditional sense, it can be said, the principles of the British economic tradition are too crude. The British tradition portrays a national economy as a system of thing-like processes, pressures, and balanced forces which look as objective and tangible as the structure of a steam-engine, chugging away successfully or perhaps racing to destruction if some vital flywheel or governor is removed. What is left out of the picture is the fact that all the agents operating an economic system are human beings with very un-thing-like minds, and that the economic aspects of life exist at all only because of people's subjective thoughts and feelings.

There exists another tradition of economic thought, founded in Austria in the 1870s and 1880s by men such as Carl Menger, professor of economics at the University of Vienna, and Eugen von Böhm-Bawerk, a member of an aristocratic Austrian family who divided his career between high government service and the academic world. This tradition places subjective human psychology at the heart of economics. From the point of view of the Austrian economists, the British tradition distorts economic reality by forgetting that human beings are full of ignorance but also full of creative potential, and that apparently rational economic behaviour is entirely driven by largely-irrational wishes and perceptions.

For many years the Austrian approach to economics was little heard of in the English-speaking world. This began to change when Nazism drove some of its leading exponents overseas, but the implications (and even the humane, un-mathematical style) of Austrian economics were so out of tune with postwar trends that for several decades the Austrians writing in English were more respected than read. In 1967 the urbane Oxford political philosopher Anthony Quinton described the *chef d'oeuvre* of the most eminent contemporary 'Austrian', Friedrich von Hayek, as a 'magnificent dinosaur stalk[ing] on to the scene'. He could not say that today. The American Israel Kirzner wrote in 1979 of 'a remarkable resurgence of the Austrian tradition'. Austrian economics has become a fashionable intellectual current, read by many who are not themselves professional economists. 'Austrian' insights are increasingly being incorporated into the body of mainstream English-language economic theory. And the Austrians give us new reasons for striving to free society from the burden of State intervention.

One of the ironies of intellectual history is that, though Britain was perhaps the least receptive of all major Western nations to Karl Marx's ideas, those ideas were to a large extent based on British theories of political economy, and British economists had no very satisfactory answers to Marx's critique of capitalism. When, quite a long time after Marx first attracted attention on the Continent, British writers turned to discussing his views, they were easily able to reject his historical determinism on the ground that it was refuted by subsequent history: Marx predicted that under capitalism the gap between rich and poor should grow steadily wider and the poor actually become poorer in absolute terms until 'bourgeois' society cracked under the strain, whereas in reality the opposite occurred. But historical prophecy was only one aspect of Marx's critique. Another aspect, perhaps the most central in terms of its influence on people's political attitudes, was Marx's idea that suppliers of capital 'exploited' workers by appropriating a portion of the rightful fruits of their labour, in the guise of 'interest' or 'profits'.

Nowadays, the average person with vague socialist leanings who hears that Marx objected to capitalist 'exploitation' of labour seems to take this as referring to harsh, inhumane mistreatment by employers of hapless workers terrified of losing their jobs in a society without State unemployment benefits or job-security laws. Such mistreatment may sometimes have occurred, though (as suggested in Chapter 2) the incidence of it has certainly been grossly exaggerated; but it has no special relevance for Marx's point of view. Marx's objection was much more precise and all-embracing. He believed that *any* element of income from investment or entrepreneurial activity was in a strict sense theft from the workers in the industry in question, because labour is the only source of value. The sale price of the products of any enterprise derives from the cost of the inputs to that enterprise (both the consumable inputs and a share of the cost of fixed assets such as machinery, which is gradually 'consumed' until it eventually wears out), together with the added value contributed by the employees of the enterprise. (The cost of the inputs in turn represents the labour which produced them, together with the cost of the inputs to those productive processes, and so back and back.) The owner of the enterprise has to pay for the inputs; so any excess of sales income over costs represents the workers' contribution, and any portion of that excess which is diverted away from employees' wage-packets is stolen from them. Even the most enlightened, humane capitalist is necessarily an exploiter.

Adam Smith could scarcely have replied to this; for him, too, value was a product of labour. The British economic tradition had little to say about interest, and tended to treat profit as a sort of wage for the work of supervising industry: yet, unlike ordinary wages, it bears no regular relationship to the work actually done. One could defend the capitalist system pragmatically by pointing out that it was a very efficient device for harnessing individuals' self-interest to the common good, by giving every controller of an asset a personal motive for seeking the use in which it would yield most benefit to consumers; but this sort of defence might (and in fact did) seem morally unsatisfying. If a certain portion of the national income has been *earned* by workers, how can arguments of expedience justify giving it instead to people who have not earned it (and who furthermore often live better than those who have)?

The classic refutation of Marx's analysis of capitalism was a book which Böhm-Bawerk published in 1896, between spells of service as Austrian Minister of Finance, as a response to the final volume of Marx's *Capital* which had appeared two years earlier.

In the first place, Böhm-Bawerk argues, it is just wrong to think of value as crystallized labour; indeed Marx contradicted himself on this point within a single chapter of *Capital*. It is quite possible for great labour to be devoted to something which proves unsaleable and useless to its maker when complete. The value of anything derives not from its past but from its future, not from the history of production but from the expectation of consumption. What someone will give for a consumer good depends entirely on the satisfaction he expects it to yield him, which is a wholly subjective phenomenon, and often an apparently irrational one. The value of the goods used in production derives at one or more removes from the consumption which they play a part in generating: the value of a steel-rolling mill, say, corresponds to the fact that it contains a million pleasant and convenient car-journeys locked in its womb. More precisely, the value of a good corresponds to the least important of the uses to which that good might economically be put. If we have blank paper in such abundance that we use it even for lighting fires, then the value of any single sheet will be its value as a firelighter even though some sheets are used for far more important purposes. In an efficient market the inputs of labour to various goods will tend to be in proportion to their values, giving Marx's theory a superficial plausibility; but the direction of cause and effect runs from value, determined by consumer psychology, to the organization of production – not from production to value.

One of the (arguably) irrational, yet universal, aspects of consumer psychology is that present satisfactions are preferred to future satisfactions. Other things being equal, a good meal now is worth more to anyone than an equally good meal in twelve months' or ten years' time. We are not bound to regard positive time preference as irrational; after all, we may not be around next year or next decade to eat the meal. But, rational or irrational, the pattern exists. And this explains the phenomenon of interest: it is a payment for postponement of consumption. If I lend someone £10 which I could spend on a meal today, it will take £11 (in real terms, ignoring the possibility of inflation) to repay me in a year's time because the £10 meal eaten then is now worth less to me. And it is possible to pay me £11 then for £10 now, because capital is fertile: investing capital in a productive process enables more consumer satisfaction to be generated per man-hour worked.

An explanation of interest is not an explanation or justification of profit. One of the achievements of the Austrians was to insist on the distinction between capitalist and enterpriser (or 'entrepreneur' for those who prefer the French word). The enterpriser may work largely or wholly with borrowed capital; and, even when enterpriser and capitalist are the same person, he makes a profit or loss in his entrepreneurial role. In his role as capitalist he simply receives the current rate of interest, which is the standard against which profits and losses should be judged. (If the standard rate of interest is positive, an enterprise which, after a year, is worth no more than was invested in it has made a loss.)

Profit and loss are a consequence of ignorance, which is a pervasive feature of human economic behaviour, though the British economic tradition did not recognize its importance.

In that tradition, the economic world is envisaged as including a large but in principle fixed set of categories of goods. Each type of good has its demand schedule – the differing amounts of the good that would be bought by consumers at different hypothetical prices (it is obvious that more pineapples would be bought than are bought now, if pineapples cost 20p each) – and its supply schedule, the differing amounts that would be produced at different hypothetical prices (if pineapples fetched £20 apiece, more resources would be switched to growing them). The two schedules can be represented as a rough X shape on a graph: if the vertical axis represents quantity and the horizontal axis price, the demand line falls, and the supply line rises, reading from left to right. The point where the two lines cross is the equilibrium, giving the quantity that will actually be produced and the price it will fetch. If trading moves away from the equilibrium point, market pressures will push it back – but movements away from the equilibrium are abnormalities caused by special situations. If participants in the market know what the schedules are, there is no reason for the production-levels and prices of goods to depart from their equilibria.

In those circumstances, there would be interest, but there would be no profits and losses. However, to the Austrians, this picture is utterly unrealistic: it portrays an ideal situation which almost never (perhaps never at all) corresponds to actual circumstances. 'Special situations' which disturb demand and supply schedules and cause movements away from equilibria are not abnormal: life is all special situations. Economic activity consists very largely not of making decisions in the light of one's knowledge of demand and supply schedules, but of trying to discover what the schedules are. It would be difficult to plot the schedules for any given good even if they were stable, because all the points except the place where they cross are purely hypothetical: what sort of answer could one hope to get to a question like 'How often would you buy pineapples if they cost 20p (but they don't)?' But, more important, the schedules are *not* stable; both demand and supply schedules for any good must be thought of as in a state of perpetual, unpredictable motion.

The schedules move, as a consequence of human creativity, which strives constantly to overcome the disadvantages of ignorance in the economic domain as it does in other domains. Someone thinks of a new method of production, and this alters the supply schedule, moving it leftwards and perhaps changing its shape. The novel idea may be a scientific invention (the inventor of the transistor obviously caused a major change to the supply schedule for radio sets), but far more often it will be a smaller-scale innovation of which consumers may be wholly unaware ('If we shift the finishing team into Shop D and use Shop F to store the reserve of widgets, we can use a cheap forklift to transport the pallets rather than replacing that clapped-out overhead conveyor.') Conversely, consumers think of new ways to lead satisfying lives, and this changes demand schedules: the introduction of papooses has shifted the demand schedule for prams. Indeed, the *set of goods* having demand and supply schedules is itself constantly changing as a result of human inventiveness: in 1960 there did not exist demand or supply schedules for word-processors. The range of marketable goods is not a fact of nature, but a creation of the human mind.

In this situation there arises the possibility of enterprise: the attempt to cause some range of inputs to produce more value than those particular inputs are commonly taken to be capable of producing. The costs of inputs to production are determined by what people *believe* they can yield in terms of consumer satisfaction, not what they actually can yield. Humanity is constantly inventing new uses for things, and since there is no reason to expect this process to stop it is meaningless to talk about what a thing might in principle be used for, independently of any given state of human knowledge. (Who would have guessed in 1700 that a smelly, dirty supply of petroleum would one day be available for its ability to speed people along roads and through the air?) Thus an enterpriser who succeeds in making given inputs yield more value than they are generally thought capable of yielding produces for himself an income after paying his costs: a profit. Conversely, if his experiment yields *less* value than could have been produced by standard uses of the inputs in question, the enterpriser loses.

The novel economic arrangement soon ceases to be profitable (that is, to yield a greater rate of return than the standard rate of interest) as others notice it and productive arrangements in general are adapted to the new discovery. An enterpriser's profits are temporary (unless they are artificially prolonged by State-backed institutions such as patent law, towards which liberals tend to be hostile). While they last, though, profits may be enormous; the bigger they are, the more the enterpriser has added to society's stock of economically-relevant knowledge. As the Austrian-turned-American Ludwig von Mises put it, 'it is absurd to speak of . . . a "normal rate of profit" or an "average rate of profit". . . . Profit and loss are, on the contrary, always a phenomenon of a deviation from "normalcy", of changes unforeseen by the majority, and of a "disequilibrium".'

However large they may be, profits belong properly to the enterpriser – they are not carved out of anyone else's share of the returns from production. The employees certainly have no claim to them; they have been paid the value of their labour, which depends on the general state of knowledge in society about the uses to which that labour can be put, so that a specially profitable use is by definition irrelevant to it. (In any case, since value depends on marginal use rather than actual use it is unlikely that general awareness of the enterpriser's innovation will significantly affect the value of labour.)

Many people instinctively rebel at the idea that enterprisers are entitled to whatever profits they can make (though they often overlook the fact that possibilities of profit are balanced by risks of loss). It seems arbitrary and unfair that someone should be able to enrich himself greatly for doing no more than stumbling across an economic opportunity that was waiting to be found, like Columbus happening on America while seeking a route to India. But to say that a novel economic opportunity was 'there all the time, waiting to be discovered' is the voice of hindsight speaking. The arrangement of English words that we call 'Wenlock Edge' was in a sense there all the time, waiting for Housman to think of it and write it down (none of the *words* were new), but we usually think of a poem as 'invented' or 'created' by the poet, not just 'found' or 'discovered'. Israel Kirzner, an economics teacher at New York University who is the leading figure among the younger generation of 'Austrian' economists, argues that the enterpriser, too, should be seen as 'inventing' or 'creating' novel uses for resources. If an enterpriser finds that

> a quantity of oranges is being sold, for eating, throughout the market at $5, while consumers would gladly pay a total of $12 for these same oranges converted to orange juice and marmalade, at a total manufacturing cost, above that of the oranges, of $4 . . . [then his] discovery of the $3 profit opportunity . . . represents the discovery of $3 value in the oranges that did not previously exist. . . . The entrepreneur

. . . may, then, be held to have created this additional value in the oranges.

Kirzner takes a hard-nosed line on the enterpriser's entitlements. Suppose three travellers are heading across a desert to an unowned water-hole that all of them know about, and one of them races ahead and charges monopoly prices for water to the others when they arrive:

> May it not be that they were less alert, entrepreneurially, to the possibility that someone else might indeed appropriate all the water than the energetic traveler? Should we not, then, say that the latter was the first to discover the true market worth of the unheld water?

Of course it may be that in such a situation the cost to the energetic traveller in terms of resentment and abuse by his companions would outweigh any cash gains, in which case no opportunity for entrepreneurial profit-making exists. But Kirzner's point is that, *if* the first man wants to make a financial killing in this way, he has a moral right to do so.

Some may feel that the water-hole example presses Kirzner's notion of entrepreneurial creation further than is plausible (in real life, if two of the travellers hang back this would probably mean not that they are unaware of the value of the water but that they suppose themselves to be living under a constitution which does not allow a water-hole to be appropriated in such circumstances). But Kirzner presents this as an extreme, and debatable, example. The example of the oranges is much more ordinary, and here it does seem reasonable to say that the enterpriser has 'created' new value, if we say that Housman 'created' 'Wenlock Edge' or that William Shockley 'invented' the arrangement of semiconductors and electrodes that we call a transistor.

Certainly the view that profits are effectively the proceeds of sale of an enterpriser's creation makes his right to them seem much solider. It is very generally taken for granted that a person is entitled to whatever he creates. The equalitarian economist Kenneth Arrow has commented, ruefully, that 'when teaching elementary economics, I have had considerable difficulty in persuading the students that [this principle – that an individual is entitled to what he creates] was not completely self-evident.'

(Inventors of commercially-valuable items are in many cases not the people who make the most money from their inventions, and this might remain true in a thoroughgoing liberal economy. But that just shows that the strictly scientific or technical inventiveness represented by a novel product is only a small fraction of all the inventiveness needed to make that product actually minister to consumers' needs. Translating an invention from the drawing-board into economic production, and marketing it, are intellectual activities in their own right, and very demanding ones. Academic intellectuals frequently affect a lofty scorn for the banal trivialities which they see the businessman's life as composed of; to which the only possible response, surely, is 'Just you try it, chum.')

To the Austrians, an economy is a network of relationships between thinking individuals; and the Austrians stress also the individuality of the non-human goods involved in economic exchanges. The British tradition tended to see economic life in terms of undifferentiated aggregates: the nation produced so many million tons of coal, a commodity with one fixed pair of demand and supply schedules, so many million tons of butter, a sharply distinct commodity with another pair of schedules – it even possessed so many billion pounds of capital, envisaged as a sort of chameleon-like substance without fixed characteristics of its own. To the Austrians, the lack of individuality in a quantity of coal or butter makes these untypical goods; and even in these cases any householder knows that in reality there is coal and coal, butter and butter. To a particular individual going shopping on a given occasion, the difference between two packets of butter may be more important than the difference between a radio set and a vase, either of which seems equally suitable as a birthday present for his aunt. Human intelligence constantly suggests new ways to substitute one good for another in order to satisfy a consumer craving, making nonsense of the idea of a fixed set of demand and supply schedules; and our cravings themselves are not constant – the Austrians are very far from accepting the Chicago postulate of fixed universal human tastes. They see individual psychology as developing in response to the individual's environment: people growing up in widely different cultures will develop widely different needs and tastes. The capital stock of a society, for the Austrians, is not a homogeneous mass, like a mountain of gold-dust, but a 'filigree' of particular things in particular places, each with its own special, quirky properties, and similar only in that they can all be used (directly or indirectly) to satisfy some consumer wants.

(From an Austrian point of view, one of the objections to Keynesian economics – not necessarily to the ideas of Keynes himself, but to the policies elaborated after his death by the 'Keynesians' who became so influential in British politics – is that they adopted a 'macroscopic' approach to economic affairs which systematically overlooked the rationale of all the numberless individual transactions of which the national picture was composed. Axel Leijonhufvud has commented on the 'schizophrenic' nature of an economic orthodoxy which explained market-clearing equilibrium in terms of individuals but sought to cure malfunctions in the system by reference to large-scale aggregates.)

Two common consumer wants are for goods that can conveniently be used as a store of value across time, and as a general medium of exchange. In a developed economy, we expect that some thing or things will take on the functions of 'money'. But 'money', to the Austrians, is an adjective, not a noun. Milton Friedman, working in the British tradition, asserts the importance of State action to limit the supply of money, but to an Austrian the doctrine of 'monetarism' ultimately makes little more sense than a suggestion that the State should limit the supply of birthday presents. If people cannot give radios, they will give vases. If willing lenders and borrowers cannot exchange pounds sterling, they will monetarize something else.

One particular implication of the Austrian emphasis on the individuality of goods is that the concept of 'monopoly' loses its importance. In the British tradition, if a given category of goods has only one producer then market forces cease to play their beneficent role, and a far smaller quantity of the goods is produced than the social optimum. The virtuous effects of the market are fully realized only in an ideal state of 'perfect competition' which is never attained in practice. To the Austrians, virtually everything is a monopoly. As Mises points out, 'Each factory turns out products different from those of the other plants. Each hotel has a monopoly on the sale of its services on the site of its premises. The professional services rendered by a physician or a lawyer are never perfectly equal to those rendered by any other physician or lawyer.' But this does not matter, because an economy is a dynamic, not a static, system. The real social need is not to push the production-levels and prices of a fixed range of known goods to their equilibria; rather, as Hayek puts it, 'The solution of the economic problem of society is . . . always a voyage of exploration into the unknown, an attempt to discover new ways of doing things better than they have been done before.' Hayek notes that the textbook definition of perfect competition presupposes a perfectly homogeneous commodity, small-scale buyers and sellers none of whom expects individually to be able to influence prices, and complete knowledge of all relevant factors by all market participants:

> Advertising, undercutting, and improving ('differentiating') the goods or services produced are all excluded by definition – 'perfect' competition means indeed the absence of all competitive activities . . . the need for competition is nowhere greater than in fields in which the nature of the commodities or services makes it impossible that it ever should create a perfect market in the theoretical sense.

Friedrich von Hayek, who has just been quoted, is without doubt the most distinguished living member of the school under discussion. He has developed 'Austrian' insights into a very wide-ranging philosophical system, which extends far beyond economics to embrace the sociological and even cognitive psychological aspects of the study of Man. By any reasonable standards Hayek must count as one of the intellectual giants of the twentieth century. The fact that, even ten years ago, his name was rather little known outside certain specialized circles just goes to show the great power of fashion to make intellectual excellence invisible.

Born in Vienna in 1899, Hayek began his career as a pure economist, working on money theory and the theory of trade cycles – he was one of the few economists to give advance warning of the great American stock-market crash of 1929. Hayek came to teach at the London School of Economics in 1931, and became a naturalized Briton a few years later (which he remains today, though he has lived abroad for thirty years). He first came to wide public attention in 1944, when he published a short book, dedicated 'to The Socialists of All Parties', which shocked the British and American publics by arguing that the evolution of British social thought and social organization which was then in its initial stages was no less than a repetition of the same evolution he had witnessed in Germany a couple of decades earlier; that the progress towards planned welfare which all around him were taking for granted as the best hope of a decent life for all was not a beneficent advance to a higher stage of society – it was, as his title described it, *The Road to Serfdom*. In Britain, the book was widely discussed, welcomed even by people one might have expected to be out of sympathy with its views (Keynes wrote: 'I find myself . . . not only in agreement with it, but in a deeply moved agreement'), but in the years that followed its message was largely ignored. (In the USA, with its low level of tolerance for intellectual unorthodoxy, the book had difficulty finding a publisher, and when published it became the target of bitter invective.)

Hayek went to the chair of Social and Moral Science at Chicago in 1950, where he produced what is perhaps the most important of his many books, *The Constitution of Liberty*. In 1962 he moved to the university of Freiburg-im-Breisgau in West Germany, where he now lives in very active retirement. Hayek's influence was probably never as great as it has become since he turned eighty. As well as his books and scholarly articles he issues a steady flow of pronouncements on current affairs, using the columns of the *Times* to lecture his pupil Margaret Thatcher on the folly of her approach to the realization of his and her shared ideals. (After Mrs Thatcher's election victory in 1979, Hayek saw it as essential for her to change the legal and economic framework of society abruptly – as Ludwig Erhard had done in West Germany after the war – so that the necessary but extremely painful period of adjustment would at least be short. He argued, rightly as it appears, that

Mrs Thatcher's gradualism would condemn Britain to massive unemployment over a long term, though he seems to have been wrong in supposing that this would render the nation ungovernable.)

The master-idea in Hayek's philosophy is that many of the most valuable social institutions are 'the result of human action but not of human design'.

Ever since Aristotle, it was a cardinal principle of Western thought that all phenomena could be assigned to one or the other of two domains: the domain of the 'natural', of things and events governed purely by the laws of science, and the domain of the 'artificial', of objects or institutions designed by an intelligent mind. According to Hayek, this is wrong: there is a very important intermediate domain of human institutions produced by gradual cultural evolution, which are not 'natural' in the sense of being biologically determined, but were never consciously designed either. An obvious example is language. English and other languages are not given to us by our biological inheritance, along with things like our organs of sense or our metabolism; but at the same time no person or committee ever sat down and invented the English language (languages like Esperanto, which were consciously designed, are exceptional curiosities rather than the norm). Another example might be the pattern of settlement in a territory, whereby towns and cities of different sizes are scattered at regular distances apart. Unless the territory was colonized quite recently it is certain that nobody planned the settlement-pattern, yet at the same time that pattern results wholly from voluntary decisions made by individual people – the pattern was not imposed on the inhabitants in the inexorable fashion in which the trajectory of a boy falling out of a tree is imposed on him by the law of gravity.

Hayek sees the artificial/natural dichotomy as not just an error but a dangerous error, because it suggests that whenever a social institution is obviously not constructed in accordance with a comprehensible, conscious plan it can advantageously be abolished and replaced by a rational, streamlined alternative. The English language (to illustrate Hayek's point with an example that is not politically contentious) is full of arbitrary-looking quirks and irregularities having no clear function or virtue, and this might seem to imply that we would do well to abandon English in favour of some perfectly regular artificial language such as Esperanto, if it were feasible to do so. Hayek would argue that this does not follow. The quirky irregularity of a culturally-evolved institution springs from the fact that its present structure emerges from many generations of trial and error by innumerable individuals, each of whom innovated in some particular respect and either found that his innovation worked out badly in practice and abandoned it or else found that it worked well and retained it, after which others imitated him.

Hayek sees a culturally-evolved institution, therefore, as encapsulating far more knowledge and experience than is or can be possessed by any single individual or small group who set out consciously to design an alternative. Where many people see irrational traditional accretions which serve no clear purpose and would be better abolished, Hayek sees solutions to practical problems that we are unaware of – solutions with which we tamper at our peril. (Who knows why it pays to have irregular verbs in a language like English? The fact that we *do not know* what advantage there is in them does not mean that the unknown advantage may not be very significant indeed. Perhaps they help to make some of our most crucial semantic distinctions easier for the hearer to pick out from the confusion of rapid speech. As a student of linguistics myself I find Hayek's point of view extremely plausible for the case of language.)

Hayek has coined the term 'scientism' for the attitude which regards consciously designed institutions as necessarily superior to institutions which grow up haphazardly. He traces the origins of the 'scientistic' passion for social engineering to eighteenth-century France, where after the revolution it expressed itself through the adoption of radically new, consciously rational approaches to everything from weights and measures to local government. In the post-revolutionary period, England was the one nation which set its face actively against French scientism; part of the anguish in Hayek's *Road to Serfdom* sprang not simply from the fact that he saw the mistakes of prewar Germany being repeated once again but from the fact that England, for Hayek, was the very country whose history and traditions should have taught it better than to go down that road. '[I]t is one of the most disheartening spectacles of our time to see to what extent some of the most precious things which England has given to the world are now held in contempt in England herself.' For, to Hayek, political liberalism and rejection of scientistic social engineering are all of a piece. Both stress the virtues of allowing social progress to emerge gradually and spontaneously from the attempts of innumerable free individuals to find the good life for themselves; both exclude the possibility that society can be planned by a central, guiding intelligence, however benevolent.

There is a close relationship between Hayek's social thought and the philosophy of his Viennese contemporary and colleague at the LSE, Karl Popper (now Sir Karl). Popper's chief theme is the process by which humanity acquires knowledge; he describes this process as one of 'conjectures and refutations'. Scientists learn about the natural world by making guesses – guesses which may be mistaken, and often are – and by testing those guesses, checking whether their implications chime with observable evidence. We weed out guesses that fail the tests we set, and what we call our 'knowledge' is nothing more or less than the totality of guesses which have not been refuted to date. There is no finality: all our beliefs are perpetually vulnerable to refutation by novel evidence. Hayek sees social life, likewise, as a process of conjectural discovery of how to use resources to best satisfy humanity's wants, and commercial activity is a central part of that social discovery procedure. (Commerce is not the only area of life to which the idea of progress through conjectures and refutations applies; we advance by trial and error also in many non-commercial aspects of human behaviour and relationships, and Hayek has a good deal to say about these. However, it is particularly in the commercial sphere that the process of social discovery is most at risk from interventionist political theories, so that is the area where Hayek's analysis is most urgent.)

An enterpriser launching a new product or experimenting with a new technique of production is like a Popperian scientist proposing a new theoretical conjecture. The scientist abandons his conjecture if it is refuted by experience; for the enterpriser, profit and loss provide the discipline which compatibility with experimental findings provides for the scientist. Capital is the fuel which enterprisers use to mount their social research projects, and profits increase the ability of talented researchers to try further conjectures. The enterpriser can never afford to relax; even if his past experiments have been so successful that he has attained a position of total dominance over his branch of commerce, it always remains open for a newcomer with a still better idea to set up in business and scoop all the big man's custom (as Einstein overthrew the seemingly-impregnable physical theories of Isaac Newton). What matters in commerce is not actual monopoly (a monopolist who tries to exploit his position by profiteering will promptly lose his market dominance to undercutters), but only artificial restraints on the entry of potential challengers, such as grants of legal monopoly or a tax structure which favours established enterprises. Just so, in the scientific domain, there was nothing wrong with the fact that Newton's physics was universally accepted for two centuries, though it would have been very wrong if Einstein's challenge had been suppressed when it was made.

For Popper, knowledge advances most rapidly and successfully if many different scientists are engaged in 'friendly-hostile' intellectual rivalry, so that they will weed out one another's mistakes as rapidly as possible and produce a constant flow of new ideas. Correspondingly, for Hayek it is important that society should contain many independent individuals with large holdings of capital prepared to use it to back their various hunches about profitable opportunities. Hayek says at one point that if there were no other method of getting large capital holdings into private hands it would be a good thing to parcel out the nation's capital resources by a lottery. In reality it is not necessary to resort to such artificial stratagems when the mechanisms of profit-accumulation and inheritance are available to do the job – provided they are not tampered with by redistributionist State policies.

States need to levy taxes in order to carry out their proper functions; and Hayek would include among those functions that of making 'provision for those threatened by the extremes of indigence or starvation due to circumstances beyond their control'. But there is a big step from levying taxes to pay for essential State functions to the use of taxation as a tool to redistribute the pattern of incomes and capital holdings. (From the taxpayer's point of view, these two kinds of redistribution are scarcely distinct; the value of capital derives from its power to yield future income, so progressive taxation of private incomes reduces the value of capital to a private owner without any direct capital levy.) To Hayek, redistributive policies are objectionable for reasons quite apart from the immorality of coerced payments which are not matched by corresponding benefits. They interfere with the process of economic discovery, in two ways.

In the first place, the more capital is drained from individual, private hands towards the central State machine, the less economic experimentation and advance can occur. A State cannot replace a mass of individuals as enterpriser, because economic advance, like scientific progress, is an essentially social, 'critical' activity. Progress comes from refuting others' conjectures as much as from making conjectures of one's own; a solitary scientist would soon become an uninteresting eccentric. If *all* economic initiatives were taken by an all-powerful State, its subjects could be fairly confident that they were getting very bad value for money indeed – though they could never demonstrate this for certain in any particular case, because one can never know in advance how successful another and cheaper way of doing things will be in practice. Real life always throws up endless complications that one could not anticipate, so the only way to establish that an economic technique is the best available is actually to put it into practice in competition with the alternatives and actually to win custom from them.

Secondly, redistribution is one of the many ways in which State intervention in the economy distorts prices, and prices are the information-transmitters in economic life, they play the crucial role which in the scientific domain is played by academic publication. The relative prices which are most directly affected by redistribution are those of current consumption *vis-à-vis* saving and investment. Redistributionist policies make current consumption artificially cheap and investment artificially expensive. If I am left with £20,000 after tax this year, then provided I spend it all on consumer goods I get a full £20,000 worth; it would take considerably more than £20,000 of investment at the prevailing rate of interest to give me an equivalent return in terms of discounted future consumption, if the interest is itself taxed at a high marginal rate (perhaps including a special extra levy on 'unearned' income), and if a proportion of the capital sum is taken when I bequeath it to my heir or even as an annual capital levy in my own lifetime. Even the prospect that some of these things *might* well happen under a future change of government is quite enough to make current consumption a better bet. Hence the fact that many Rolls-Royces are to be seen in the West End, at the same time as richer Englishmen are heard to complain bitterly about the punitive UK tax structure. Expensive cars, in particular, are often even cheaper than ordinary current consumption, since the tax system makes them an allowable expense for many people. Socialists sometimes point to the luxury cars as evidence that the rich like to squander their money on conspicuous consumption, so that it is morally justifiable forcibly to divert their funds to worthier uses. This is like opening a chain of State butcher's shops selling steak at a heavily subsidized price and then complaining that people are greedy. Never mind what the ideals behind redistributive taxation may be: its objective effect is to encourage people to use resources in ways that benefit only themselves, rather than benefiting society at large by investing them.

State economic intervention distorts many price-relativities other than that of investment versus current consumption. For instance, various forms of long-distance transport are currently subsidized in different ways and to different extents, so that it is simply impossible to know what is actually the socially-optimal method to achieve any particular movement of goods or people. The rail network is entirely operated as a State enterprise, only a proportion of whose costs are covered by fares and freight charges; road users pay taxes which are unrelated to the costs of maintaining roads or to the intangible costs borne by people who live near heavy traffic; air freight is, I believe, relatively free of State intervention in either direction, while air passenger fares are kept artificially high by a State-backed cartel. One can guess that it would pay society on balance to close down most of the rail network and make more use of roads and air transport, but we cannot be sure of this – it might turn out that if users had to pay the true marginal costs of an upgraded road system they would find it cheaper to move back to rail in many cases. We just cannot tell. When the State plays as large a role in the economy as is normal in contemporary Western societies, the decisions of individual economic agents (each aiming simply to minimize costs and maximize income in his own case) are often influenced almost wholly by the consequences of political decisions and scarcely at all by what is actually the most economical use of resources in current circumstances.

Thus, for Hayek, interventionist politics deserves the special odium which is incurred by book-burning regimes: it destroys knowledge. Prices on a free market perform an all-important task: they filter out, from the unmanageable total mass of economically-relevant facts, just that information which an economic agent needs in order to serve consumers' needs at least cost in terms of other needs unserved or served less well (and they give him a motive to act accordingly). 'Prices have work to do,' but State intervention distorts prices and prevents them carrying out their tasks. And State intervention goes hand in hand with confiscation of private holdings of capital, which fuel economic experimentation: the State both discourages the advancing of novel commercial conjectures and makes it difficult or impossible to discover whether such conjectures are refuted. We hate governments which put libraries to the torch, because they destroy some of the noblest adventures of the human spirit. But the kind of knowledge which is attacked by economic interventionism, while it perhaps seems less inspiring in the abstract, is in practical, human terms far more important. It is knowledge not about remote issues like the shape of galaxies or the deeds of heroes long dead, but about how to keep ourselves fed, housed, and able to lead our daily lives satisfyingly, today and tomorrow.

All this may be water off a duck's back to someone for whom material equality is a supreme political good. I wonder how many people would be sincerely willing to 'buy' greater material equality at the cost of a significant general impoverishment of society. But to Hayek it is irrelevant whether people have this political preference, since his reply is that it is a contradictory preference which cannot be achieved. We cannot compare individuals' standards of living unless we are given the yardstick of free-market prices. The more a State interferes with the price structure, the less comparisons of individuals' money spending tell us about their relative economic positions. In the Soviet Union, someone whose tastes run to sport and education can get far more satisfaction for the same expenditure than someone who prefers pleasant accommodation or the convenience of a private car, because the Soviet State happens to have chosen to make everything to do with sport and education artificially cheap, and cars and good housing artificially expensive or otherwise difficult to obtain. (We know that the Soviet price-relativities are artificial, because we can compare them with the still fairly freely-determined prices for comparable goods in Western nations.)

At the extremes, admittedly, we might feel safe in saying that a tramp sleeping in a doss-house is enjoying less consumer satisfaction than someone in a mansion surrounded by manicured lawns, without needing to enquire into the details of money expenditures. But if one wants to take material equality seriously one has to think about much more than just the extremes of inequality. How do we compare a fairly spacious house requiring a lot of upkeep and cleaning, situated in a lonely rural position, with a cramped but modern flat in a fashionable area of a town? Or a word-processor, with an elegant dining-room table? In the abstract, we can't. Tastes differ. Some people hate isolation and would put up with a great deal of inconvenience to live in towns, others positively prefer remoteness. Some people care little about the quality of their furniture, others would not give a thank-you for a word-processor. The price system of a free market gives us a way of balancing all these intangible factors and comparing the total bundles of goods consumed by different individuals; and there is no other way.

The choice is not between equality and a higher average income. It is between a higher average income in a dynamic society allowing free rein to individuals' creative urges, which at any time possesses a known degree of inequality, and a lower, stagnating average income in a society that systematically frustrates creativity *and possesses an unknown degree of inequality* (which might in practice be just as high, or much higher).

What I have said of Hayek so far may make him sound like an uncritically loyal advocate of business interests, a kind of unpaid propagandist for the CBI. This he is not. Like other liberals, Hayek often makes the point that businessmen themselves are by no means reliable supporters of the free enterprise system. Often they greatly prefer the cosy world of State subsidies and protection to the chilly atmosphere of free trade which forces their activities to serve the general welfare. But, more than that, Hayek objects to aspects of the legal framework within which commerce currently operates – not just to recent, socialist-inspired aspects, but to aspects one thinks of as commercially-inspired. Hayek is certainly *not* just naively saying that we only need to turn the legal and political clock back to 1910, or 1870, or 1830, and all will be well.

For instance, Hayek objects to the way in which commercial enterprises are incorporated under the law as 'legal persons', with many of the rights of persons, such as the right to own property. A firm is simply a device through which individuals (its shareholders) seek to achieve their purposes, Hayek argues, and it cannot properly be treated as an independent agent with goals of its own. Thus it is illogical and wrong to allow one firm to buy shares in and gain control of another – a point Hayek made well before the asset-strippers of the 1960s led many people to become dubious about this aspect of our current private enterprise system. Likewise, Hayek criticizes the system by which the directors of a company decide how much of its profits to distribute in dividends and how much to plough back into expanding the company's activities. All the profits, so far as Hayek is concerned, properly belong to the shareholders, and he finds it as odd to treat the firm as entitled to retain them as it would be to let my typewriter retain a portion of the royalties I use it to earn. If the directors believe the firm needs to increase its working capital, they ought to have to persuade owners of capital to lend it, just as any enterprise must do when it starts up.

It is interesting that this latter criticism coincides in its effect with a criticism of the present commercial system made for different and much more pragmatic reasons by Milton Friedman. Friedman argues that the tax system (he is discussing the USA, but the point would apply with equal or greater force to Britain) makes it artificially cheap for shareholders to allow a company to retain profits rather than to take the profits as dividends and reinvest them elsewhere. Thus the structure of taxation encourages the expansion of existing firms, even when these are relatively inefficient, at the expense of new and potentially more efficient entrants to the field; in yet another way, the State promotes harmful oligopoly or monopoly. Friedman's solution is to assess shareholders to tax on their share of a company's profits irrespective of whether they receive them; for Hayek, they should have the right to receive them. Both of these figures whom socialists see as bogey-men agree in arguing for a radical innovation in commercial law which would remove one of the features of the business world which socialists find most objectionable.

That said, it could be argued that Hayek does not go nearly as far in this direction as the logic of his position suggests. Thus, I find it difficult to see a principled liberal rationale for limited liability. The standard arguments used to justify the introduction of limited liability were that industrial progress would be severely damaged by shortage of capital, if investors in a firm risked not just their investment but their entire property, and that nobody's freedom was abridged since the letters 'Ltd' told everyone entering into a contractual relationship with a limited company where he stood. But these arguments, like arguments for a Welfare State in the 1940s, seem much weaker now we have experience of their practical consequences. Modern critics of big business charge that it overrides and damages the interests not particularly of individuals in a contractual relationship with business firms, but – much more strikingly and objectionably – of the general public. Although this sort of complaint is often greatly exaggerated, one must admit that there is something in it. Big firms represent such massive concentrations of power that they can sometimes manage one way or another to get away with things that the small man could not, and shareholders have insufficient motive to restrain a firm's rapacious pursuit of profit when, however badly the firm behaves, their own losses are limited to their investment.

The situation is much worse when power is concentrated in the State, since then there is ultimately *no* legal recourse when an individual's interests are overridden. Individuals can and do sue giant firms, and sometimes they win. But even when industry is in private hands, under the present system the situation is unsatisfactory. Firms would surely act very much more cautiously and decently, if shareholders were personally responsible for any damage awards against them. (P.S. Atiyah has commented on the 'low level of sophistication' of the debates that preceded the Limited Liability Act of 1855: 'Nobody . . . seems to have raised the question of tort liabilities. Was the victim of a tort also to be deemed to have "dealt" with the company on the terms that its members were to have limited liability?') Yet, despite his objection to the treatment of firms as legal persons, Hayek never, as far as I know, calls into question the principle of limited liability (except for one brief and ambiguous allusion). To abolish that principle probably would have serious effects on the overall level of investment in public companies (and still more on *how* resources were invested); but liberals are used to making radical proposals, and it is not clear why they should shrink from radicalism in this particular respect. To my mind it is not excluded that a genuinely liberal Britain might be materially much poorer than the society of today. Freedom versus equality is a phoney opposition, but freedom and opulence are perhaps less straightforwardly compatible than liberals commonly assume.

Friedrich von Hayek is an intellectual of the old school, soberly cultivated in demeanour and dress, ranging in his prose with easy familiarity over the sweep of European history and culture. Perhaps it is not surprising, then, if his liberalism seems at times to verge on conservatism. Hayek is no friend of the anarchic, self-willed approach to life. For him, civilization depends crucially on the acceptance by individuals of general rules of behaviour whose rationale will often be obscure (since they have been shaped by a myriad forgotten events during the course of cultural evolution) and whose consequences in a particular situation may even be adverse. To take an example outside the economic domain: during most of human history, nobody understood the genetic mechanisms which imply that matings between close kin give a high probability of deformed offspring, yet humanity succeeded in evolving incest taboos without understanding their function. Probably there will have been many individual brothers and sisters whose chromosomes in fact contained no pair of harmful recessive genes, so that no harm would have come if they had been allowed to develop sexual feelings for one another and marry; but such cases were (and still are) impossible to identify, so it was far better to maintain the general rule even though in some particular instances much good might have come from its relaxation. Hayek is totally hostile to 'situational morality', to the outlook which Keynes ascribed to his elite circle of Cambridge 'Apostles' in the years before the First World War: 'We entirely repudiated a personal liability on us to obey general rules,' settling moral decisions case by case thanks to the enlightenment conferred by their 'colossal moral superiority' to the ordinary population. Hayek condemns Freud for having 'destroyed culture' by encouraging people to liberate themselves from traditional emotional shackles. We are often ignorant of the good achieved by our repressions, but this is no reason to suppose that they achieve no good.

There is a severe tension between this stress on preservation of tradition despite personal inclinations, and the liberal emphasis on progress through innovative experimentation.

Hayek denies that his position is ambiguous. A postscript to *The Constitution of Liberty* is entitled 'Why I am not a conservative', and argues that it is inconsistent to be a conservative (with a small 'c', of course) if one advocates – as Hayek does – radical changes in the structure of society. For Hayek, a conservative

> does not object to coercion or arbitrary power so long as it is used for what he regards as the right purposes. He believes that if government is in the hands of decent men, it ought not to be too much restricted by rigid rules. . . . he is essentially opportunist and lacks principles. . . .

Hayek would claim that there is no incompatibility in his

arguing for the desirability of free innovation with respect to particular economic or social arrangements, at the same time as he urges us to treat with quasi-religious awe the constitutional framework within which those innovations occur. The constitution of a liberal society, for Hayek, is one in which the actions even of government itself are constrained by laws framed in general terms, without a view to their implications for any particular person or situation, by a legislature independent of and uninfluenced by the executive. These laws should be guided by the principle that coercion is permitted only in pursuance of what Hayek calls 'the three great negatives: peace, justice, and liberty'. Laws may not be directed to achieve specific positive purposes, because in normal circumstances the members of a society do not share common purposes. The Britain of 1941 was extremely abnormal in the extent to which its inhabitants agreed on the overriding priority of one goal, the defeat of the Axis. Normally, each individual member of a society has his or her own range of goals which differ greatly from the goals of others, so the most a State can do is to prevent people hindering one another in the pursuit of their respective goals.

Yet in practice, surely, it will not always be easy to decide whether a proposed innovation should be regarded as changing the framework of untouchable rules or as a desirable experiment without 'constitutional' consequences. Furthermore, if cultural evolution tends to produce good rules that can only be because the worse makes way for the better – if past evolution was a good thing, why end it now? Consider a concrete case: a man who finds that he has homosexual inclinations. Should he feel free to indulge them, and thus help society to discover whether the gay way of life is a valid, satisfying alternative to the traditional choice of heterosexuality or celibacy? Or should he repress his urges in conformity with the deeply-entrenched cultural taboo on homosexuality? For most liberals it is axiomatic that anyone should feel free to do as he wishes with a willing partner. A conservative might mindlessly insist that homosexuality is wrong because it has always been seen as wrong. Hayek, I suspect, would in practice side with the conservative, not mindlessly, but on the ground that homosexuality may have highly deleterious consequences which twentieth-century science knows nothing of, and that the traditional taboo is an unconsciously-evolved response to these. The homosexual might understandably find this argument less than wholly convincing.

It is not as if Hayek's own practical suggestions for a liberal political constitution are marked by an attempt to preserve continuity with Britain's (or anyone else's) traditions. Hayek is an economist and a sociologist, not a practising politician, and during most of his career he has discussed his political ideals in strictly abstract terms. In a passage within a three-volume work published in his old age, however, he turns his hand to the design of a concrete institutional framework capable of fulfilling his requirement that government and legislature should be strictly separated. Whether Hayek's utopia would be workable, I cannot say, but it is certainly novel. Laws will be enacted by a set of *nomothetae*, new members of which are elected annually from among their number by the class of all citizens reaching the age of forty-five in that year; each nomothete serves for one term of fifteen years and is thereafter guaranteed an honourable sinecure. Wise choices of lawmaker will be aided by a corporate spirit fostered in each age-cohort through the formation of clubs of contemporaries. It is hard to repress a giggle when Hayek goes on to suggest that these clubs could be made more attractive by modifying the age rule so that 'men of one age group were brought together with women two years or so younger,' and then the old boy solemnly discusses how this might be engineered 'without any objectionable legal discrimination'.

Practical politics is not Hayek's *forte*. It was perhaps rash of him to embark on constitution-building, and unkind of me to draw attention to a short, untypical section in a long and rich work. But if his essay in this area involves an institutional iconoclasm which is difficult to reconcile with his emphasis on the virtues of culturally evolved forms of life, his suggestion that a liberal State will offer an economic safety-net to rescue the unfortunate from indigence seems to reveal a streak of the paternalistic aspect of conservatism. Hayek appears reluctant, here, to face up to the implications of his liberal concept of justice. Hayek often argues that the modern concept of 'social justice' is senseless; justice or injustice is a feature only of individual dealings, and if these are all just there is no room for a further question about whether the society as a whole is just. On the face of it, coercing some individuals to part with their property in taxes in order to provide a welfare safety-net for other individuals looks like a doubly unjust proceeding: the first group are forced to give something for nothing, the second group are given something for nothing. We saw that Milton Friedman, too, accepted the concept of a State guarantee against indigence, but then Milton Friedman's liberalism is highly pragmatic. He is chiefly concerned to argue that the market will achieve society's goals more efficiently than the command system, whatever those goals happen to be, so if a belief in the desirability of an economic safety-net is widely shared (as it currently is) then it is reasonable for Milton Friedman to incorporate it into his model society. Hayek's liberalism is more radical and principled, so that one might expect him to insist that relief of poverty should be left to voluntary charity – as younger radical liberals would commonly regard as axiomatic.

When Hayek was writing *The Constitution of Liberty* in the 1950s it may be that the idea of offering *no* State welfare provisions was just too extreme to be included in a book intended to be taken seriously by men of influence in the world. When I took up the issue with Hayek more recently I formed the impression that he perhaps now sees the economic safety-net as a kind of insurance premium against insurrection by those at the bottom of the social pyramid, in which case taxation for welfare could be justified on 'public good' grounds like taxation for national defence. If this really is Hayek's current view, it seems implausible: surely, revolutions are not made by the starving? And it suggests, too, an odd lack of confidence in his own persuasive arguments that free-market relationships lead to a general rise in living standards rather than to great wealth for a few. I prefer to see the 'safety-net' aspect of Hayek's thinking as a blemish, caused by his belonging to a generation in which it was near-impossible to free one's mind of all traces of socialist ideology.

But these flaws – if they are flaws – are small things, set against the overall sweep of Hayek's social philosophy. Hayek's writings are far too extensive to do justice to in a few pages. Again and again they open up novel ways of looking at familiar human and social phenomena, and although Hayek, like all of us, is fallible, the overall picture of Man and society that emerges from his work is one that I find more believable and satisfying than any alternative I have encountered. The details of Hayek's ideal constitution may be contrived and impractical, but he is surely right in stressing the need to separate lawmaking from government. We must somehow deprive our rulers of the power to use law as a tool for bribing voters.

7/Utopia for Sale

Among professional philosophers, by far the best-known member of the liberal movement is Robert Nozick, a young Harvard Professor of Philosophy who in 1974 published a book called *Anarchy, State, and Utopia*.

Nozick's book was in part a response to a long and extremely influential volume published three years earlier by his Harvard colleague John Rawls, *A Theory of Justice*, which was one of the first fruits of the new willingness among professional philosophers of the 1970s to bring their intellect to bear on the real problems that confront humanity, after a couple of decades during which philosophy in the English-speaking world had been a sterile matter of analysing the meanings of words. Rawls asked what properties a society must have in order to be a just society, and he concluded that justice imposes a presumption in favour of equal distribution – of tangible income, as well as of abstractions such as liberty. The presumption can be overridden in particular cases, but only provided that the effect of a particular inequality is to benefit the less-favoured. Thus it would be allowable for managers of industry to be paid a higher than average income, but only if the consequence of failure to do so would be that industry is run too incompetently to produce cheaply the consumer goods that the lower-paid need. In other words, Rawls's theory of justice provides a moral underpinning for the kind of mild, 'mixed-economy' socialism which was (and is) the consensus position in the East-Coast American academic circles he and Nozick inhabit, as it is in their British equivalents.

Nozick, initially, shared that consensus view. His *Anarchy, State, and Utopia* grew out of encounters during the 1960s with early proponents of liberal politics, who interested him sufficiently to make him want to refute them. He found he

could not; 'with reluctance,' as he says, he found himself
becoming converted to liberalism while attempting to confound
it. The reluctance in due course fell away. In *Anarchy, State,
and Utopia* Nozick argues with relish and passion for a fairly
extreme liberal position, a 'minimal state' which protects its
citizens against force and fraud and otherwise leaves them free
to prosper, or to starve. 'How *dare* any state or group of
individuals do more,' he concludes.

On its publication, the book was greeted by the philosophical
community with near-universal applause, even on the part of
writers who strongly disagreed with its conclusions. 'In contrast
to the moderate and conventional ideological stance of John
Rawls,' another American philosopher has said, ' . . . Nozick's
work announced a thesis so out of joint with its times that the
critical acclaim accorded it by many of its reviewers must have
astounded its author as much as it baffled its critics.'

Nozick remains personally somewhat aloof from the rest of
the liberal movement. He is a professional academic first and
last, and seems to have no inclination towards political activism.
And his case for liberalism is in several respects unusual. Most
obviously, Nozick's case is made entirely in moral terms.
Nozick alludes to the economists' 'invisible hand' argument
about the material benefits that flow from economic freedom,
but he takes this for granted rather than discussing it in detail.
For Nozick, I think it is fair to say, a liberal form of society
would remain morally imperative even if he believed that its
inhabitants would all be far wretcheder than they would be
under socialism. Most other members of the liberal movement
tend to treat moral principles as axiomatic and concentrate on
the material consequences of various systems of society –
perhaps because, realistically, that is the likeliest way to convert
the public. There is a fair amount in Hayek, for instance, about
the moral advantages that derive from individual economic
independence, but these are, as it were, simply part of the
package of benefits offered as an inducement to opt for the free
society. (Hayek also writes a great deal of good sense about the
spurious morality of socialism, but negative arguments are
never the most persuasive.)

The drawback about political arguments based mainly on

economic considerations is that, while they may have considerable appeal to the average working man, they sometimes cut little ice with opinion-formers, university teachers and the like, who are the people most likely to encounter them and best placed to publicize them. These people tend to be comfortable enough in their own circumstances to be able to despise arguments appealing to the pocket (unless they happen to specialize in the dismal science of economics themselves). Thus Nozick's approach could potentially fill a largish gap in the liberal armoury of argument.

Nozick's strategy undermines Rawls's discussion of the type of structure which justice requires us to impose on our society, by denying that we have a moral right to impose any structure on society at all. A State can only be allowable, he argues, if it could have emerged as the end-result of a series of voluntary bargains between free individuals who began their interactions with one another in a 'state of nature' lacking coercive political institutions. In fact, Nozick believes, a State *would* emerge from such a morally-impeccable trading process, but it would be a particular, rudimentary kind of State which certainly would not engage in such Rawlsian activities as enforcing a society-wide incomes policy. Only the minimal State which could arise in this way, Nozick claims, is ethically acceptable.

Anarchy, State, and Utopia is a young man's book – it is difficult to believe that Nozick was ever quite as reluctant as he suggests to espouse views which flout all the decencies of the Ivy League mandarinate. And his writing, as Nozick himself points out disarmingly in his preface, is couched in the rather unattractive, flashy mode that has become a house-style of much modern professional philosophy – half of it gratuitously mathematical formalizing of matters that could have been expressed with equal precision in plain English, half of it flip, grotesquely implausible examples used to support arguments about important human realities. We commonly feel it is fair to demand recompense for benefits conferred, but 'suppose,' says Nozick, 'that your best way of getting exercise is by throwing books into people's houses' – can you ethically charge for the books? We usually treat human welfare as taking precedence over the welfare of animals, but what if 'you felt like snapping your fingers, perhaps to the beat of some music, and you knew that by some strange causal connection your snapping your fingers would cause 10,000 contented, unowned cows to die after great pain and suffering' – would it still be OK to snap? 'Listen, chum,' the reader may be tempted to respond, 'I've got a family to keep, a mortgage to pay, and I'm not too sure about the future of my job – why should I waste my time indulging your daft fantasies?' And the average voter is not likely to be reassured when he moves on from Nozick's remarks about finger-snapping to a passage such as ' . . . the upper limit of what one may use in self-defence against a doer of harm H is $f(H) + r \times H$. . . . When $r = 0$, $f(H) + r \times H$ reduces to $f(H)$.' But such things do not offend Nozick's academic audience – his style is what they are used to; so let us not be side-tracked by Nozick's manner from getting to grips with the substance of his argument for freedom.

Nozick's ideal is what he often calls a 'night-watchman State' – the term alludes to a famous nineteenth-century description of the liberal State as an organization that simply guarded private property against criminals and invaders without playing any active part in its management. The central strategy of Nozick's book is not to argue that the night-watchman State is better than the kind of State we now have (although Nozick does do this in his later chapters), but rather to argue that the night-watchman State (and nothing else) is a morally legitimate alternative to anarchy.

This strategy is perhaps an inevitable consequence of Nozick's decision to argue in pure moral terms. In those terms, it is not very interesting to compare some ideal type of State with what we (or Nozick's American compatriots) actually have now. Few people would imagine that the particular form of State that happens to have emerged out of the continuing processes of political struggle and compromise in North America or Britain in 1974, 1984, or whenever is a perfect realization of anyone's moral ideals; and accordingly it would not be very surprising to learn that a hypothetical form of State invented by a philosopher was superior to it. What *is* potentially impressive is a demonstration that this form of State is as unobjectionable on moral grounds as a wholly stateless society in which no one and no organization claims the right to coerce another. We all, surely, agree that pushing people around against their will is a bad thing; and a State, when the chips are down, is a monopolist of coercion – that is what we *mean* by the word 'State', even if contemporary States carry out many other functions too. So one might suppose that, if it were *possible* for humans to live together without a State at all, that must be a morally unrivalled form of civil society: people commonly see the State as an unfortunate necessity.

For his initial postulate Nozick borrows the seventeenth-century philosopher John Locke's device of a hypothetical 'state of nature' in the dawn of history, when men had not yet provided themselves with any State-like structure of government or law and simply confronted one another as equals, each possessing the same natural rights to engage freely in behaviour that did not harm others and to defend themselves against others' aggression. Now, Nozick argues, whenever people make a voluntary bargain with one another to exchange things they possess, the situation which results from the exchange is morally indistinguishable from the situation before it. If I own an apple and you own a pencil and I want to write and you want to eat, there can be nothing wrong with our doing a swap. In some special cases, admittedly, this principle is not self-evident: for instance, many people object violently to individuals swapping quantities of heroin for sums of money. But what we object to in such cases is only incidentally the procedure of swapping, and more centrally the heroin which is swapped, and the fact that the possibility of getting money for it encourages pushers to persuade people to get hooked who otherwise might not. The commodity Nozick is interested in, on the other hand, is the defence of the individual against unjustified aggression, and this lacks the obnoxious features of a commodity like heroin. People agree that individuals have a natural right to self-defence, and it seems good that aggression should be prevented.

But now, Nozick says, if people have a right to self-defence and a right to swap whatever is theirs, then we can be sure that ordinary commercial considerations will lead to the formation of 'protective agencies': firms that specialize in providing defence services (and, by virtue of specialization, defend people more efficiently than they could themselves, just as specialist tailors make suits better and at less cost in time and resources than the average man could if he had to make his own). These agencies will be paid by individuals, whether in money or kind, to exercise those individuals' rights of self-defence on their behalf. That is, there will be many voluntary, morally-unobjectionable exchanges in which an individual gives to a protective association payment and the right to defend him, and receives in return a guarantee that he will be defended if the need arises. The relationship between these protective agencies and their customers is a perfectly normal commercial one. An agency will offer different levels of protection to suit different clients' budgets; it will do its best to attract custom by undercutting others' rates, by clever advertising, and so forth; and of course it will be entirely up to each individual whether to take out a policy with any given agency or remain sturdily independent of the lot of them.

A society in which various protective agencies compete for individuals' custom is still far short of being a State, or even a collection of States. One of the most distinctive things about the kind of 'protective agency' called a State is that the Inland Revenue does not ask whether individuals require the State's services before sending in a bill. But Nozick proceeds to claim that the same morally-unobjectionable commercial trading process will go on to convert a state of nature containing protective agencies into a true State.

For one thing, the situation in which many protective agencies compete for customers in the same territory is commercially unstable. Protection, Nozick suggests, is a 'natural monopoly' like telephone service, where part of what the customer pays for is the size of the total system. Nobody will want to sign up with a small protective agency if they can take their custom to a bigger one, because a relatively small protective agency must be a weak protective agency. Nozick assumes that, if the clients of two protective agencies come into conflict, the agencies will make an honest attempt to assess the rights and wrongs of the matter (as an agency obviously must do when the parties to a conflict are both on its books), rather than each automatically taking its own client's part. (If protective agencies operated in the latter fashion, the moral basis which is essential for Nozick would be lost: it is crucial that what a customer entrusts to an agency is only the right to use force to protect him from – or obtain compensation for – *unjustified* invasion of his person or property, since this is the only right of coercion that an individual possesses in the first place.) Nevertheless, it is sure that agencies will often take different views of the merits of a given case: judges are frequently in honest disagreement in our own society, where they are each interpreting the same body of law, and in Nozick's state of nature there are no general laws – each protective agency must codify individuals' natural rights as best it can. If each of two independent agencies believes its own client is in the right, then they can resolve the matter only by doing battle, and of course if one agency is much weaker than the other it will lose. So people will abandon small agencies and sign up with the biggest they can find. Either just one large agency will survive in any given territory, or else perhaps various agencies will agree among themselves to establish a neutral court of appeal and to abide by its decisions – either way, a territory ends up being dominated by a single unified rights-protection system.

This 'dominant protective agency' is not yet a State, though: it is not monopolistic, and its coverage is not universal. It is not monopolistic, because it makes no claim to be the only agency entitled to exercise protective coercion in its territory. Perhaps it succeeds in putting all rival agencies out of business, but it has (and claims) no right to *prevent* them competing, if they can manage to do so. It is in the nature of a State, on the other hand, to object forcibly to any sign that its citizens are transferring their allegiance and tax payments to a rival concern in the same territory (as has been happening in parts of Northern Ireland). Furthermore it is unlikely that everyone in the territory of a dominant protective agency will become a paying customer, because not everyone will be able to afford the premiums. If protection of individuals' rights is a purely commercial enterprise, then an agency can apparently have no reason to protect anyone who does not pay its fees (and – as Nozick does not add – if protection is a 'natural monopoly', then presumably the standard advantages of a monopoly situation will cause a dominant protective agency to price its premiums well above what some people can afford).

This is where Nozick pulls out of his hat a most ingenious philosophical trick. Consider those 'independents', Nozick says – the individuals who, either because they cannot afford the premiums or possibly just because they prefer to remain aloof from the world of commercial protection, sign up with no agency and still enforce their own rights in person. We can imagine them as being in the main fairly backwoodsy types, isolated from the mainstream of society by poverty or choice and perhaps working all the hours God sends in order to make both ends meet. Even if some of them are more prosperous, notice that when they do find themselves in a conflict they must somehow find the time, strength, and resources to work out what justice requires and, if they decide that they have in fact been wronged, to impose their solution on the other party by force. They must do all this in the middle of a busy working life, while a successful protective agency will have its own full-time, well-trained lawyers, policemen, gaolers, soldiers, and so forth who enable the agency to enquire minutely into the merits of a case and to impose a carefully-graded scale of punishments and compensation payments. The independent's reaction to someone who crosses him may be to poleaxe him first and ask questions later, not necessarily because the independent is reckless of moral subtleties but because he simply lacks the resources to run a subtler and fairer self-defence system.

Now, Nozick argues, clients of a powerful protective agency will want to be defended against this sort of rough justice; *and they will have the right* to buy such defence. No one has any moral duty to submit to a crude system of justice if subtler, juster justice is available. So the protective agency is allowed to prevent the 'independents' from exercising their inherent right of self-defence *vis-à-vis* its clients – and, of course, it will be able to enforce this ban without difficulty. But the agency must compensate the independents for this encroachment on their rights. The simplest method of compensating them fairly will be to supply them with its own protective services, to replace the protection they are no longer allowed to provide for themselves. If they cannot afford the fees, then the agency must supply at least its cheapest level of coverage free, though Nozick argues that the protective agency is entitled to demand premiums from those former independents who can afford them.

And there we have it: a State protecting all within its realm and brooking no rival agent of coercion, which has emerged from pure anarchy by a series of transactions none of which, arguably, can be morally faulted. For centuries it was supposed that men must submit to the rule of States because, wretched creatures that they are, they cannot conduct social life otherwise. Now we are invited to see the State as a successful market response to consumer needs, like cornflakes.

Nozick's State is indeed a minimal one, as he says. It protects its inhabitants from each other and from outsiders; and it redistributes just one commodity from rich to poor, namely protection (we have seen that people too poor to pay the protective agency's premiums have to be provided with protection services anyway, and, since these services must be paid for somehow, they are paid for by increasing the premiums of those who *can* pay above the level that would otherwise be charged). Beyond that, this State does nothing whatever; it does not limit the bargains people make with one another in any way, and in particular it does not redistribute anything *other* than protection – it allows incomes and property-holdings to become as unequal as they may through the differential commercial success of different individuals. Any State which does more than this, according to Nozick, can have no moral right to exist, since it not only has not but *could not have* emerged via morally-acceptable transactions from a morally-acceptable initial state of nature.

For Nozick, a discussion such as John Rawls's about what principles make a pattern of income or property distribution 'just' does not get off the ground, since individuals' rights over themselves and over particular bits of the non-human world are so complete that they leave no free play for abstract, global principles of justice to get a purchase. As Nozick puts it, the notion of 'redistribution' in order to achieve greater fairness suggests that some central agency has already 'distributed' things to the various members of society once, but it got its task a bit wrong, so that we need to arrange for an institution of our own making to correct the errors of the first distribution. But there was no first distribution. If we ignore the very small fraction of a modern society's total wealth that corresponds to the natural environment it inhabits – the value its territory would have if it were unimproved waste-land, and the value of raw materials still buried in the earth – then any particular thing was produced by someone out of materials produced by someone else out of materials produced by someone else again. . . , and, provided that all the transfers of goods and contributions of labour were voluntary exchanges or gifts, then the current holders of the things are their rightful owners. 'The situation is *not* one of something's getting made, and there being an open question of who is to get it. Things come into the world already attached to people having entitlements over them.' Nothing can legitimately be 'redistributed' because everything is already spoken for, morally speaking.

Rawls's theory of justice began by suggesting that individuals ought to settle on a pattern of distribution for their society as if from behind a 'veil of ignorance' which conceals from them which particular position in that society they are destined to occupy. Even quite selfish people might well agree to the principle that only those inequalities are permitted which improve the lot of the worst off, if they did not know whether they themselves would turn out to be among the relatively well-off or among the relatively badly-off members of the society. Rawls's notion of the 'veil of ignorance' is attractive as an attempt to give concrete meaning to the idea that fair principles of social organization must not be tailored to suit a particular individual or a particular class of people. But, Nozick says, the veil that Rawls weaves has another and less innocuous consequence. Not only does it hide from us our identity with a particular member of society, but by confining us to contemplation of society's resources at a particular time it hides from us the fact that those resources have histories – it divorces the question of consumption of goods from their production, treating them as if they were manna from heaven just lying round needing to be consumed by *someone*. (Likewise, Rawls's approach divorces the receipt of gifts from the act of giving: he argues that individuals are not entitled to receive large bequests from wealthy parents, for instance, but overlooks the fact that rightful owners of property are entitled to give it to whomever they wish – that is part of what ownership means, and if a State adopts taxes on transfer of capital then in reality, though not in law, it is partially expropriating the *original owner* of what is properly his.) It is pointless to try to work out what would be a fair pattern of distribution for a society, since no society has pieces which can fairly be made available for the building of any particular pattern.

Rawls claimed to be implementing the famous moral principle of the eighteenth-century philosopher Immanuel Kant, that people are always to be treated as ends in themselves and never as means only. To 'impose . . . lower prospects of life' on some people 'for the sake of the higher expectations of others' would be to regard the former group as means, tools to be used for others' satisfaction. But this cannot be taken seriously, Nozick suggests: Rawls has already pointed out that his principles of justice imply 'an agreement to regard the distribution of natural talents as a common asset. . . . The naturally advantaged are not to gain merely because they are more gifted, but only to cover the costs of training and education and for using their endowments in ways that help the less fortunate as well.' What is this, Nozick asks, but an agreement to use people as means? What *is* a person, other than the sum of his particular talents, abilities, special characteristics and so forth, all of which may be relevant to his earning power but all of which equally are part of his identity? There is no 'fairness' about the distribution of natural talents, agreed, but to treat them as a communally-owned resource is scarcely distinguishable from treating people as slaves.

Furthermore, what redistributive principle justifies treating only mental qualities, such as marketable talent, as a common resource? Most people have two functioning eyes, but some have none at all. If medical technology makes it feasible, Nozick suggests, a consistent redistributionist should surely demand that some two-eyed people give up at least one eye for transplantation into the blind, perhaps after they have enjoyed the use of both for many years. Nobody ever suggests compulsion in such matters, but surely the two kinds of redistribution are difficult to distinguish morally?

No State is permissible, then, other than the minimal State into which a commercially-successful protective agency is entitled to mutate. But that is no bad conclusion to reach, since by a happy coincidence (as Nozick presents it) just that State is the 'framework for Utopia'. Like other liberals, Nozick stresses that no one particular way of life can be ideal for the vastly diverse range of human natures and tastes; but the minimal State provides the maximum of opportunities for different groups to experiment with different ways of life, abandoning experiments that prove unsuccessful and converging on solutions that manage to fulfil individuals' aspirations.

Some groups may opt for social structures that are highly paternalist or collectivist in the conduct of their internal affairs; yet no individual is forced to join or to remain in membership of a particular community, so while he remains a member of an illiberal community his surrender of his rights is voluntary and thus unobjectionable. It might be that *every* community was thoroughly communistic, Nozick suggests, so that an individual who wanted to get any of the benefits of social life would be forced to surrender very many of his rights, perhaps much against his will: but he could not complain about this, as he could if the State enforced a communistic way of life – nobody has any right to require others to cooperate in enabling him to be a non-conformist.

This raises an obvious question about why Nozick sees such a crucial distinction between the current, morally-abhorrent situation in which the world is parcelled out among a number of States each of which violates its citizens' rights heavily, and a hypothetical, morally-impeccable situation in which the world consisted of one huge, wholly free minimal State containing a number of large 'communities' corresponding to present-day countries, each of which practised a greater or lesser degree of illiberal coercion (as contemporary States actually do). In this alternative to current reality, the world-State would intervene to prevent, for instance, East German border guards interfering with emigrants to the West; but it is difficult to see any role it would play in connexion with 'communities' comparable to the present UK or USA, which do all sorts of objectionable things to their inhabitants but allow them to leave fairly freely if they wish to jump out of the frying pan into a neighbouring fire.

At this point in his book, Nozick seems to run out of steam, failing to provide the answer which the general tenor of his discussion suggests as appropriate – namely, that the crucial difference between the two situations depends not on the minor contrasts between their current postulated arrangements but on their history. Except for the communist border guards, the present world would be unobjectionable for Nozick *if* it had resulted from a series of voluntary, rights-respecting decisions and actions from an earlier state of natural freedom. But it didn't. Nozick would no doubt add that it is very unlikely that the kinds of States that now exist could have emerged and survived, if they had had to attract individuals to adhere to them voluntarily when alternatives involving significantly greater individual freedom were available; and, surely, he would be right.

The appeal to history perhaps does not wholly solve the problem here. What answer would it be to say to a child, complaining about the oppressive character of the community into which he was born, 'Don't worry – we were scrupulous about not overriding anyone's rights when we set things up fifty years ago'? But I shall not pursue this issue, because questions about the virtues of the Nozickian minimal State arise only provided we accept the heart of Nozick's thesis, namely his argument that market forces constrained by moral principles will lead from anarchy to a State. Impressive though many philosophers have found Nozick's argument, I cannot see that it gets off the ground.

In the first place, the thing that Nozick sees a 'dominant protective agency' turning into, which he calls a 'minimal State' and identifies with the 'night-watchman state of classical liberal theory', is a travesty of any State known to the eighteenth- and nineteenth-century tradition of political liberalism. There are several reasons for saying this. The most striking is the fact that, like any commercial insurance organization, the protective agency sells different levels of protection to suit the pockets of different citizens. Nozick makes it quite explicit that this feature continues after the dominant protective agency has converted itself into a State. What the agency is obliged to provide for impoverished former independents is only an 'unfancy' protection policy, comparable presumably to some American medical insurance plan that pays for the holder's body to be patched up in emergency but certainly does not stretch to any fal-lals such as anaesthetics where it is possible to get by without them.

Remarkably, none of Nozick's critics in the professional philosophical world seem to have drawn attention to this strange feature of Nozick's 'State'. My problem with it is not so much that differential protection would have been regarded as intolerable by classical proponents of the minimal State – though that is certainly true – but that I cannot understand what in practice it would *mean*.

One of the chief functions of a minimal State is defence against foreign aggression. Suppose England were Nozickland, and I had bought a cheap policy from Securibrit ('Your Friendly Protectors – Ring This Number for a Free Estimate'), while my neighbour in our Yorkshire village had lashed out on a more lavish deal. Does this mean that Securibrit personnel would perhaps allow one smallish Russian sailor to get ashore from the North Sea and rampage up Wensleydale and across the fells to my garden (always carefully steering him across land belonging to my fellow cheapskates), while ensuring that he did not lay a finger on my neighbour's fence? Or, again, the other central function of a minimal State is the provision of judges to settle internal disputes. How can it be arranged that my neighbour's cases are better tried than mine? Suppose he and I are the two parties to a lawsuit: will the judge perhaps be instructed to lean towards him – not blatantly ignoring my side of the case (since I too have a Securibrit policy to flourish, if only of the cheap and cheerful kind), but perhaps being specially careful to tune in his hearing aid when the other man's advocate speaks, coming down hard on points of order when my side is presented, and so on? (The two sides could be represented by advocates of different degrees of skill: but neither in a classical liberal State nor, I think, in Nozickland will barristers' services be a 'public' expense.)

Nozick's central mistake here is to suppose that the functions of a minimal State are services to identifiable individuals, which could in principle be charged out to the individuals who receive them. He gets greatly exercised about the question of why it should be all right to 'redistribute' protective services by forcing richer inhabitants to fund policies for the poor, although other forms of redistribution are wrong. But in reality this question never arises; what national defence forces produce are services to society *taken as a whole*, and only incidentally to individual members of society. It is not merely that preventing invasions is a 'public good' in the technical sense, meaning that the benefits cannot be withheld from individuals who opt out of paying for them. It is not a service to individuals at all, whether to payers or non-payers. The reason why a State must resist foreign invaders is that successful invasion destroys the very social institutions which it is the State's task to maintain. Invasions also do a lot of damage to private property along the way, but if that were the only problem there would be no need for State defence forces: it would be sufficient for the civil courts to enforce compensation payments by the invaders after the event. Likewise, justice (particularly criminal justice) is more naturally viewed as a service to society rather than to individual members of society.

Apart from this misunderstanding of the nature of the classical liberal State, there is a peculiarly *ad hoc* quality about the moral principles on which Nozick's argument is based, baffling in a writer who chooses to derive his political prescriptions exclusively from moral considerations and not at all from issues of expedience. Remember that the 'dominant protective association' will turn into a State, providing protection for all within its territory, only if it acknowledges the moral duty to compensate 'independents' properly for its interference with their freedom. In real life a commercial firm possessing unrivalled physical power, and outside the reach of any overarching framework of law, would be very unlikely to give two hoots about abstract moral obligations towards individuals who found themselves unable to pay for protection. Nozick realizes this perfectly well: he does not claim that his story about the emergence of a State from anarchy is an account of what actually did or could occur in reality, but only of what *would* occur if, implausibly, moral duties were always accepted. It is this hypothetical possibility that gives Nozick's State the legitimacy he ascribes to it. But, in a hypothetical world in which people obeyed moral rules without being forced to, why would any protective agencies ever arise? Their only *raison d'être* is to prevent people from breaking moral rules by violating others' rights. Surely Nozick is not asking us to envisage a scenario in which individuals often act as immoral bullies but powerful commercial coercion-agencies are always lily-white?

Only if moral rules are violated can a protection agency emerge; only if they are obeyed will it become a State. Nozick says that he assumes merely that people 'generally act as they ought,' not that 'all people act exactly as they should.' But what lies behind his 'generally', it seems, is an assumption that people act as they ought just when they need to do so in order to create a State. In arguing that a State will emerge from anarchy, Nozick reasons in a circle.

Still, none of these points are in human terms the most damning flaws in Nozick's thesis. Some readers may prefer to overlook the subtle logical difficulties in Nozick's argument, but even they must surely lose patience with Nozick's strange view of history. Nozick repeatedly stresses that his approach to politics is one which focusses on the fact that society has a history which imposes constraints on its present arrangements. He insists that we must not hide that history behind a Rawlsian veil of ignorance and treat society as a new-found land to be patterned as we see fit. Yet Nozick's argument manifests a bizarre failure of even minimal feeling for historical realities.

Reading Nozick's account of how local protection monopolies could develop through commercial processes, one envisages a villein on the doorstep of his mediaeval hovel chatting politely to a rep from a protective agency striving to open up new territory. 'We're with Earl Richard's mob, actually. We do find his premiums very reasonable, only a hundred days' corvée labour a year – and the *jus primae noctis* of course but Alysoun thought we could afford that all right, didn't you darling, ha ha. And they turn out ever so promptly when there's any trouble with Welsh raiders – you'll see a row of bodies hanging from the battlements now, as a matter of fact. I'm afraid we really aren't interested in switching. So sorry you had a wasted journey; but thank you for calling anyway.' Real life, one feels, was never and *could* never have been remotely like that. Surely it is very unlikely that a travelling salesman from a Nozickian protective agency making his pitch in a pre-modern society could ever have got his prospects to understand what he was talking about; and, if some mediaeval peasant did manage to grasp that his visitor was coolly proposing renunciation of his rightful duty to his liege lord in exchange for a cash saving, the response would not have been a weighing of the economic advantages but horrified flight, followed shortly by the capture and disembowelment of the would-be salesman. Adam Smith believed that 'the propensity to truck, barter, and exchange one thing for another' was common to all men, and that may be correct; but people think of bartering only what is theirs to exchange, and the right to defend an individual's freedom against all comers is in human history the very last thing that people think of converting into private property, not one of the first.

My point is not that the postulation of an anarchic initial state of nature is illegitimate. To that extent, Nozick's scenario is actually quite realistic, provided one goes far enough back in time. According to the anthropologist Harold Barclay, 'Ten thousand years ago everyone was an anarchist' – meaning not that our remote ancestors consciously believed in the desirability of life without the State, but that no social institutions identifiable as States had yet emerged anywhere in the world. Many anarchic human communities survived into modern times, and a few still do although their mode of life is rapidly eroding as they become drawn into economic and political relationships with subjects of States. But the anthropological evidence suggests that primitive anarchies are very far from the communities of free and independent men imagined by John Locke three hundred years ago. The anarchic way of life seems to be associated mainly with a nomadic, hunting-gathering method of subsistence, involving few

personal chattels and little or no improvement of the natural
world such as is practised by agriculturalists. (There is
therefore little motive for anyone to define property rights.)
Social relationships are not marked by fluidity and experiment;
on the contrary they tend to be governed by rigid codes of
precedent which prescribe individual behaviour to a far greater
extent than even fairly repressive modern States. Fear of
sanctions that we would regard as 'supernatural', fear of being
ridiculed or ostracized by the community, and sheer inability to
conceive of behaviour for which there is no precedent, can
jointly be quite enough to render members of such a society
highly conformist without any need for a coercive agency to
suppress deviance.

In a society like ours, where no one knows personally more
than a tiny fraction of his compatriots, and where many points
of view, alternative moralities, different concepts of the good
life and so forth are constantly circulating, many individuals
would break many laws and invade many of the rights of other
individuals if they were not afraid of the State-enforced
consequences. This leads us to overlook the extent to which,
even today, people often do obey the criminal laws and abstain
from violating others' rights without any thought of sanctions,
simply out of inbred respect for law and their fellow-men. In
'face-to-face' societies untouched by the urge to technological
progress, the psychological force of custom backed up by public
opinion can be overwhelming. One does not need to go as far as
the hunter-gatherers of the Australian outback for an example.
The inhabitants of the island of St Kilda, fifty miles west of the
Hebrides, formed an anarchic community (until the island was
evacuated in 1930), running their affairs through daily
communal discussions between equals. On one occasion, a St
Kildan whose earth floor was more than averagely damp and
uneven imported some cement in order to concrete it over. This
dangerous departure from precedent was deemed
unacceptable; the cement left on the boat which had brought
it.

The life led by our remote ancestors in economically-
primitive societies was not necessarily a wretched one. Another
anthropologist, Morton Sahlins, has assembled evidence to
suggest that early hunter-gatherer communities formed 'the

original affluent society', providing abundantly for their material needs in what would now count as a very short working day. (If *nowadays* the life of Australian aborigines or Southern African Bushmen is hard, that is unsurprising: economically-advanced societies have forced them off the fertile lands into marginal, desert areas.) Some people argue that the whole of economic development, not just industrialization but the replacement far earlier of the hunting-gathering way of life by agriculture, was a vast and tragic mistake: perhaps men were happier in the easygoing routine of hunting and gathering than they have ever been since. Maybe so; but what boots it to ask the question, since the road we took can never be retraced? For better or for worse, we are people who are not content to devote our lives to maintaining some changeless, traditional pattern of society in which every intimate detail is prescribed by ritual. Even if the notion attracted us, we have no particular pattern to maintain. It is axiomatic for us that life involves an endless, active search for ways to better our lot. Modern life keeps presenting us with choices, willy-nilly; we must strive to find the choices which are good in terms of whatever values we hold, since a life without choices is no longer available. Even the man who becomes a monk chooses to take the vows, and these days he continues to be faced with the choice of asking for release from them.

It is this choicefulness of economically-developed life which creates both the possibility of freedom and the tendency to evolve States which limit that freedom. If individuals are constantly taking initiatives in a search for a better life, then from time to time they are sure to get in one another's way and some system of resolving conflicts will inevitably emerge – even if the system is merely that the strongest man decides. So long as everyone takes it for granted that the purpose of life is to maintain a traditional social pattern for its own sake, then – particularly if the necessities of life are as easy to come by as Sahlins suggests – conflicts of interest may not be frequent or serious enough to call for the creation of a conflict-resolving agency.

The relevance of all this to Nozick is that it reduces his account of the growth of a State in a society of free men to absurdity. Men were not free before they had a State: they were a good deal less free than almost anyone is now, though since they knew no other way of life this did not worry them. The *possibility* of freedom arose only with the developments that led to the creation of States; as I understand the anthropological and historical record, States emerged from these developments first and a degree of freedom only much later. The power of early States was limited by the current level of technology, but among all the cultures of the ancient world only the Greeks, so far as I know, evolved any concept that it might be good to constrain State power below what was technologically possible. (When the Chinese encountered the Western notion of 'freedom' in the nineteenth century the concept was novel to them, and it was not easy for them to grasp that Europeans regarded it as a desirable thing.) Rousseau's slogan that 'Man is born free' is the opposite of the truth: freedom is a novel invention of the human spirit, and still awaits its fullest realization.

Nozick's account of the emergence of a minimal State is admittedly purely hypothetical; he does not pretend that any State *actually* came into being that way. But Nozick's hypothesis is an anthropological impossibility. Men who are capable of bargaining with one another to develop commercial institutions must already have left the stage of primitive anarchy behind; free market behaviour may lead to the modification or, perhaps, even to the dismantling of the State, but certainly not to its first creation. Nozick's fable shows nothing, because it is based on a contradiction. For Locke or Rousseau to reason in an anthropological vacuum about the actions of men in the dawn of history was excusable, but a philosopher today has an obligation not to advance arguments that are inconsistent with the known facts.

A particularly remarkable feature of Nozick's political theory is that – having argued forcefully and with passion against a State which redistributes economic benefits from one individual to another – he then effectively takes the argument back. The propertied are morally entitled to the benefits that property provides, Nozick argues, provided their property can be traced back through a chain of rights-respecting exchanges and/or gifts to its first creation. But this will almost never be possible. In Nozickland all exchanges may be voluntary, but if Nozickland is to be built in America or Britain then most property that already exists at the time of the revolution will have previously been transferred from owner to owner under immoral laws which failed to safeguard individuals' natural rights. In such cases, Nozick says, we must work out who ought by rights to possess the item and arrange for the State to enforce its return, or payment in lieu: ' . . . to introduce socialism as the punishment for our sins would be to go too far, [but] past injustices might be so great as to make necessary in the short run a more extensive state in order to rectify them.' Nozick alludes to a specific example: the rights of Africans brought to America as slaves were grossly violated over a long period, and arguably the non-black American community should be required to pay 'reparations'. Since it is possible that relative poverty correlates with descent from victims of rights-violating actions, Nozick even suggests that State-enforced systems of redistribution from rich to poor, such as a progressive tax system, might be justifiable as 'rough rules of thumb' for approximating to a rectification of past injustices.

The mind boggles at the implications of this idea. For me (as for many people) my most valuable piece of capital is my house, which is built on a third of an acre of land that has been improved from its virgin condition for, I would guess, at least two millennia. I occasionally hear something of what archaeologists and historians are discovering about the early history of the area, a topic in which I have a mild interest. Come a Nozickian revolution and I will presumably develop a very much acuter interest in these matters, since they will become highly relevant to my family's welfare. There is a current controversy about whether the Germanic-speakers who settled here in the Dark Ages moved in peacefully and occupied mainly vacant land, or whether they forcibly dispossessed the earlier, Celtic-speaking inhabitants. I had better hope that the former view proves well-founded, since otherwise I am likely to be sitting on stolen goods, and I will have little claim to retain them since my own ancestry is largely Germanic. (There is also the point that, if various rights-violating events in the Dark Ages had not taken place, very likely *I* would not exist; I am not clear what Nozick would require me to do about that.)

Why Nozick believes that the extension of State power needed to rectify such past violations of rights will be a short-term thing is quite mysterious to me. Under his system of justice, history, archaeology, and genealogy would rapidly develop into the most lucrative and expansionist professions, as everyone looked further and further back to uncover long-forgotten injustices to their ancestors. Like any other research, this would have no natural end: one can always increase one's knowledge by looking harder, and if the State can reasonably entertain claims dating back a century or two in the case of American blacks it can have no principled reason not to hear claims going back a millennium, or several millennia.

Any such proposal is silly. It overlooks the fact that we cannot possibly know 'what would have happened if. . . . ' It is odd to see that Nozick has published an article on Austrian economics, recommending it to his philosophical colleagues as offering valuable insights into human behaviour; seemingly he has not taken to heart the central Austrian theses about ignorance and unpredictability. Any present action is for the Austrians a gamble whose consequences are unknowable until they occur; by the same token, if we suppose that this or that past event had not occurred in the way it did, we cannot know how the present situation would be affected. Given that black Americans did not sell their labour in a free market in the eighteenth century, how can we possibly say what their economic circumstances, or those of plantation owners, or others connected indirectly with the cotton trade, would have been if slavery had not existed? If we cannot know even that, then certainly we cannot know what the consequences would be for individuals now living who count some of those people among their ancestors. When civil law reverses an individual unjust act soon after it is committed, it is reasonable to regard the final situation as similar to what would have been if neither injustice nor compensation had occurred; but any action initiates a ramifying, ever more remote and unpredictable chain of consequences, so that in time it becomes meaningless to think of rectifying an injustice.

Austrian liberals, such as Hayek, never argue for a free society in terms of (hypothetical or real) past history, but in terms of future results. It seems odd to describe a brash, up-to-the-minute, and historically naive young American such as Nozick as backward-looking in contrast to an elderly scholar like Hayek, conservative in style and widely versed in traditional culture and learning. Yet Nozick is unique among liberals in the emphasis he lays on how current situations arose (or might hypothetically have arisen). Hayek never suggests that the present distribution of wealth or incomes has any particular historical justification: he knows that such a claim would be utterly implausible. Hayek is not interested in how resources happen to be distributed *now*; what matters for him is that we should as far as possible liberate the holders of resources from artificial constraints on their *future* exchanges, because this will make the economy dynamic and fluid, it will allow individuals who discover ways of serving society well to increase their capital holdings fast, it will expand the total wealth of society and cause the arbitrary, unjust economic differentials which existed under the old, illiberal regime to be swamped by new and ever-changing patterns of just differentials which do correlate with real differences in people's contributions to society. Hayek, again, is not interested in the morality of the various events out of which our present society has emerged; we all know that many features of our and others' history were morally abominable, but we must work with what we have. What Hayek cares about is the idea that adoption of free institutions will lead to moral growth in the future, as individuals learn to take control of their lives and cease to blame society's ills on a nameless 'them'.

Surely, if we want liberal politics to become more than an academic exercise confined to the philosopher's study, then only future-oriented approaches such as Hayek's can hope to succeed? I suggested earlier that the liberalism of some contemporary politicians has not yet been fully recognized for what it is, because it is mistaken for a nostalgic harking back to some vaguely-defined good old days. The abstract political and legal framework of a future liberal Britain would involve reversing many developments of the last fifty or a hundred years; but the concrete kinds of life that develop within that political and legal framework will have no particular

relationship with the way people lived fifty or a hundred years
ago, and we should not aspire to them if they had. Ordinary
people do not want to mull endlessly over the past, as Nozick
bids us do. We can learn lessons from the past, but we are
heading towards the future, and that is what most of our mental
energies must be focussed on.

Nozick's politics seem to me to exemplify the blight of
professionalization which has come to dominate the practice of
philosophy as it dominates so many other contemporary
activities. The quality of Nozick's argument is such as to leave
anyone who lives his life in the world of practical affairs
unmoved. Nozick is almost aggressively intellectual for the sake
of being intellectual, facetiously logic-chopping, unrealistic. A
philosopher in the late twentieth century has no motive to
appeal to an audience outside the ivory tower: philosophers
nowadays are salaried State employees, who seek their
audiences and the benefits that audiences confer from within
the army of fellow university teachers of philosophy. Even
inconsistency with the findings of another academic discipline
need not worry a philosopher: philosophers work in Philosophy
Departments, anthropologists in Anthropology Departments,
and department does not speak unto department.

Happily, the liberal movement as a whole seems to be
relatively free of the sterile academicism that infects much of
modern thought, now that the expansion of higher education
has swept so many thinkers into university posts. Many leading
liberals work outside academe: before Nozick, the philosopher
most discussed by American libertarians was Ayn Rand, a
screenwriter and novelist by career rather than an academic.
(Ayn Rand, born in Saint Petersburg in 1905, emigrated to the
USA a few years after the Russian Revolution. Her novels, *The
Fountainhead* and *Atlas Shrugged*, have been instrumental in
bringing many American college students to 'libertarianism' –
though this arguably tells us more about American college
students than about Miss Rand's virtues as a writer. She
published a series of philosophical works advocating her own,
'objectivist' version of liberalism, before her death in 1982.)
Furthermore, many liberals who are academics by vocation
seem to maintain more links with and awareness of the 'real

world' outside academe than do some of their professional colleagues. Nozick, though in academic circles he is often seen as the representative liberal, is a very untypical one indeed.

8/Anarchism with a Capitalist Face

If the effects of State action are as undesirable as liberals claim, and if human beings have a natural right not to be coerced, then the ultimate political ideal must be anarchism: society without any agency of legitimized coercion at all. Very many political thinkers concur in seeing anarchism as a theoretical ideal, though most of them add in the next breath that it is an unattainable one – States are an inevitable consequence of Man's fallen nature, and the best we can hope to do is to provide ourselves with States that rule us as beneficently as possible. For classical, nineteenth-century liberals that meant: States which rule us as *little* as possible. Some contemporary liberals, on the other hand, believe it is practical to take the process of State-shrinking to its logical conclusion and abolish government outright.

It is a puzzling truth that, historically, anarchists saw themselves as essentially on the same side as socialists, and had little respect for commercial relationships. The first man to call himself an anarchist, P.-J. Proudhon, is best known for the profoundly anti-liberal remark 'Property is theft,' and the history of nineteenth-century anarchism is thoroughly tangled up with the history of socialism. I find this puzzling, because to reject *both* the command *and* the market solutions to the problem of social coordination seems truly irrational. I have tried to show why a command economy is obnoxious; and I think I understand why many people have sincerely feared the consequences of untrammelled capitalism, though I believe what frightens them is a set of unreal phantasms rather than genuinely plausible possibilities, or else real problems which are mistakenly blamed on the market system. But decisions about use of resources, techniques of production, distribution of consumer goods have to be made *somehow*.

Socialist anarchists seem to postulate a dream-world in which such issues mysteriously and conveniently resolve themselves as fast as they arise, with goodwill on all sides. But goodwill alone cannot do it. We have innumerable specific economic choices that need to be settled: what is to become of the coal mined tomorrow at the Aberdare pit, for instance? To say 'Let's not fight about it, life will be sweeter if we all agree to help one another' gets us no further forward. It might be marvellous if we could manage it, but the question would remain: how is that coal to be used? None of the leading nineteenth-century anarchists seem to have come close to defining the goal they were aiming at, and one recent expositor of traditional anarchism, Terry Perlin, has been reduced to describing it as 'less a political philosophy than it is a temperament'.

Anarcho-capitalism, the new, liberal variety of anarchism, may contain fatal flaws (as I believe it does), but it is far more satisfactory than this. The anarcho-capitalists tell us just how they envisage the Stateless society of the future resolving the economic and political issues that will confront it. They deal with the obvious objections which occur to people brought up to take States as axiomatic; they explain why their ideal form of social organization will be superior to rule by even a liberal, minimal State; and sometimes they discuss in an intelligent and practical manner what are the best strategies for moving towards Statelessness.

The anarcho-capitalists begin by pointing out that people are grossly unimaginative about the possibility of privatizing functions that happen at present to be carried out by States. For instance, it is widely taken for granted that the issue of money must be a State monopoly, but there is no law of nature decreeing this. Friedrich Hayek, himself very far from being an anarchist, has written a great deal on the desirability of privatizing currency, so that rather than all using pounds some of us would choose to set our prices and keep our savings in natwests, others in barclays or billglyns (each unit based on whatever basket of commodites the issuing bank thought appropriate – gold, oil, coffee, or most likely a mixture of many things). Hayek argues that this offers an automatic method of eliminating inflation, without some of the difficulties involved in other anti-inflationary measures.

What is true of money is more obviously true of many other current State functions. Take streets and roads, for instance. There are a few private toll roads in Britain, but almost all roads are 'the Queen's highway', built and maintained from taxation and provided for general use under laws which permit passage and forbid obstruction. Quite a few people who in general support free-market institutions are inclined to feel vaguely that roads have to be maintained by the State because they are a prerequisite for the operation of a market system – they are part of the apparatus by which buyers and sellers get together, rather than a 'good' which the system of exchange produces. By this argument, the classified-ad columns of newspapers would have to be a State enterprise, which they are not. But roads seem more 'crucial' than newspaper advertisements. If the road outside my house was in private hands and the owner took agin me, it looks as though he could reduce my family to starvation by preventing us getting out or deliveries getting through.

It would not work like that in practice, though. Consider first of all the case where a new street or system of streets is built, providing access, say, to a new estate of houses being built speculatively.

Under anarchism, the obvious thing for the builder to do is to sell the houses in a package deal including a binding covenant to permit access along the streets in perpetuity for the householder and his visitors, in exchange for an annual maintenance charge to cover upkeep. Certainly, in a Stateless society the builder would be free to offer a different sort of package, in which he retained the right to veto passage by inhabitants: but that would be a quick way to put himself out of business – who would buy on such terms? Even if someone trusted the builder not to make difficulties in his own case, lack of an access covenant would make the resale value of the house so low that he would not buy it except at a giveaway price. What businessman would think of choosing the reality of present bankruptcy for the sake of retaining the right to work off some hypothetical future grudge against the owner of a house he built? (If the grudge already existed, the buyer would be specially careful to check the access guarantee.)

That is not to say that the access covenants of all new houses would provide for such unrestricted access as applies to State roads in contemporary Britain. Some up-market estates might bring their builder a higher profit if the conditions of sale included a guarantee by the builder that he would *restrict* access to residents, their personal guests, and only such other *bona fide* visitors as his gatekeepers deemed acceptable. There is nothing fanciful about this; such housing estates, surrounded by walls and with guarded gates, exist now in the USA. I am not sure that I would want to live in one, but then I would not have to; it would certainly be cheaper to live in a general-access estate where the management charges covered only road maintenance. You pays your money and you takes your choice.

Trunk roads, motorways, and the like would be built as an ordinary speculative investment, financed by tolls collected at access points, or by charges for licences which the road-owner would require users to display on their vehicles. This, after all, is how the first modern roads, the turnpikes, were built in the eighteenth century (although the construction and charging arrangements of the turnpikes were regulated by the State in a way that would not happen under anarchism). One might expect rather fewer new roads this way than under the State system, because there would be no compulsory purchase; unless a would-be road-builder could pay enough to induce the owners of the land he needed to sell of their own accord, the road could not be built. If a lot of people felt strongly about the undesirability of desecrating some lovely landscape with a motorway, they could put their money where their mouth was and seek to buy landowners' signatures on covenants not to allow their land to be used that way. Bodies like the National Trust and the Council for the Preservation of Rural England might become regular channels through which individuals would fund the protection of rural beauty. On the other hand, if a beautiful area was uniquely convenient as the site for a new road, it would pay haulage interests to get together with the road-builder in order to improve on the conservationists' offer. Thus roads would tend to get built where the good achieved by building them (as reflected in builders' and users' profits) outweighed the harm (as reflected in what conservationists were willing to pay to protect scenery) and would tend not to get built where the opposite was the case. I say 'tend' – the bargaining process would never work perfectly; but then, who believes that State decisions about road-building are perfectly judicious?

What about existing roads, which in a heavily populated country like ours must remain the great majority? This is a question not about how an anarcho-capitalist society would work, but about how we might make the transition to it. In general, presumably, the rule should be that, in moving towards a fully-privatized situation, public property ought to be converted into private property in a fashion which comes as close as possible to preserving citizens' existing rights over it. When an ordinary road was sold off to a private buyer, one condition of sale would be a permanent obligation to provide access along it to residents at, say, a price no higher than charged to any other class of customer. (Don't say: residents previously had the right to use it for nothing. They did not; they had to pay their rates and taxes, which would cease under anarchism, and a portion of these were used for road-maintenance.) One might want to go further and specify, say, that the buyer of a motorway would be required to provide licences at concessionary rates for all those living within five miles of an access point, because their previous right to use that particular motorway was more valuable to them than the share the State required them to pay towards its upkeep. These are matters of detail, and probably there is no answer to them that is perfect in the sense that it quite exactly preserves everyone's existing rights without reducing or increasing their value. But, if anarchism is in other respects a good thing, we surely cannot reject it on the ground that the changeover would involve some unfairnesses which we cannot assess. (If we could quantify them, we could compensate for them.) Nobody argued against the introduction of decimal currency on the grounds that it entailed losses for owners of cash-registers and gains for their manufacturers.

(In many cases the 'redistribution' entailed by privatization would tend to rectify existing injustices. For instance, privatized postal services would almost certainly charge more for collections from remote rural areas than within cities – letters posted in rural postboxes would require more stamps, say. At present, people like myself who live in the country enjoy the advantages of rural life while – in this and many other ways – we do not pay the true costs: urban users of the postal service are forced to subsidize us. What justice is there in that?)

If money and roads can be privatized, so, obviously, can the many 'welfare' functions of modern States. Education, medical services, provision for old age and the like are often arranged privately now and it is difficult to doubt that consumers would get better value if they were entirely privatized. But we have not yet touched on the central problems of anarchism. I have talked about parcelling up this and that area of public property into private property rights, but how are these rights to be enforced? Irrespective of how people managed in the pre-agricultural dawn of history, surely modern life makes States inevitable at least as devices to provide law? And how could private enterprise keep the Russians at bay?

The most impressive answers to these questions, in my view, are those provided by David Friedman, an economics teacher in Virginia (and son of Milton Friedman). In fact, if someone wanted to read just one book about the modern liberal movement, David Friedman's book *The Machinery of Freedom* is the one I would recommend. Before I read David Friedman, it seemed to me too obvious to be worth arguing about that States were for all kinds of reasons an unavoidable necessity. After exposure to Friedman's shrewd and subtle reasoning, though I remained a 'statist' my faith was severely shaken. It might be very difficult to 'get there from here', to make the transition from our current situation to anarchism; but David Friedman makes a powerful case for the view that, if we got there, we could stay there. Anarchism in his version would not be the unstable thing it is usually taken to be, doomed to perish of its internal contradictions as fast as it is achieved.

Let us start with the judicial function. It is clear that we do not need State judges to decide conflicts arising under contract law; private arbitration agencies already exist and are heavily used in the commercial world because they offer a cheaper and much faster service than the State judicial system. Contracts include clauses specifying what agency will be asked to arbitrate any dispute arising under them. At present the results of such arbitration are enforceable by the State, but Friedman suggests that to a large extent they would be self-enforcing in an anarchist society. A key commercial service in such a society would be the publication of reference works akin to current credit-rating lists, showing individuals' and firms' records of obedience to arbitration awards made against them. Anyone with a poor record would find it difficult to enter into new contracts except on punitive terms, and contract would be such a pervasive feature of an anarchist society that this would be a major sanction.

Still, surely there would be cases where arbitration awards had to be enforced; and many conflicts arise outside any contract, so that it is unclear how arbitration could apply to them. If I run into your car, you have a claim for damage against me, but there is no private contract between us specifying how liability is to be assessed.

Here Friedman invokes the notion of the protection agency, with which we are familiar from Nozick's writing (undoubtedly, Nozick derived his use of the idea from the anarcho-capitalists). Each of us would be paying premiums to a commercial organization that looked after our rights *vis-à-vis* the rights of others, and although you and I have no contract specifying how liability for our collision should be assessed, your protection agency and mine would have a contract specifying how conflicts between their respective clients are to be arbitrated. No overarching State would *require* them to have such a contract: there would be nothing to stop the two agencies simply going to war with one another – but it would not pay.

Nozick might argue that war between protection agencies *would* pay one of them – the one which conquers the rest and emerges as coercion-monopolist, or State. David Friedman would not accept Nozick's view that rights-protection by commercial protection agencies must lead to monopoly, whether through peaceful competition or warfare. Friedman's society of the future is one in which many competing protection agencies continue to coexist, and none of them acquires even somewhat State-like tendencies. What would stop them?

Ultimately, Friedman concedes, nothing short of armed resistance by the populace could stop them. But in practice there are other safeguards.

After all, our present police departments, national guard, and armed forces already possess most of the armed might. Why have they not combined to run the country for their own benefit? Neither soldiers nor policemen are especially well paid; surely they could impose a better settlement at gunpoint.

The complete answer to that question comprises nearly the whole of political science. A brief answer is that people act according to what they perceive as right, proper, and practical. The restraints which prevent a military coup are essentially restraints interior to the men with guns.

It is the shared beliefs of a society which set bounds to what political developments are feasible and what are not. In Latin America, army coups are regarded as realistic possibilities, and they happen; in Britain, the idea is not taken seriously, and they do not happen, though I imagine there would be no greater physical barriers to such an event here than there. If an anarcho-capitalist form of society were suddenly to be imposed on contemporary Britain or the USA by visiting Martians, it would quickly collapse, because people would have little understanding of or commitment to it. Anarchism works only if the people who live under it expect it to work and to some extent want it to work, but that does not make it unrealistically utopian – the same can be said about constitutional democracy. Radical political change requires political education.

Given a population who believe in anarchism, then David Friedman argues that an anarchist society would actually be safer than Britain or the USA from the risk of a violent coup.

In our society, the men who must engineer such a coup are politicians, military officers, and policemen, men selected precisely for the characteristic of desiring power and being good at using it. They are men who already believe that they have a right to push other men around – that is their job. . . . Under anarcho-capitalism the men in control of protection agencies are 'selected' for their ability to run an efficient business and please their customers. It is always possible that some will turn out to be secret power freaks as well, but it is surely less likely than under our system. . . ?

It is a point of view, though I do not myself see senior British politicians and military officers in peacetime as being such experts in naked aggression as Friedman suggests. The people who do the really dirty work of State coercion tend to be far down the hierarchy, and they have little real chance of organizing a coup. A commercial protection system might be much less top-heavy administratively, so that the men in charge would be closer to the sharp end of physical force.

Still, Friedman has another argument: under his system there would be a *lot* of protection agencies, and if 'any group of them start acting like a government, their customers will hire someone else to protect them against their protectors.' Friedman argues that the number of agencies will be determined simply by whatever is the best size for an economically-efficient service: 'My own guess is that [in the territory of the USA] there will be nearer 10,000 agencies than 3. If the performance of present-day police forces is any indication, a protection agency protecting as many as one million people is far above optimum size.'

Nozick, as we have seen, argues that there is no natural limit to the size of a protection agency: the bigger the better, from the customer's point of view. That is because he envisages the agencies as emerging from a primordial Hobbesian 'war of all against all', so that the customer needs might as well as right on his side. But Friedman is oriented towards anarchism as a future evolution from ordinary, largely-peaceful present-day society. His protection agencies will grow out of existing organizations like Securicor and its competitors, as the State gradually abdicates from more and more of its prerogatives and private enterprise picks up the baton. Such organizations do not currently spend their time fighting one another or the law-abiding public at large, and – provided the population act intelligently – there is no reason why they should ever begin. The price of liberty is eternal vigilance; if the citizenry lose their taste for anarchism, they will soon find themselves living under a State.

But what laws will David Friedman's protection agencies enforce? At first they might take over the body of law that the State has been promoting up to the point at which it pulls out of the judging business. In the British case, it is worth noting that important parts of that legal corpus were not *produced* by a State (the Common Law and Law Merchant evolved respectively from Germanic folk-customs and from merchants' own rules), and one specialized manifestation of the current liberal trend of opinion is the view expressed widely nowadays in the legal profession that we ought to be moving to greater reliance on Common and less on Statute Law. Some anarcho-capitalists would advocate pressing this point of view to its logical conclusion, and abolishing the legislative role of the State without providing any replacement. David Friedman does not take this line. Instead, he argues that just as car makers provide a range of cars to suit their customers' preferences, so private-enterprise legislators should produce whatever brands of law there is a market for. The particular legal system or systems operated by an arbitrator would be an aspect of the product offered by the arbitrator to its clients, the protection agencies, and would in turn be a feature of the service which the protection agencies advertised to their customers.

At first blush this sounds crazy. A conflict between two parties cannot be judged under two rival systems of law; one system or the other must prevail. Yes indeed. But the conflict between laws is settled in advance of the conflicts that have to be adjudicated between individuals, when protection agencies make contracts with one another about which arbitrators they will use when their clients are in dispute. These decisions will emerge from a bargaining proeess governed by ordinary commercial pressures, and (unlike our present system) will allow diverse legal preferences to be reflected by diversity in law.

For instance, suppose – realistically – that some citizens strongly favour capital punishment for certain crimes while others feel strongly (as I do) that capital punishment for any crime is immoral. Protection agencies patronized by the former group might advertise 'Fullest possible use of the rope protects YOU against violent crime,' while the latter group would favour agencies that boasted 'Not a penny of your premium usurps God's privilege of taking life.' When a pro-hanging protection agency and an anti-hanging agency agreed a legal system to be applied in disputes between their clients, one agency would have to give way on hanging, in exchange for getting its own way on some other legal preference – or, Friedman suggests, possibly in exchange for a cash payment which would allow the agency that gives way to lower its premiums enough to compensate its clients for failure to universalize their preference on the hanging issue.

It sounds disgusting, perhaps, that commercial bargaining should settle questions as solemn as whether an offender shall in cold blood be deprived of life. But how are they settled now? Many MPs who voted to bring back the rope in 1983 certainly were swayed by their constituents' preferences – my own Member was quite frank about this. On that occasion the 'civilized' side outvoted the hangers, but suppose it went the other way as, one day, it probably will: would one be happy that one's own objections to capital punishment went for nothing, provided that what overwhelmed them was skilled and vociferous political agitation by those who feel differently? In David Friedman's system, if a substantial minority reject hanging as immoral, at least they can use their economic strength to reduce the incidence of capital punishment in their society even if they cannot eliminate it altogether. Under Friedman's system 'the customer's legal preference . . . [is] a major factor in determining the kind of law he does live under. It cannot completely determine it, since accused and accuser must have the same law.'

My example concerned a method of punishment, but legal systems would differ also on what actions were criminal, and on the details of civil law. Under English law the rule in house-buying is *caveat emptor*; Scottish law imposes a duty of disclosure on the seller. In David Friedman's world, such an issue would be decided not by the location of the house but by the arbitrator agreed between the buyer's and seller's protection agencies.

(In case the reader wonders who the accuser would be in a murder case, the answer is that a protection agency which was not seen to pursue vigorously the killers of murdered clients would have difficulty in retaining living ones.)

It might seem that criminals would use *their* economic power to bend a private-enterprise legal system to their own ends, pumping money into protection agencies whose laws treated their crimes as no crimes. But, unless they represented a truly massive proportion of society, there is no chance that Mafia-type groups could get murder, grievous bodily harm, and the like legalized; ordinary citizens would have a very strong economic motive to press their protection agencies not to accept such legal codes. If criminal types really do comprise a large fraction of the population, then things are likely to go badly under *any* political system; if there is a State, the criminals can get control of that.

The one fatal objection to purely free-enterprise law, surely, is that protection agencies or arbitrators would respond to commercial logic in individual cases by covertly favouring the side which could afford to pay best. On this point David Friedman is uncharacteristically glib. He simply says that such behaviour 'would be suicidal; unless they maintained a reputation for honesty, they would have no customers.' This I fail to see. It seems that private legal agencies would lose poor clients by 'selling' verdicts, but gain rich ones – an excellent exchange, commercially speaking. Indeed one can apply a standard liberal economic argument by pointing out that an organization which bribes a legal agency has a concentrated motive for doing so, while those harmed have only a dispersed motive for discovering what is happening and placing their custom elsewhere – the bribing organization may have conflicts with many other organizations or individuals, each of which taken singly has only a limited exposure to dealings with the briber. True, *other agencies* would have a strong motive for exposing the misdeeds of their commercial rivals, but it is not obvious that this would be enough to ensure honesty. (It may be that contemporary private arbitration agencies are honest, but Friedman himself points out that these agencies are normally used for contracts about 'matters where it is more important that a decision be immediate than what the decision is'; there is little reason to bribe them.) States have many obnoxious features, but at least they have no motive to take sides in civil suits. No subject can bribe a State when the State can steal all it wants in taxes.

The State seems indispensable in its judicial role, alas. But that means only what it says: it does not imply any wider objections to David Friedman's arguments. Even if the State has to provide the judges, there is no reason why it should also provide the law or even that the law should necessarily be uniform for all subjects – free enterprise legislation seems quite compatible with a State judicial system. Will it be objected that judges could not cope with alternative legal systems? But I personally do just that as a matter of routine. Like hundreds of other senior British academics I serve as an 'external examiner' for various universities, meaning that I am paid to ensure that the respective institutions observe their own complex and subtly-different rules for granting degrees, whatever those rules may be. What academics can do, I hardly think judges would be incapable of.

David Friedman's case for anarchism is restrained and undogmatic in tone. His view of the ability of an anarchist society to avoid relapsing back to statism is one of 'guarded optimism' – and surely this is more convincing than any stronger statement would be, given the obvious problems. On the issue of defence against foreign aggression, Friedman is more cautious still. He examines a number of ways in which defence of the territory of the USA might be financed non-coercively, noting for instance that the job could be done for only about ten to twenty times the annual total of all the tips Americans give voluntarily to taxi-drivers, waiters, and the like – so that it might not be out of the question to run defence as a charity, with people shaming one another into contributing to it. He has some other suggestions too; for instance, foreign States would probably treat a national defence agency as a 'State' for the purpose of issuing passports, so the defence agency could finance itself partly through the sale of passports.

Under Friedman's system, as he admits, defence would be chronically under-funded. There is no more than symmetrical with the problem that under a State, for reasons discussed in Chapter 4, defence is chronically over-funded. Nevertheless, all Friedman's suggestions about non-coercive funding of defence services scarcely add up to a believable case for a free-market nuclear umbrella, and ultimately it would seem that Friedman is resigned to a State which forces citizens to pay taxes for this purpose alone – until the day when the problem solves itself because all other societies manage to evolve anarchist institutions too. But Friedman insists that limited government is a very poor second best to anarchism, because limited government will not stay limited. Government has its own dynamic, as we saw in Chapter 4: it is in the nature of government to grow. As Friedman says, referring to the American experience, 'It took about 150 years, starting with a Bill of Rights that reserved to the states and the people all powers not explicitly delegated to the federal government, to produce a Supreme Court willing to rule that growing corn to feed to your own hogs is interstate commerce and can therefore be regulated by Congress. . . . Anarchy at least might work; limited government has been tried.'

The restraint which is such an attractive feature of David Friedman's work is notably absent in the writings of the other leading anarcho-capitalist: Murray Rothbard, an economic historian who combines teaching at the Brooklyn Polytechnic Institute with an immensely productive writing career. Rothbard, a jolly, wrinkled gnome of a man who speaks Brooklynese in a combative, high-pitched whine, seems to see no reasons other than bad faith or brute stupidity for the failure of all the rest of us to concede the case for anarchism immediately. He brushes aside worries about breakdown of law and order, saying semi-seriously 'I'm a New Yorker; we already have the war of all against all and, believe me, it woiks fine.'

Rothbard is a more central figure in the American 'libertarian' movement than David Friedman, and he has many interesting ideas that are quite different from Friedman's. I find the hectoring tone of his writings offputting, not just in its own right but because its authoritarian flavour seems to consort badly with its anti-authoritarian content. Rothbard's style is sometimes uncomfortably reminiscent of the kind of hard-left ranting most liberals want to get away from. Still, others feel that my reaction to Rothbard is unduly donnish, that liberalism needs ranters as well as academics; and Rothbard's occasionally tortured syntax may be excusable as the result of a struggle to get onto paper the products of an exceptionally fertile mind.

National defence, the problem that virtually defeats David

Friedman, seems scarcely a problem at all to Murray Rothbard, who sees it as absurdly contradictory for the advocates of a classical-liberal minimal State to 'sanction and advocate massive invasion of property [i.e. taxation] by the very agency (government) that is supposed to defend people against invasion!' How can one seriously look to the State for help against invasion in view of 'its black historical record as *the* great engine of invasive violence'?

Rothbard has a serious point here. As I said earlier, individuals do not declare wars. Virtually all States have a far worse record of criminal violence than any individual (using 'criminal' in a vague, moral sense – obviously wars are not 'criminal' in terms of the technical legal codes of the States waging them). I readily concede the point made by both Rothbard and David Friedman, that if the whole world were converted to anarchism then wars would become impossible: there would be no units to make war with one another.

But I cannot see that the minimal-State position is as naively paradoxical as Rothbard suggests. Surely, most classical liberals have been well aware that what they advocate is acceptance of the least evil, not because it is good but because alternatives are worse? They aim for a State which does just enough bullying to prevent its subjects being exposed to worse bullying, and where is the illogic in that? As David Friedman puts it, the State is a gang of criminals, but useful criminals.

Rothbard implies that, because States are our chief coercers, all we need to do is to remove our States and we would cease to be coerced. But, if the British State (say) were magically to vanish tonight, without any change in the mentality of the population, then we certainly would not cease to be coerced. Never mind the Russians; within Britain, individuals and groups with a taste for pushing their fellow-men around (and we all have a bit of the bully in us) would find that nobody was preventing them indulging their taste, small gangs would grow into big gangs, and fairly soon we would be in a much worse situation than now – whether we *called* the protection rackets that controlled us 'States' or not. Rothbard concedes that 'there can be no absolute guarantee that a purely market society would not fall prey to organized criminality,' but for him that is no argument against it because 'the worst that could possibly happen' would be re-establishment of the present system of State power. If Rothbard really thinks that the current situation (whether in Britain or even his own New York) is the worst possible form of society, then he is deeply unimaginative.

Returning to the issue of defence against foreign aggression: Rothbard comes close to suggesting that an anarcho-capitalist society would be safe from foreign conquest because, as it were, there would be nothing there to conquer. If Germans had invaded Britain in the 1940s and managed to seize control of the Houses of Parliament, the King, and a few other central institutions (including radio transmitters to tell the rest of us what they had done), that would pretty well have been that. Very likely the rest of the British population would have thrown in the towel and regarded itself as 'conquered', without necessarily having seen a single field-grey uniform in their own street. Under anarcho-capitalism there are no Houses of Parliament, and, to an inhabitant of Northumberland or Somerset, the fact that a Berkshire man called George Windsor has been taken prisoner by some men speaking German would have no personal implications. 'Conquering' an anarchist territory would mean conquering each individual household separately, so it would be impractical. Rothbard suggests that 'the idea of inter-State war against a libertarian country or geographical area would most likely disappear.' He refers to problems the British faced in extending imperial rule to cover anarchic tribes of the kind discussed on pp. 201-2.

But British empire-builders solved those problems – not in very pretty ways, but they did solve them even when doing so required teaching their new subjects what government meant. I do not believe German or Russian invaders would find any problems at all in conquering a modern anarchist society, given that its population would be perfectly well aware of how government works. David Friedman concurs. 'It is all very well to fantasize about fighting the invader village by village. . . . A serious invader would inform each unit that if it resisted or failed to pay tribute, it would be destroyed. . . . After the invader proved that he meant business, the citizens of the surviving communities would be eager to create the institutions

. . . necessary to give the invader what he wanted.'

However, it is perhaps unfair to concentrate so heavily on the points where Rothbard's ideas are weakest. Much more interesting are Rothbard's views about the structure of laws and property-rights that would govern behaviour in an anarcho-capitalist society, assuming that the society did succeed in maintaining itself against internal and external statist threats.

For David Friedman, laws should be a consumer good reflecting whatever consumer preferences happen to be. For Rothbard, on the other hand, laws are an expression of morality. A liberal society, if it functions at all, must be a society in which the population at large subscribes to the liberal moral principles that an individual is entitled to be free of coercive aggression against his person and his property, and to defend himself against such aggression. Law will be, not a collection of arbitrary statutes, but a body of judicial practice giving tangible expression in various practical circumstances to the agreed fundamental principles – which is what Rothbard sees both English Common Law and the original Roman Law as having been, before they were contaminated by 'statist accretions'. Like David Friedman, Rothbard envisages the market as selecting among rival arbitrators, but Rothbard sees consumer choice as acting to select judges who most accurately and efficiently realize the shared legal principles, and certainly not as acting to select individual laws just because people fancy them.

To illustrate the distinction, consider for instance the question of legislation on drugs.

Liberals in general are hostile to the existing panoply of laws criminalizing the manufacture, sale, and/or consumption of ('soft' or 'hard') drugs, together with laws defining other 'victimless crimes', such as those concerning prostitution and pornography. Even if it is true that pornography predisposes men towards rape, the liberal response is that people should be prosecuted for committing rape but not for producing material that might or might not lead to someone else committing rape. Liberals object to such laws in the first place on moral grounds: it is not for any third party to interfere between a willing buyer and a willing seller, and, although many of us may agree that taking heroin is an extremely foolish activity, there is no principled line to be drawn between State banning of heroin and, say, State censorship of reading-matter expressing views that deviate from the Thirty-nine Articles of the Church of England. No individual or group of individuals can decide what is the good life on others' behalf; we are all entitled to go to Hell in our own fashion. But liberals also have an important argument of expedience tending the same way. If heroin addiction is a widely feared problem in cities like New York, this is very largely not because of the horrific consequences for the individuals who get hooked but because their need for money to support their habit creates a very high level of crimes of other sorts, muggings and burglaries. These crimes are almost entirely caused not by addiction in itself but by the criminality of heroin, because it is this that forces up the price; if the stuff could be manufactured and sold as openly as barley-sugar, the price would be very modest (unless the State chose to live off immoral earnings by taxing it) and junkies could maintain their ghastly habit without troubling the rest of us. Nobody is arguing that heroin is a good thing, but surely this situation might on balance be preferable to the current reality?

(According to the Chicago economists George Stigler and Gary Becker, it is futile to reply that criminalizing drugs at least reduces consumption; economic theory implies that this effect can be significant only in the case of 'beneficial addictions', such as 'addiction' to classical music.)

Under David Friedman's system, it would be an open question whether laws reflected this liberal presumption in favour of freedom to take drugs, or not. Addicts would try to subscribe to protection agencies which used legal systems that were silent about drugs; convinced prohibitionists would patronize agencies using legal systems forbidding drugs. Friedman envisages the likely result as a geographical split: in a place like New York, where there are many addicts willing to pay heavily for the right to take heroin, probably most agencies would subscribe to laws that were liberal in this respect; in other areas, where there are only a sprinkling of addicts whose economic power is small relative to that of the many people who strongly oppose hard drugs, no protection agencies would treat heroin as legal. Once again, the free market increases choice: you can live in New York if you want to take heroin yourself, and you can live somewhere else if you do not want anyone round you to be allowed to take it.

For Rothbard, on the other hand, there can be no question of any part of an anarchist society having laws criminalizing drugs; interference with the manufacture, sale, or consumption of drugs is an invasion of personal liberty, therefore illegal, and that is the end of the matter. Rothbardland has nothing comparable to criminal law; all lawsuits are civil suits, so no one would have any standing as plaintiff in a case against a drug-dealer or user.

In one way this seems a much more consistent line than David Friedman's. If coercion is wrong, then how can it be right to throw a drug-addict – or a drug-peddler – into gaol simply because the pattern of economic choices made by other members of the society he inhabits have yielded laws against drugs? At that rate one risks having to say that any excesses of a tyrannical regime are perfectly OK from a liberal point of view, provided they result from choices made by consumers. It would be truly disgusting to say that what was wrong with Nazi Germany was that its laws did not accurately reflect consumers' preferences. What was wrong was that the Nazi regime legalized things that nobody ought ever to be allowed to do to anyone, irrespective of any voting either in the marketplace or in polling booths. (To which I think David Friedman would reply that he does not pretend that free-market laws will be morally ideal, but that the best practical means of getting morally good laws is to get them on the market.)

The trouble with Rothbard's approach, though, is that he assumes it is reasonably straightforward to decide what the abstract principles of liberalism imply for the diverse concrete issues which law is used to resolve. But this is very far from straightforward, even with respect to aggression against the person – let alone with respect to the definition of property rights over the non-human environment. It just is not true that the complexities and arbitrarinesses of actual legal systems are all 'statist' distortions of principles which are otherwise simple and pure (though, certainly, there is a lot of this). Rothbard himself draws out the implications of liberal principles with no sense of hesitation or doubt; but that would not help, in a real anarcho-capitalist society, unless everybody else agreed with his interpretation of liberal ideals, and I do not believe for a moment that they would.

Consider, for instance, his position on the status of children and on abortion.

Like many radical liberals, Murray Rothbard objects to the way in which human beings below an arbitrarily-fixed age are deprived of ordinary civil rights and treated legally as something akin to their parents' property, much as Negroes used to be treated in the southern USA, and married women in England. For Rothbard, children are free agents just like everyone else, and if they choose to 'run away' from home and seek foster parents, or try to make their way in the world independently (whether successfully or not), neither natural parents nor anyone else has any right to interfere. Some liberals would qualify these rights as coming into existence at a particular age, much lower than the present age of majority – David Friedman suggests nine – on the ground that a very young child is not yet really a 'human being'. To Rothbard this is illogical (if twenty-one or eighteen is wrong, why is nine right?). He treats the act of leaving home as itself decisive in showing that the child has become a free agent and is entitled to be treated as such, so a child may leave at any age he likes – in characteristic Rothbardian language, 'it is totally impermissible enslavement and an aggression upon his right of self-ownership for [the parents] to use force to compel him to return.' (There is nothing arbitrary in saying that the child becomes free just when he leaves home; before that point, he is a guest on the parents' private property, and in that situation anyone, child or adult, must obey his host's orders.) As Sean Gabb has put it, criticizing a British advocate of civil rights for children, the radical position involves 'demanding the right of a child of three to run away from home after being refused a second helping of rice pudding. . . .'

One might expect, then, that Rothbard would be hostile to abortion. Many liberals favour the 'woman's right to choose', arguing that no ecclesiastical or other guardians of morality can impose their views on the individual; but Rothbard feels that this represents far too 'brusque' a dismissal of the unborn child's countervailing rights. Nevertheless, Rothbard concludes that women should indeed be free to procure abortions, *despite* the human rights of unborn children, because no human – born or unborn – has a 'right to live, unbidden, as a parasite within or upon some person's body'. Abortion is 'the expulsion of an unwanted invader', comparable to the act of a farmer who turns campers off his land.

I do not know what my answer is to the grave question of whether, and if so when, abortion is justifiable. Since I am a man, some may say that it is inappropriate for me to have a definite opinion on the matter. But to anyone who has cradled a young child in his own arms, who has seen and felt for himself what a piece of work a newborn baby is, it must surely argue a degree of moral blindness for Rothbard to settle the matter in a couple of sentences in terms of the law of trespass?

To Rothbard it is all but self-evident that a child can be killed at will before birth, but may not even be restrained from signing a contract with a white slaver once old enough to lift a pen; perhaps this is right, but it is very easy to imagine someone else starting from the same fundamental liberal principles and reaching quite different conclusions – on these, and many other issues. (To give a less directly personal example: according to Rothbard any clause in a contract specifying penalties for non-performance is necessarily invalid, something with which few other liberals, I believe, would agree.) If such disagreements are possible, I do not understand how a coherent system of law could subsist in Rothbardland. It is difficult to repress the suspicion that in practice Rothbard would regard deviation from his own version of liberal law as crypto-statism, to be eliminated coercively.

Rothbard would, I believe, reply that sincere differences of opinion about the correctness of laws are indeed possible among liberals, but that such differences can be resolved almost as objectively as scientific research resolves differences of opinion about the physical world. Quoting mediaeval philosophers, he argues that study of human nature reveals the 'natural law' applicable to our species. However, like Marx and Hayek among others, I do not believe in a fixed 'human nature'; it seems to me that members of different cultures have very different natures, so I find this reply unpersuasive.

Murray Rothbard is a learned man, versed in many unusual byways of history and philosophy. But he has a large share of the romanticism often found in socialists, allowing him to believe in gross implausibilities if they are convenient for his case. Most anarchists concede that the only functioning anarchic societies that have endured for any significant period have been the economically very primitive societies discussed in Chapter 7; but Rothbard believes that Ireland was a sophisticated anarchy for a thousand years, until it was conquered by England in the seventeenth century. I would find it easier to believe that he might be right about that, if I did not know that Rothbard, like a number of other American 'libertarians', also subscribes to the doctrine which they call 'the Myth of the Six Million', that is the view that Nazi Germany never carried out mass exterminations of Jews, gypsies, and others – the stories about the death camps are said to have been cooked up to suit various groups' ulterior purposes. Rothbard needs this to be true, since – if orthodox history is right – it is difficult not to regard the Second World War as just, and wars between States are never just; they are disgraceful manifestations of State terrorism at its worst. (And British wars are specially bad; there is a strong streak of Anglophobia running through Rothbard's thinking, so that for instance he takes it for granted that the current situation in Northern Ireland is nothing more or less than a case of the brave, freedom-loving lads of the IRA using whatever methods they can find to throw off the vicious yoke of British imperialism.)

Rothbard's romanticism is unexpected in a liberal. The liberal outlook is normally marked by a grey literalness about human relationships, a refusal to indulge in mystification or pretty fairy-stories about what makes people and societies tick. Yet in the USA, where adherents of the liberal movement are perhaps thicker on the ground than anywhere else, Rothbard with his forceful personality and untiring appetite for work appears to have captured the role of chief guru to the movement. American 'libertarians' make respectful nods towards Hayek (allusions to his Nobel Prize come in handy when sceptics treat libertarianism as a far-out frivolity by a bunch of youngsters); but Hayek's soberly intellectual prose is tough going for the average twenty-year-old in a small-town American college, Hayek is not on hand in America to inspire by his presence, and in any case the moderation of his views makes them less thrilling to radical youth. There is a certain panache in declaring oneself an anarchist, but not in arguing for constitutional separation of legislature and executive. Rothbard's name seems near-ubiquitous in the publications of American libertarianism.

(A word about the terminology problem, already alluded to on pp. 19-23. In America – and in Britain too – those who call themselves 'libertarians' commonly claim that the term covers both anarchists and believers in a minimal State, but in my experience they usually are themselves anarchists anxious not to alienate potential minimal-statist allies. People who want the process of reducing State power to stop anywhere much short of Nozick's truly exiguous State usually call themselves liberals rather than libertarians.)

The central role that is currently allotted to Murray Rothbard makes the anarcho-capitalist case look weaker than it really is. At present it is easy to make fun of anarcho-capitalism; but, if we heard a lot more of David Friedman and less of Rothbard, I believe many of us might find it difficult to go on insisting that States are indispensable. Even Friedman's case contains flaws, but what political theory escapes that criticism? There are some apparent impracticalities in Friedman's anarchism, but they strike me as considerably less glaring (and less crucial) than the impracticalities in any version of socialism that I know of.

David Friedman's anarchism seems to me impractical because I cannot understand what balance of economic pressures could lead his private-enterprise judges to be impartial (though on this point it may be that he has simply not been explicit enough), and more seriously because I do not believe that Friedmanland could defend itself against foreign conquest. The other issue on which none of the anarcho-capitalists seem satisfactory is that of public goods and bads. It is difficult not to believe that an anarcho-capitalist society will seriously underproduce public goods such as rabies control, because there is no way of withholding the benefit from an individual who chooses not to pay for it, and will seriously overproduce public bads such as air pollution, because there is no way of withholding the disbenefit from an individual who chooses not to accept compensation for suffering it.

The main libertarian strategy towards the public good/bad problem is to invoke the ability of modern technology to convert public into private goods. For instance, there is no way to prevent a non-subscribing mariner seeing a lighthouse of the traditional kind, but one could easily arrange nowadays for 'lighthouses' to broadcast some electronic signal which could be detected only by an apparatus that mariners would rent for a fee. City streets are seen as a public good because it would be impossibly inconvenient for cars to stop at tollgates every few hundred yards, but nowadays one might charge for usage by burying some apparatus at intervals in the road surface which would trigger a meter in passing vehicles. And so forth.

(Libertarians, incidentally, tend to be strongly enthusiastic about technology and everything to do with it. For instance, libertarians are often avid readers of science fiction, and a surprising number of leading science fiction writers, including Robert Heinlein, Poul Anderson, and others, are themselves radical liberals and incorporate liberal politics into some of their novels. Almost to a person, libertarians favour nuclear power and pooh-pooh fears about the risks. Perhaps this linkage is natural, given that libertarians are committed to a belief in advance through industrial progress. However, I do not see anything inevitable about it; if liberalism is worth believing in it is because it enables individuals better to realize their own particular values *whatever* those values happen to be. I am grateful to industry because, by producing cheap personal transport, it lets me pursue my career while living in the countryside, far from the feverish atmosphere of twentieth-century technology.)

The trouble with the appeal to technology is that it assumes that scientific problems will always have politically-convenient solutions. Sometimes, what used to be public goods will indeed be converted into private goods by advances in technical knowledge, but there is no reason to suppose that that will always happen. Protection against rabies would become a private good if a pill were invented that conferred immunity on the swallower, but such a pill may be a biological impossibility. Indeed, sometimes technology does the opposite. Books used to be a clearcut private good, but the introduction of photocopying technology has made them much more public-good-like. If an expensive book exists in one copy in a library it is near-impossible to prevent readers running off photocopies, and if copying technology becomes even cheaper books may become virtually pure public goods, with serious consequences for their production. I take the point that *some* public goods will be produced even by the market (a lighthouse might be so valuable to a particular shipping company that they would build it even though they could not charge other users); but the question is not about whether some categories of goods will be totally absent under anarchism, it is about whether the socially-optimal quantity will be produced. Surely, it will not. Under States the production of public goods is usually far from optimal also, but at least the Virginians show us how in principle States might be made to solve this problem; anarcho-capitalism seems to offer no solution.

Another approach suggested by some anarcho-capitalists, particularly for the mirror-image problem of control of 'public bads', is the American legal concept of the 'class action', in which a civil lawsuit is prosecuted not by an individual or a named set of plaintiffs but in the name of a wide group identified by the fact of having suffered from the circumstance giving rise to the suit. Thus, a pharmaceutical company may be sued by the class of all people who have suffered unexpected side-effects from a new drug. (In existing American law I believe the *defendant* is always an individual rather than a class, but anarcho-capitalists envisage actions against as well as actions by classes.) Thus the British libertarian David Ramsay Steele, replying to my objection that anarcho-capitalism offers no better remedy than current arrangements for Scandinavians whose interests are damaged by acid rain caused by British industrial pollution, has suggested that a class of Scandinavians could sue English factory-owners as a class. But the concept of 'class actions' seems highly anti-liberal. A lawsuit in which neither party can appear in person must surely yield a travesty of justice; and if it is not possible to factor out accurately the contributions of individual polluters and the damages sustained by individual sufferers, then there can be no fair way of apportioning responsibility for – or receipts from – an award made in such a case.

David Friedman's response to the public goods problem is to say that 'I am perfectly willing to accept a slightly less than optimal production of a few public goods in exchange for the security of there being no government to expand into the 95 percent of human affairs where it can do nothing but damage.' This is a reasonable answer, *if* there is reason to suppose that the deviation from optimality will be 'slight' – but is there? Murray Rothbard virtually ignores the problem; 'public good/bad', 'externality', 'free rider' (the standard terms that economists use to discuss these issues) are not to be found in the indexes of his books. And some libertarians are very naive in this area. I once asked an Irish libertarian of some standing what the anarchist response would be to the loss of amenity I would suffer if large advertising hoardings were erected across the hillside which rises a few miles in front of my living-room windows. 'Easy,' he replied, 'sue the advertiser for trespass by light-waves.'

I continue to believe that an anarcho-capitalist society, if it survived at all, would be even more encumbered by industrial poison, filth, and ugliness than much of modern, statist England; that, if we are talking about political *ideals*, we ought to permit the State a carefully circumscribed role with respect to public goods and bads, and be more vigilant than twentieth-century Americans have been in combating the perpetual danger of State gigantism. The American Supreme Court could not have made rulings such as the one about pig feed cited by David Friedman (p. 223 above), if Americans in general had not come to believe that the constraints on Federal action laid down in the Bill of Rights were undesirable. One cannot elevate the American example into a universal rule. The Swiss Confederation is three and a half times older than the USA, but its share of political power in its territory – while greater than it used to be – is very much smaller than the share of political power in the USA possessed by the American Federal government.

Arguably, there is little reason to stress the shortcomings of the anarcho-capitalist position. Our society contains so much *genuinely* unnecessary and maleficent coercion that liberals and anarchists will be on the same side for the foreseeable future. We can go on dismantling the State for a long time before we get to the bits worth keeping. There should be no need for liberals to define the differences between themselves and the anarcho-capitalists too rigidly, provided that what the latter are developing is a serious political movement. I have some anxieties on that score, though.

In the USA, anarcho-capitalism or 'libertarianism' has become a highly visible movement. There is an array of libertarian institutes of various sorts – the Cato Institute and the Institute for Humane Studies in California, and the Center for Libertarian Studies in New York, for instance; and a range of publications, often glossy, expensively-produced magazines: *Reason, Inquiry, Libertarian Review* are a few titles. At first sight the American libertarian scene presents the appearance of a galaxy of separate groups linked only by belief in an idea whose time has come.

The aura of glossy success is somewhat dimmed when one looks closer and realizes the extent to which American libertarian groups are linked into a network with overlapping membership, and a network which is very heavily subsidized by one or two super-rich individuals. There is a strong atmosphere in the American libertarian movement of too much money chasing too few ideas. After I became publicly associated with liberalism a few years ago I became used to fielding a succession of air-mail letters, cables, and excitable transatlantic phone calls proposing vague projects which seemed in the end to lead nowhere.

In Britain, 'libertarianism' made its first formal appearance with the foundation in 1979 of the Libertarian Alliance, a group of people mainly in their twenties and early thirties who used as their headquarters the Alternative Bookshop in Covent Garden

– an excellent institution which stocks publications on all aspects of freedom and liberal thought and policies, without limiting itself to any particular 'party line'. (It is worth making the point, parenthetically, that there exists by now a truly massive literature on the various ideas touched on in this book. I am sure it will frequently have occurred to the reader that I have totally overlooked this or that major practical problem that liberal politics would engender, and clearly there is a severe limit to the number of topics that can be treated in a book of this size. But other writers have covered what I have not; the reader may disagree with their conclusions, but I should be quite surprised if he can think of any specific topic which has not been analysed in detail by some liberal writer or writers.) The Alternative Bookshop is managed by Chris Tame, who became the central figure in the Alliance, and his wife Judy Englander was the first editor of the Alliance's magazine *Free Life* (a reassuringly un-glossy, small-format quarterly production). In contrast with the USA, where libertarians formed their own political party, the Libertarian Alliance in Britain preferred to concentrate on infiltrating liberal ideas into society at large, including the existing political parties.

Like American libertarians, the British Libertarian Alliance claims to embrace both anarcho-capitalist and minimal-statist positions, and certainly some of its members have been minimal-statists. However, I believe it is true to say that most of the leading members are anarchists, and the last of its four declared Principles is 'Elimination of coercive intervention by the state, the foremost violator of liberty' – which is close enough to a statement of anarchism to have caused a number of the radical liberals who are beginning to emerge in British public life to have held aloof from Alliance membership.

For several years the Alliance did valuable work, publicizing liberal thought through a stream of publications of various kinds, by holding discussion meetings both for the 'in-group' and for the larger public, by presenting the liberal case to the media and to Royal Commissions, and so forth. Unfortunately, in 1982 the Alliance was split apart by a factional row which reached quite astonishing depths of violent acrimony. (Perhaps one of the economists of politics could explain why destructive in-fighting is relatively cheap for members of small and extreme political groupings, since what the Alliance went through seems to be a familiar syndrome.) At the time of writing (late 1983) the somewhat absurd result is that there are now two organizations called the Libertarian Alliance led respectively by Chris Tame and David Ramsay Steele, each of which refuses to recognize the existence of the other, two *Free Life* magazines (the early post-split issues even included one or two of the same articles), and, for the time being, half as much impetus towards liberalism being generated as before.

The two groups are very different in style. David Ramsay Steele (the Ramsay is important – it is an odd quirk of current British politics that we have a Liberal Party which is not liberal and a Libertarian Alliance which is liberal, both led by a man called David Steele) is everyone's idea of a young anarchist, gaunt, shabbily-dressed, and he has no interest in keeping lines open to lukewarm sympathizers who compromise radical liberalism with practical politics. Steele's strategy is to build up a small nucleus of dedicated, hard-line libertarians until . . . not being one of their number, I cannot say until what. Chris Tame's anarchism is *salonfähig* (he and his wife have indeed been received at 10 Downing Street); and he believes in the steady drip which wears away the stone: he makes no secret of his own extreme views, but he will spend time putting the liberal message across even to unpromising audiences. Tame and Steele differ in their attitudes to American libertarianism; Steele and his group seem to have given up on it as an essentially frivolous movement which has made so many compromises in order to court popularity that it no longer offers a radical alternative to mainstream politics, while Tame's group has affiliated to a US-sponsored 'Libertarian International' which held its first convention in Switzerland in 1982 and is due to meet in London in 1984. How British libertarianism will develop, in view of the split between these men, is very hard to guess.

Evidently, I am not an anarcho-capitalist. Anarcho-capitalism represents liberalism pushed to its logical extreme. Some anarcho-capitalists seem perversely determined to revel in the paradoxes which that extreme produces (as when Walter

Block hails blackmailers as heroes of entrepreneurship, supplying silence to customers who value silence highly and helping society to become more tolerant of deviance by spilling the beans when some wretched sexual nonconformist can no longer pay). Extreme positions in any domain are attractive to people with a logical, systematic cast of mind. But in human affairs it is important to understand that logically-pure, extreme positions are not always the right ones to adopt. If it really were possible to construct a society as totally free as the anarcho-capitalists suggest, while avoiding the disastrous consequences that statists predict, then I doubt that our species would have spent so many millennia wrangling about politics as it has – a solution so perfect and simple would quickly have been accepted. We wrangle, because no political system is perfect, and good systems are messy compromises between many conflicting ideals. Human life, unlike mathematics, seems to involve an irreducible minimum of woolly inconsequentiality.

Nevertheless, although I believe the anarcho-capitalists' views are ultimately untenable, their work remains immensely valuable. By setting out to 'think the unthinkable', they succeed in showing how private enterprise might well replace the State over a much wider domain than liberals setting out from statist axioms have ever thought possible. The anarcho-capitalists' errors teach us far more than mainstream writers' truisms.

9/Parting Words

'OK, I agree that modern Britain is far too authoritarian, and getting worse. But do you really think that a society in which everything depends on money wouldn't be ten times worse still – except for the few who could afford to indulge their whims in callous indifference to the sufferings of the rest?'

Yes, I do believe it really will be, not just no worse, but far better. It won't be paradise, and concerned citizens will be wringing their hands and telling each other that they are ashamed of their own society – until their historians remind them how things were, back in the twentieth century. For decades now we have been brainwashed into thinking that any measure of interference with individuals is excusable, if it can be claimed to remedy the fact that someone, somewhere, is a bit poorer than someone else. This is cant; it is just the fashionable way of concealing an ulterior motive. Money is a marvellous instrument of emancipation, and people low in society's pyramid benefit from it as much as or more than others. They may have less to spend than the rich in a society based on money, but in a society based on political authority welfare-differentials are far greater. If someone is worse off than you in a money-based society, there are a thousand avenues by which he can try to catch up or pass you. In a power-based society he might as well throw in the towel, 'You can't fight City Hall.' The worst thing for a person is not to be poor but to be constantly frustrated in his attempts to improve his lot. Perhaps the poor man fails at whichever of the thousand opportunities he tries; if he fails he fails – that is not your fault and there is no reason why you ought to feel guilty about it, but if it *does* worry you the remedy lies in your pocket.

If you are relatively poor yourself, remember to compare your position not just with richer contemporaries but with your predecessors. What Africa and India are now, materially speaking, we were once – you aren't as poor as *that*, and it is free enterprise which has brought us to the position where a poor Englishman would count as a rich Tanzanian. As Milton Friedman has pointed out, the rich have gained little from material progress – for the wealthy in ancient Greece, 'running servants replaced running water'. It is the masses who have benefited hugely from the fruits of capitalism.

('Ah, but material welfare isn't everything.' No, but you can't have it both ways. If it doesn't matter that you haven't got much of what money buys, then all you are being deprived of is a fair share of political power, and that is what I am trying to remedy. If money isn't your problem and power isn't your problem, then I'm afraid your problem lies inside you, and you really have to sort that out for yourself.)

'Does it never occur to you that your liberal ideas may be quite wrong?'

If I didn't have doubts, about everything, probably what I write would be scarcely worth reading. Of course I am not so arrogant as to think that the ultimate Truth about politics has been vouchsafed to me. Precisely because I know what a fallible thing the human intellect is, I want to see a world in which people have maximum freedom to experiment with different conceptions of the good life. It is the collectivists who feel so sure they know what is best for their fellow men that they can force everybody into a few approved moulds.

'If you like naked free enterprise so much, why don't you go and live in America?'

You guess right, I would not want to live in the USA (I tried it for several years, and have no desire to repeat the experience). But I do not see the USA as a uniquely close approximation to the liberal social ideal. Liberty in America is the State religion – they write it on their coins, schoolchildren take a daily oath in liberal wording to the American flag; in these and many other ways Americans persuade themselves that their society is uniquely free, and since most Americans have little experience of other countries they believe it and often get the rest of us believing it too. Yet it would be hard to argue that the USA is in fact a freer society than Britain on balance: there are particular respects in which it is, but there are also many respects in which Americans are more regulated than we are, in the whole spectrum of life from commerce to the most intimate relationships. And the instinct for freedom at the personal level strikes me as weaker among Americans than among Britons. Switzerland, where I have also lived, strikes me as a freer society than either Britain or America, and given the opportunity I could well see myself emigrating there – if I hesitated it would be for family and language reasons, things that are no fault of the Swiss Confederation. (Even to a political animal, freedom is not the *only* thing that matters about a society – far from it.)

'You are right, in theory. Your liberal society would be a healthier, happier place to live. But it is an impossible dream. The State has its own dynamic; now we have computers and all the other sophisticated technologies of social control, there is no way that they will not be used against us.'

In my lifetime, the men who ran the British State have abdicated from control over hundreds of millions of Asians and Africans, sometimes in favour of quite vicious thugs, not because they lacked the technical or economic ability to retain control but simply because it became fashionable to think that this was the right thing to do. If we can get people to understand that liberalism is a moral imperative, are you seriously telling me that the successors of those men will refuse to abdicate from control over us, in our own favour – just because they are physically *capable* of retaining and deepening their control? The people who hold high positions in the British State do not strike me as cunning, Bismarckian types ruthlessly determined to hang on to power. On the contrary, they are rather wet. (Down at the lower echelons there may be a fair amount of ruthlessness about, but subordinates in the State salariat do what their superiors tell them to do; they don't determine how our nation evolves.) The people at the top – who would probably achieve reasonably fulfilling careers under almost any political dispensation – will destroy the computer files and rewrite the laws fast enough, if we can manage to seize the ideological initiative. Even in ten years, we have won a lot of ground.

It is just a question of keeping up the pressure, and increasing it. Whenever you hear someone laying down in the plummy-toned voice of authority what shall be done for people or to people for their own good, make it obvious that you recognize his arrogant pretensions for what they are. Join a political party, and make it clear to your parliamentary candidate that talk of 'compassion' is a quick way to lose votes in your constituency – in politics, 'compassion' is code for using other people's earnings to provide cushy salaried jobs for the middle classes. Don't let friends get away in casual chat with loose talk of people 'owing' so much in taxes (nobody 'owes' the taxes that are levied nowadays, they simply lack the power to prevent themselves being taxed) or of someone not being 'qualified' to do a given job (pieces of paper don't fit people to do jobs, skills and abilities do).

There is a case for being ruthless; for instance, for grabbing every advantage one can from the Welfare State while showing that no level of benefits will ever satisfy one, so that its functionaries sicken of their work as it becomes increasingly obvious that the system must break down. No doubt this advice goes against the grain, since many people who help to operate the Welfare State are very decent people. But the Indians and Africans who fought for 'independence' – meaning rule by people of roughly the same skin-colour as themselves – hardened their hearts against their knowledge that many of their British rulers were enlightened and admirable men, for the sake of what they saw as a greater good. Do we not owe it to ourselves and our descendants to be equally unyielding in pursuit of genuine independence for Britons?

Get people to understand that it is dangerous to grow dependent on the State, because the State may not be able to go on handing out its welfare bribes indefinitely. At present Conservatives are bemoaning the fact that the rising proportion of old people in the population is making long-term reductions in public spending seem unachievable. This should be a golden opportunity. We ought to be saying to people who are now young or in early middle age, 'Think how much of their earnings today's children would have to hand over if you are to get a State pension at present-day levels. Seeing how social attitudes are changing already, you're likely to wind up pretty hungry in the year 2020. Are you really going to risk it, or are you going to organize your own pension from your own earnings?' The more people decide that they don't dare rely on the State, the more votes there are for politicians who offer to stop the State purloining the earnings they need to provide for themselves.

Spread the word. Don't let up. It is our own lives we are fighting to take control of. If you help, we can win.

References

The following list includes works on which I have drawn to a significant extent in writing this book. It is not a general bibliography of the liberal movement; to readers looking for that, I recommend the catalogue of the Alternative Bookshop, 3 Langley Court, Covent Garden, London WC2E 9JY.

Publication details often correspond to recent paperback editions, so dates are not necessarily those of first publication. The place of publication is London except where noted in brackets.

Allsopp, Bruce, *Towards a Humane Architecture*, Frederick Muller, 1974.

Barclay, Harold, *People Without Government*, Cienfuegos Press (Sanday, Orkney), 1982.

Bauer, P.T., *Reality and Rhetoric*, Weidenfeld & Nicolson, 1984.

Becker, Gary, *Human Capital*, National Bureau of Economic Research (New York), 1964.

Becker, Gary, *The Economic Approach to Human Behavior*, Chicago University Press, 1977.

Block, Walter, *Defending the Undefendable*, Fleet Press (New York), 1976.

von Böhm-Bawerk, Eugen, *Karl Marx and the Close of his System (Reprints of Economic Classics series)*, P.M. Sweezy (ed.), Augustus M. Kelley (New York), 1966.

Bosanquet, Nick, *After the New Right*, Heinemann, 1983.

Bradshaw, John, *Doctors on Trial*, Paddington Press, 1978.

Brittan, Samuel, *Capitalism and the Permissive Society*, Macmillan, 1973.

Buchanan, James, Burton, John, and Wagner, R.E., *The Consequences of Mr Keynes* (Hobart Paper 78), Institute of Economic Affairs, 1978.

Buchanan, James, Rowley, Charles, et al., *The Economics of Politics*, Institute of Economic Affairs, 1978.

Buchanan, James, and Tullock, Gordon, *The Calculus of Consent*, University of Michigan Press (Ann Arbor, Michigan), 1962.

Chapman, Leslie, *Your Disobedient Servant*, Chatto & Windus, 1978.

Coase, R.H., 'The Lighthouse in Economics', *Journal of Law and Economics*, vol. 17, pp. 357-76, 1974.

Demsetz, Harold, 'Toward a Theory of Property Rights', *American Economic Review*, vol. 57, *Papers and Proceedings*, pp. 347-59, 1967.

Demsetz, Harold, 'The Private Production of Public Goods', *Journal of Law and Economics*, vol. 13, pp. 293-306, 1970.

Dore, Ronald, *The Diploma Disease*, Allen & Unwin, 1976.

Freidson, Eliot, *Profession of Medicine*, Dodd, Mead & Co. (New York), 1970.

Friedman, David, *The Machinery of Freedom*, Arlington House (New Rochelle, N.Y.), 1973.

Friedman, Milton, *Capitalism and Freedom*, University of Chicago Press, 1962.

Friedman, Milton and Rose, *Free to Choose*, Secker & Warburg, 1980.

Hayek, Friedrich, *The Road to Serfdom*, Routledge & Kegan Paul, 1944.

Hayek, Friedrich, *Individualism and Economic Order*, Routledge & Kegan Paul, 1949.

Hayek, Friedrich (ed.), *Capitalism and the Historians*, Routledge & Kegan Paul, 1954.

Hayek, Friedrich, *The Counter-Revolution of Science*, Collier-Macmillan, 1955.

Hayek, Friedrich, *The Constitution of Liberty*, Routledge & Kegan Paul, 1960.

Hayek, Friedrich, *Studies in Philosophy, Politics and Economics*, Routledge & Kegan Paul, 1967.

Hayek, Friedrich, *Law, Legislation and Liberty* (3 vols.), Routledge & Kegan Paul, 1973.

Hayek, Friedrich, *Denationalisation of Money* (2nd ed.), Institute of Economic Affairs, 1978.

Hewitt, Patricia, *The Abuse of Power*, Martin Robertson (Oxford), 1982.

Hirsch, Fred, *Social Limits to Growth*, Routledge & Kegan Paul, 1977.

Illich, Ivan, *Deschooling Society*, Penguin, 1973.

Illich, Ivan, *Limits to Medicine*, Penguin, 1977.

Jefferson, J.M., 'Industrialisation and Poverty: in Fact and Fiction', in R.M. Hartwell et al., *The Long Debate on Poverty* (2nd ed.), Institute of Economic Affairs, 1974.

Jewkes, John, *Delusions of Dominance* (Hobart Paper 76), Institute of Economic Affairs, 1977.

Kennedy, Ian, *The Unmasking of Medicine* (2nd ed.), Paladin, 1983.

Kirzner, Israel, *Perception, Opportunity, and Profit*, University of Chicago Press, 1979.

Klein, Rudolf, *Complaints Against Doctors*, Charles Knight, 1973.

Le Grand, Julian, 'The Distribution of Public Expenditure: the Case of Health Care', *Economica* vol. 45 (n.s.), pp. 125-42, 1978.

Leijonhufvud, Axel, *Keynes and the Classics*, Institute of Economic Affairs, 1969.

Lepage, Henri, *Demain le capitalisme*, Livre de Poche (Paris), 1978.

Luard, Evan, *Socialism Without the State*, Macmillan, 1979.

Mingay, G.E., 'The Transformation of Agriculture', in R.M. Hartwell et al., *The Long Debate on Poverty* (2nd ed.), Institute of Economic Affairs, 1974.

von Mises, Ludwig, *Human Action*, William Hodge, 1949.

von Mises, Ludwig, *Socialism* (2nd ed.), Jonathan Cape, 1951.

Niskanen, William, *Bureaucracy and Representative Government*, Aldine, Atherton (Chicago), 1971.

Niskanen, William, 'Bureaucrats and Politicians', *Journal of Law and Economics*, vol. 18, pp. 617-43, 1975.

Nove, Alec, *The Economics of Feasible Socialism*, Allen & Unwin, 1983.

Nozick, Robert, *Anarchy, State, and Utopia*, Blackwell (Oxford), 1974.

Papps, Ivy, *For Love or Money?* (Hobart Paper 86), Institute of

Economic Affairs, 1980.

Pappworth, M.H., *Human Guinea Pigs*, Penguin, 1969.

Paul, Jeffrey (ed.), *Reading Nozick*, Blackwell (Oxford), 1982.

Pawley, Martin, *Architecture Versus Housing*, Studio Vista, 1971.

Perlin, Terry (ed.), *Contemporary Anarchism*, Transaction Books (New Brunswick, N.J.), 1979.

Pinchbeck, Ivy, *Women Workers and the Industrial Revolution 1750-1850*, Routledge, 1930.

Popper, Karl, *The Poverty of Historicism* (2nd ed.), Routledge & Kegan Paul, 1961.

Popper, Karl, *Conjectures and Refutations* (3rd ed.), Routledge & Kegan Paul, 1969.

Rawls, John, *A Theory of Justice*, Oxford University Press, 1972.

Rothbard, Murray, *Power and Market* (2nd ed.), Sheed Andrew and McMeel (Kansas City), 1977.

Rothbard, Murray, *For a New Liberty* (2nd ed.), Collier Macmillan, 1978.

Rothbard, Murray, *The Ethics of Liberty*, Humanities Press (Atlantic Highlands, New Jersey), 1982.

Sahlins, Marshall, *Stone Age Economics*, Tavistock, 1974.

Schrag, Peter, and Divoky, Diane, *The Myth of the Hyperactive Child and Other Means of Child Control*, Penguin, 1981.

Senior, Derek, *Your Architect*, Hodder & Stoughton, 1964.

Smith, Adam, *The Theory of Moral Sentiments* (ed. by D.D. Raphael and A.L. Macfie), Clarendon (Oxford), 1976.

Smith, Adam, *An Inquiry into the Nature and Causes of the Wealth of Nations* (2 vols, ed. by R.H. Campbell, A.S. Skinner, and W.B. Todd), Clarendon (Oxford), 1976.

Sowell, Thomas, *Knowledge and Decisions*, Basic Books (New York), 1980.

Stigler, George, 'The Economics of Information', *Journal of Political Economy*, vol. 69, pp. 213-25, 1961.

Stigler, George, 'Director's Law of Public Income Redistribution', *Journal of Law and Economics*, vol. 13, pp. 1-10, 1970.

Stigler, George, and Becker, Gary, 'De Gustibus non est Disputandum', *American Economic Review*, vol. 67, pp. 76-90, 1977.

Sugden, Robert, *Who Cares?* (Occasional Paper 67), Institute of Economic Affairs, 1983.

Szasz, Thomas, *The Myth of Mental Illness*, Paladin, 1972.

Szasz, Thomas, *Law, Liberty, and Psychiatry*, Routledge & Kegan Paul, 1974.

Tullock, Gordon, *The Vote Motive*, Institute of Economic Affairs, 1976.

Watkin, David, *Morality and Architecture*, Clarendon (Oxford), 1977.

West, E.G., *Education and the State* (2nd ed.), Institute of Economic Affairs, 1970.

Zola, Irving, 'Medicine as an Institution of Social Control', *The Sociological Review*, vol. 20, pp. 487-504, 1972.

Index